My Message

By

Evangelist Edward Adeoye Shobanke

How beautiful upon the mountains are the feet of him that **publisheth truth** *and* **salvation.**

Isaiah 52:7 KJV

1

Other book by the author:

- Exploits of Faith: *An Autobiography of my Walk With God*
- Jesus the Healer: My Testimonies

ISBN: 9798334687783

Unless otherwise stated, all scripture quotation are from the King James Version of the Bible.

Christ Ambassadors Holiness Church

Kemta, Idi Aba, Ajebo Road, Abeokuta, Ogun State, Nigeria.

E-mail: adeshobanke1@yahoo.com

Tel: +234-9012413346

.

Credits.

I extend my heartfelt gratitude to Pastor Matthew Erinola and Pastor Dr. Isaac Hunyinbo for their invaluable editorial guidance and support throughout the creation of this book. Their wisdom and insights have profoundly shaped the narrative and ensured its authenticity.

I also wish to express my sincere appreciation to Caleb Kuye, a gifted writer, for his exceptional contributions to this project. Caleb's expertise and dedication have brought clarity and depth to the text, significantly enhancing the reader's experience.

FOREWORD

I wept. I had faced bereavements before, but there was no occasion I wept like that. As soon as I would want to retire to bed, I would weep, and as soon as I got up from bed early in the morning, I would weep again. The weeping lasted for a whole week in that manner.

The word of our Lord Jesus Christ that when the Holy Spirit comes, "He will reprove the world of sin, of righteousness, and of judgment," became fulfilled in me. For four days of the Holiness Convention titled "Beware of the Error of the Wicked" organized by Christ Ambassadors Holiness Church, Abeokuta. I sat on the pew listening to the red-hot, Spirit-inspired messages of Evangelist Edward Adeoye Shobanke, who caused me to weep and experience revival. It was a series of weeping that revived me and set me on fire for ministry as a rural missionary. Glory to God for using him to bless me and many others I know through his messages and prayers.

Evangelist Edward Adeoye Shobanke lives in the presence of God and is always full of the Holy Spirit and power. Some years back, I called him on the phone to tell him that I would bring an insane person for his prayers. He obliged me. I did bring the fellow the following day. We met him in his house, the entrance to which he wrote, "Temporary Abode, Philippians 3:20." He prayed and, in Jesus' name, broke the spell and restored the sanity of the person, who, by God's grace, is preaching the gospel of Christ up to this moment.

To read printed messages of such a man of God will be a great blessing to the readers. By my closeness to him, I know his way of life; one that offers the attractiveness of biblical faith, love, holiness, and power. His familiar refrain since I knew him is, "God can do anything." He lives the simplicity of a quiet Christian life, yet he is a powerful voice for holiness.

For a mentor calling on his mentee to write the first word in his book shows Evangelist Edward Adeoye Shobanke's humility and self-effacing lifestyle. This deed teaches me humility. It cannot be hard for the blessed Holy Spirit of grace to associate with such a one in his life and ministry.

I can assure you of being impacted for a great visionary work for the Lord in your ministry if you care to study his messages, but only with the spirit of meekness.

Pastor Dapo Adeoye,
Crucified Life Mission,
Moba,
Badagry Riverine,
Lagos State.

FOREWORD

E. Ade Shobanke has been a welcome guest to my home and Church when he visits the United States of America. His ministry built up the faith of our congregation. Many times, people would be healed in the services he preached at Fairland Holiness Church. Brother Shobanke is a man of prayer, faith, and holiness. As I read his book "My Messages" I was impressed by how his life was poured into these sermons. I remember some of them being preached in full at my Church. He has given us the outlines of the fuller message. Young preachers can learn the art of sermon building by reading this book. Any preacher or believer can benefit from these faith building, Bible based, challenges to the Church. I am honored to know Brother Shobanke, and can say his life lives up to his preaching. It is as if he prepared his life before he delivered the sermon. That is the essence of powerful preaching; when a preacher prepares his life to serve God and then delivers the message that burns from his soul.

Pastor Lloyd Shuecraft

Fairland Holiness Church,

USA

Contents

INTRODUCTION.

Welcome to **"My Messages"**, a compilation of sermons that have guided, inspired, and challenged hearts throughout my ministry. Each message contained within these pages is a reflection of my journey in faith, a evidence to the transformative power of God's Word, and a beacon of hope for those seeking direction to the heart of God.

In this collection, you will find sermons that address a diverse range of topics, each inspired to illuminate the path of righteousness, deepen your spiritual understanding, and encourage a closer walk with God. From the themes of revival and obedience to the power of prayer and the importance of unwavering faith, these messages are more than mere words; they are an invitation to experience the living power of the Gospel in your own life.

The sermons within **"My Messages"** capture the essence of the Christian walk, from the exhilarating highs of spiritual awakening to the sobering lows of life's trials. Each message is designed to provoke thought, stir the soul, and inspire action. As you sweep through these pages, you will discover practical applications that can lead to a more vibrant and purposeful Christian life.

These messages have been delivered in various settings. As you read through these sermons, may you be blessed, inspired, and transformed. I assure you that you will catch the fire of revival; when you do, I encourage that you do not only keep the fire, but spread it.

Let me spark something good by letting you read or sing the following old hymns:

1. When we walk with the Lord
In the light of His Word,
What a glory He sheds on our way;
While we do His good will,
He abides with us still,
And with all who will trust and obey.

Chorus: Trust and obey,
For there's no other way
To be happy in Jesus,
But to trust and obey.

2. Not a shadow can rise,
Not a cloud in the skies,
But His smile quickly drives it away;
Not a doubt or a fear,
Not a sigh or a tear,
Can abide while we trust and obey.

3. Not a burden we bear,
Not a sorrow we share,
But our toil He doth richly repay;
Not a grief or a loss,
Not a frown or a cross,
But is blest if we trust and obey.

4. But we never can prove
The delights of His love,
Until all on the altar we lay;
For the favor He shows,
And the joy He bestows,
Are for them who will trust and obey.

5. Then in fellowship sweet
We will sit at His feet,
Or we'll walk by His side in the way;
What He says we will do;
Where He sends, we will go,
Never fear, only trust and obey.

Revival: The Only Solution.

Text: Psalm 85:6 - *"Wilt thou not revive us again, that thy people may rejoice in thee."*

Definition: Revival - The return of the joy of God, joy of salvation back to the church.

Why do we Need Revival?

A. Love Growing Cold.

Iniquity abounding leads to cold love. Text: Matthew 24:12 *And because iniquity shall abound, the love of many shall wax cold.*

B. Departure from Faith. Text: 1 Timothy 4:1, *Now the spirit speaketh expressly, that in the latter times, some shall depart from the faith, giving heed to seducing spirits and doctrines of devils – Luke 18:8b. Nevertheless when the son of man cometh shall he find faith on the earth?*

The prophecy of faithlessness in latter times. Text: *Nevertheless when the son of man cometh shall he find faith on the earth?*

C. Lack of Signs in the Church.

Text: Psalm 74:9: *We see not our signs, there is no more any prophets, neither is there among us any that knoweth how long.*

Hindrances to Revival.

What hinders revival? Sin, Iniquities, Worldliness.

II Chronicles 7:14 1. *If my people which are called by my name, shall humbly themselves, and pray, and seek my face, and turn from their wicked ways, then will I hear from heaven, I will forgive their sins and will heal their land*

Condition for revival: Humility, prayer, seeking God's face, turning from wicked ways.

IV. How to Achieve Revival.

No prayer, No Revival. Prayer is the key.

Luke 24:49 - *"Tarry ye in the city of Jerusalem until ye be endued with power from on high."*

No prayer, no revival.

Conclusion.

A. Emphasize the necessity of prayer for revival.

B. Call to action: Commitment to prayer for personal and corporate revival.

The Powerful Name of Jesus.

Text: Proverbs 18:10 - The *name of the Lord is a strong tower: the righteous runneth into it, and is safe.*

The name of Jesus is God's given and holds immense power.

I. The Power in the Name of Jesus:

Philippians 2:9-10 – "*Wherefore God also hath highly exalted him, and given him a name which is above every name:* [10] *That at the name of Jesus every knee should bow, of things in heaven, and things in earth, and things under the earth;*"

Luke 10:17 - *And the seventy returned again with joy, saying, Lord, even the devils are subject unto us through thy name.*

- Salvation and healing through His name:

  Romans 10:13, "*For whosoever shall call upon the name of the Lord shall be saved.*"

  Acts 4:12, "*Neither is there salvation in any other: for there is none other name under heaven given among men, whereby we must be saved.*"

  Mark 16:17, "*And these signs shall follow them that believe; In my name shall they cast out devils; they shall speak with new tongues;*"

II. Demonstrations of power through the name of Jesus:

- The enemies of the Gospel know the power in the name of Jesus:

  Acts 4:18, "*And they called them, and commanded them not to speak at all nor teach in the name of Jesus.*"

  Acts 3:6-7: *Then Peter said, Silver and gold have I none; but such as I have give I thee: In the name of Jesus Christ of Nazareth rise up and walk.*

  [7] *And he took him by the right hand, and lifted him up: and immediately his feet and ankle bones received strength.*

III. Conclusion:

- Encouragement to invoke the name of Jesus in faith for salvation, healing, and victory.

The Able God

Text: Daniel 3:17 - *If it be so, our God whom we serve is able to deliver us from the burning fiery furnace, and he will deliver us out of thine hand, O king.*

Affirmation of God's ability to deliver His people.

I. Knowing God's Power.

Philippians 3:10 – *"That I may know him, and the power of his resurrection, and the fellowship of his sufferings, being made conformable unto his death;"*

Jeremiah 33:3 – *"Call unto me, and I will answer thee, and show thee great and mighty things, which thou knowest not."*

Psalm 50:15 – *"And call upon me in the day of trouble: I will deliver thee, and thou shalt glorify me."*

II. Importance of seeking and acknowledging God's power.

Examples of God's Deliverance:

- Daniel's trust in God's ability:

Daniel 3:17 - *"If it be so, our God whom we serve is able to deliver us from the burning fiery furnace, and he will deliver us out of thine hand, O king."*

- Assurance of God's provision:

Philippians 4:19 – *"But my God shall supply all your need according to his riches in glory by Christ Jesus."*

III. Conclusion:

- Encouragement to trust in God's ability to intervene in every situation.

Great Faith

Text: Matthew 8:10 – *"When Jesus heard it, he marvelled, and said to them that followed, Verily I say unto you, I have not found so great faith, no, not in Israel."*

Definition: Great faith means obedience to God's Word.

I. Characteristics of Great Faith:

Matthew 8:8-9 – "*8 The centurion answered and said, Lord, I am not worthy that thou shouldest come under my roof: but speak the word only, and my servant shall be healed.*

9 For I am a man under authority, having soldiers under me: and I say to this man, Go, and he goeth; and to another, Come, and he cometh; and to my servant, Do this, and he doeth it."

Obedience as the essence of faith:

James 1:22 – "*But be ye doers of the word, and not hearers only, deceiving your own selves.*"

Luke 6:46 – "*And why call ye me, Lord, Lord, and do not the things which I say?*"

II. Examples of Great Faith:

- The Centurion's faith in Jesus' authority:

Matthew 8:13 – "*And Jesus said unto the centurion, Go thy way; and as thou hast believed, so be it done unto thee. And his servant was healed in the selfsame hour.*"

- There is power in the word:

Matthew 8:13 – "*And Jesus said unto the centurion, Go thy way; and as thou hast believed, so be it done unto thee. And his servant was healed in the selfsame hour.*"

John 11:39-40 – "*39 Jesus said, Take ye away the stone. Martha, the sister of him that was dead, saith unto him, Lord, by this time he stinketh: for he hath been dead four days.*

40 Jesus saith unto her, Said I not unto thee, that, if thou wouldest believe, thou shouldest see the glory of God?

III. Challenge to Obedience:

- Urging believers to align their actions with their faith.

We See Not Our Signs.

Text: Psalm 74:9 – "*We see not our signs: there is no more any prophet: neither is there among us any that knoweth how long.*"

Acknowledgment of spiritual blindness due to unbelief and lack of prayer.

I. Consequences of Unbelief and Prayerlessness:

Matthew 17:20-21 – *"And Jesus said unto them, Because of your unbelief: for verily I say unto you, If ye have faith as a grain of mustard seed, ye shall say unto this mountain, Remove hence to yonder place; and it shall remove; and nothing shall be impossible unto you.*

21 Howbeit this kind goeth not out but by prayer and fasting."

Luke 24:49 – *"And, behold, I send the promise of my Father upon you: but tarry ye in the city of Jerusalem, until ye be endued with power from on high."*

Luke 18:8 – *"I tell you that he will avenge them speedily. Nevertheless when the Son of man cometh, shall he find faith on the earth?"*

- Hindered prayer and lack of faith hindering the manifestation of God's power.

II. Revival Through Persistent Prayer:

The example of the early Church's prayer:

Acts 1:13 – *"And when they were come in, they went up into an upper room, where abode both Peter, and James, and John, and Andrew, Philip, and Thomas, Bartholomew, and Matthew, James the son of Alphaeus, and Simon Zelotes, and Judas the brother of James. 14 These all continued with one accord in prayer and supplication, with the women, and Mary the mother of Jesus, and with his brethren."*

Acts 2:1-4 – *"And when the day of Pentecost was fully come, they were all with one accord in one place.2 And suddenly there came a sound from heaven as of a rushing mighty wind, and it filled all the house where they were sitting.3 And there appeared unto them cloven tongues like as of fire, and it sat upon each of them.4 And they were all filled with the Holy Ghost, and began to speak with other tongues, as the Spirit gave them utterance."*

- Importance of perseverance in prayer until breakthrough.

III. Conclusion:

- Encouragement to stay connected to God through unceasing prayer for revival.

Obedience.

Text: Jonah 2:10 – *"And the Lord spake unto the fish, and it vomited out Jonah upon the dry land."*

Emphasis on obedience as crucial for experiencing God's blessings and favor.

I. The Nature of Obedience:

Definition and importance of obedience to God's Word.

Isaiah 1:19 – *"If ye be willing and obedient, ye shall eat the good of the land:"*

John 2:5 – *"His mother saith unto the servants, Whatsoever he saith unto you, do it."*

II. Obedience and Faith:

- Connection between obedience and great faith:

Matthew 8:9-10 – *"⁹ For I am a man under authority, having soldiers under me: and I say to this man, Go, and he goeth; and to another, Come, and he cometh; and to my servant, Do this, and he doeth it.*

¹⁰ When Jesus heard it, he marvelled, and said to them that followed, Verily I say unto you, I have not found so great faith, no, not in Israel."

John 11:39-40 – *"³⁹ Jesus said, Take ye away the stone. Martha, the sister of him that was dead, saith unto him, Lord, by this time he stinketh: for he hath been dead four days.*

⁴⁰ Jesus saith unto her, Said I not unto thee, that, if thou wouldest believe, thou shouldest see the glory of God?"

III. Challenge to Obedience:

- Invitation to examine one's obedience to God's commands.

Christ the Healer.

Text: Isaiah 53:5 – *"⁵ But he was wounded for our transgressions, he was bruised for our iniquities: the chastisement of our peace was upon him; and with his stripes we are healed."*

Recognition of Jesus as the ultimate source of healing and restoration.

I. The Healing Power of Jesus:

1 Peter 2:24 – *"²⁴ Who his own self bare our sins in his own body on the tree, that we, being dead to sins, should live unto righteousness: by whose stripes ye were healed."*

Psalm 103:2-3 – "² Bless the Lord, O my soul, and forget not all his benefits: ³ Who forgiveth all thine iniquities; who healeth all thy diseases;"

John 14:12-13 – "*12 Verily, verily, I say unto you, He that believeth on me, the works that I do shall he do also; and greater works than these shall he do; because I go unto my Father.*

13 And whatsoever ye shall ask in my name, that will I do, that the Father may be glorified in the Son."

Mark 16:20 – "*20 And they went forth, and preached every where, the Lord working with them, and confirming the word with signs following. Amen.*"

II. Demonstrating Faith in Healing:

- Examples of faith-filled actions leading to healing miracles.

   Matthew 10:7-8 – "*7 And as ye go, preach, saying, The kingdom of heaven is at hand. 8 Heal the sick, cleanse the lepers, raise the dead, cast out devils: freely ye have received, freely give.*"

III. Conclusion:

- Encouragement to trust in Jesus as the healer and proclaim His healing power.

The Move of God.

Text: 2 Chronicles 7:1 – "*Now when Solomon had made an end of praying, the fire came down from heaven, and consumed the burnt offering and the sacrifices; and the glory of the Lord filled the house.*"

Anticipation of God's manifested presence and power.

I. The Power of Prayer in Initiating God's Move:

   Luke 24:49 – "*49 And, behold, I send the promise of my Father upon you: but tarry ye in the city of Jerusalem, until ye be endued with power from on high.*"

The role of prayer in preparing the ground for God's intervention.

II. The Impact of God's Presence:

- Examples of the tangible manifestation of God's glory and power.

   Acts 2:1-4 – "*And when the day of Pentecost was fully come, they were all with one accord in one place*

   2 And suddenly there came a sound from heaven as of a rushing mighty wind, and it filled all the house where they were sitting.

³ And there appeared unto them cloven tongues like as of fire, and it sat upon each of them.

⁴ And they were all filled with the Holy Ghost, and began to speak with other tongues, as the Spirit gave them utterance."

III. Conclusion:

- Call to continual prayer and expectation of God's move in revival.

Stay on the Line.

Text: Luke 24:49 – *"⁴⁹ And, behold, I send the promise of my Father upon you: but tarry ye in the city of Jerusalem, until ye be endued with power from on high."*

The Divine Outlet: Connecting to God's Strength Through Prayer

I. Persistent Prayer and Its Results:

Psalm 50:15 – *"¹⁵ And call upon me in the day of trouble: I will deliver thee, and thou shalt glorify me."*

Acts 1:14 – *"¹⁴ These all continued with one accord in prayer and supplication, with the women, and Mary the mother of Jesus, and with his brethren."*

II. Examples of Persistent Prayer:

- Elijah's perseverance for rain.

1 Kings 18:43-44 – *"⁴³ And said to his servant, Go up now, look toward the sea. And he went up, and looked, and said, There is nothing. And he said, Go again seven times.*
⁴⁴ And it came to pass at the seventh time, that he said, Behold, there ariseth a little cloud out of the sea, like a man's hand. And he said, Go up, say unto Ahab, Prepare thy chariot, and get thee down that the rain stop thee not."

- The disciples' prayer in the upper room.

Acts 2:1-4 – *"And when the day of Pentecost was fully come, they were all with one accord in one place.*
² And suddenly there came a sound from heaven as of a rushing mighty wind, and it filled all the house where they were sitting.
³ And there appeared unto them cloven tongues like as of fire, and it sat upon each of them.

4 And they were all filled with the Holy Ghost, and began to speak with other tongues, as the Spirit gave them utterance."

III. Conclusion:

- Encouragement to maintain a posture of prayer without ceasing.

Prayer is the Master Key.

Text: Matthew 18:18 – *"18 Verily I say unto you, Whatsoever ye shall bind on earth shall be bound in heaven: and whatsoever ye shall loose on earth shall be loosed in heaven."*

Affirmation of prayer's authority and effectiveness.

I. Unlocking Faith Through Prayer:

John 14:13 – *"13 And whatsoever ye shall ask in my name, that will I do, that the Father may be glorified in the Son."*

Psalm 50:15 – *"15 And call upon me in the day of trouble: I will deliver thee, and thou shalt glorify me."*

Ephesians 3:20 – *" 20 Now unto him that is able to do exceeding abundantly above all that we ask or think, according to the power that worketh in us,"*

- Provide testimonies of answered prayers in Scripture.

II. The Power of Corporate Prayer:

- Example of the praying Church:

Acts 12:5 - 7 *"5 Peter therefore was kept in prison: but prayer was made without ceasing of the church unto God for him.*

6 And when Herod would have brought him forth, the same night Peter was sleeping between two soldiers, bound with two chains: and the keepers before the door kept the prison.

7 And, behold, the angel of the Lord came upon him, and a light shined in the prison: and he smote Peter on the side, and raised him up, saying, Arise up quickly. And his chains fell off from his hands."

Act 12:10 *"10 When they were past the first and the second ward, they came unto the iron gate that leadeth unto the city; which opened to them of his own accord: and they went out, and passed on through one street; and forthwith the angel departed from him."*

- The authority given through prayer:

Matthew 16:19 – *"¹⁹ And I will give unto thee the keys of the kingdom of heaven: and whatsoever thou shalt bind on earth shall be bound in heaven: and whatsoever thou shalt loose on earth shall be loosed in heaven."*

III. Conclusion:

- Invitation to engage in fervent and expectant prayer.

Salvation Plus.

Text: Matthew 6:33 – *"³³ But seek ye first the kingdom of God, and his righteousness; and all these things shall be added unto you."*

Priority of seeking the kingdom of God and righteousness.

I. Salvation First:

- Importance of being born again and becoming children of God.

- Significance of righteousness in exalting a nation.

II. The Plus of Salvation:

- Liberation from sin's reproach:

Romans 3:23 – *"²³ For all have sinned, and come short of the glory of God;*

Romans 6:23 – *"²³ For the wages of sin is death; but the gift of God is eternal life through Jesus Christ our Lord."*

- God's abundant provision:

Romans 8:32 - *"³² He that spared not his own Son, but delivered him up for us all, how shall he not with him also freely give us all things?"*

John 3:16 - *"¹⁶ For God so loved the world, that he gave his only begotten Son, that whosoever believeth in him should not perish, but have everlasting life."*

John 1:12 – *"¹² But as many as received him, to them gave he power to become the sons of God, even to them that believe on his name:"*

III. Hindrance to Receiving the Plus:

- Overcoming unbelief:

Matthew 17:20 – *"²⁰ And Jesus said unto them, Because of your unbelief: for verily I say unto you, If ye have faith as a grain of mustard seed, ye shall say unto this mountain, Remove hence to yonder place; and it shall remove; and nothing shall be impossible unto you."*

Receiving the "plus" through prayer:

Matthew 17:21 – "*²¹ Howbeit this kind goeth not out but by prayer and fasting.*"

Mark 10:27 – "*²⁷ And Jesus looking upon them saith, With men it is impossible, but not with God: for with God all things are possible.*

Philippians 4:19 – "*¹⁹ But my God shall supply all your need according to his riches in glory by Christ Jesus.*

God Can Do Anything.

Text: Mark 10:27 – "*²⁷ And Jesus looking upon them saith, With men it is impossible, but not with God: for with God all things are possible.*"

Affirmation of God's omnipotence and sovereignty.

I. The Impossibilities with Men, Possible with God:

- All power belongs to God as the creator:

  Luke 1:37 – "*³⁷ For with God nothing shall be impossible.*"

- God's mission of giving life and salvation:

  John 10:10 – "*¹⁰ The thief cometh not, but for to steal, and to kill, and to destroy: I am come that they might have life, and that they might have it more abundantly*"

  Luke 19:10 – "*¹⁰ For the Son of man is come to seek and to save that which was lost.*"

II. Overcoming Unbelief for Miracles:

- Accessing the miraculous through faith and prayer.

The Death of Lazarus.

Text: John 11:25 – *"25 Jesus said unto her, I am the resurrection, and the life: he that believeth in me, though he were dead, yet shall he live:"*

Declaration of Jesus as the resurrection and the life.

I. Jesus' Command and Promise:

- Command to remove the stone despite doubt:

  John 11:39-40 – *"39 Jesus said, Take ye away the stone. Martha, the sister of him that was dead, saith unto him, Lord, by this time he stinketh: for he hath been dead four days.*

  40 Jesus saith unto her, Said I not unto thee, that, if thou wouldest believe, thou shouldest see the glory of God?"

- Belief leading to witnessing the glory of God:

  John 11:43-44 – *"43 And when he thus had spoken, he cried with a loud voice, Lazarus, come forth.*

  44 And he that was dead came forth, bound hand and foot with graveclothes: and his face was bound about with a napkin. Jesus saith unto them, Loose him, and let him go."

II. Standing in Faith and Believing for Miracles:

- Examples of faith leading to miraculous outcomes:

  Luke 9:1-2 – *"Then he called his twelve disciples together, and gave them power and authority over all devils, and to cure diseases.*

  2 And he sent them to preach the kingdom of God, and to heal the sick.

  Mark 16:17-18 *"And these signs shall follow them that believe; In my name shall they cast out devils; they shall speak with new tongues;*

  18 They shall take up serpents; and if they drink any deadly thing, it shall not hurt them; they shall lay hands on the sick, and they shall recover."

<u>More Than Enough.</u>

Text: Ephesians 3:20 – *"Now unto him that is able to do exceeding abundantly above all that we ask or think, according to the power that worketh in us,*

Acknowledgment of God's ability to exceed expectations.

I. God's Abundant Provision:

- His love and salvation:

  John 3:16 *"For God so loved the world, that he gave his only begotten Son, that whosoever believeth in him should not perish, but have everlasting life."*

  Matthew 6:33 *"But seek ye first the kingdom of God, and his righteousness; and all these things shall be added unto you."*

  Psalm 103:2-3 *"Bless the LORD, O my soul, And forget none of His benefits;*

  3Who pardons all your iniquities, Who heals all your diseases;

- Examples of miraculous provision:

  Luke 9:10-17 – "When the apostles returned, they gave an account to Him of all that they had done. Taking them with Him, He withdrew by Himself to a city called Bethsaida. *11But the crowds were aware of this and followed Him; and welcoming them, He began speaking to them about the kingdom of God and curing those who had need of healing. 12Now the day was ending, and the twelve came and said to Him,* "Send the crowd away, that they may go into the surrounding villages and countryside and find lodging and get something to eat; for here we are in a desolate place." *13 But He said to them,* "You give them something to eat!" *And they said,* "We have no more than five loaves and two fish, unless perhaps we go and buy food for all these people." *14(For there were about five thousand men.) And He said to His disciples,* "Have them sit down to eat in groups of about fifty each." *15They did so, and had them all sit down. 16Then He took the five loaves and the two fish, and looking up to heaven, He blessed them, and broke them, and kept giving them to the disciples to set before the people. 17And they all ate and were satisfied; and the broken pieces which they had left over were picked up, twelve baskets full."*

II. The Key of Prayer:

- Accessing God's abundance through prayer:
- Hebrews 4:16 – *"Let us therefore come boldly unto the throne of grace, that we may obtain mercy, and find grace to help in time of need."*

Confession of Faith.

Text: Romans 10:9 – *"That if thou shalt confess with thy mouth the Lord Jesus, and shalt believe in thine heart that God hath raised him from the dead, thou shalt be saved."*

Joel 3:10 - *"Beat your plowshares into swords, and your pruninghooks into spears: let the weak say, I am strong."*

Introduction:

- Emphasis on the power of confessing faith in Jesus.

I. Faith in Action:

- Preaching and living by the Word of Faith: Romans 10:8 - *"But what saith it? The word is nigh thee, even in thy mouth, and in thy heart: that is, the word of faith, which we preach."*

- The substance and evidence of faith: Hebrews 11:1 – *"Now faith is the substance of things hoped for, the evidence of things not seen."*

  2 Corinthians 5:7 – *"For we walk by faith, not by sight."*

II. The Power of Confession:

- Using words to align with God's promises: Proverbs 18:21 – *"Death and life are in the power of the tongue: and they that love it shall eat the fruit thereof."*

Unchangeable God.

Text: Malachi 3:6 - *"For I am the Lord, I change not; therefore ye sons of Jacob are not consumed."*

Introduction:

- Recognition of God's unchanging nature and omnipotence.

I. Knowing the Unchangeable God:

- His eternal nature and power: Hebrews 13:8 – *"Jesus Christ the same yesterday, and today, and forever."*

John 17:3 – *"And this is life eternal, that they might know thee the only true God, and Jesus Christ, whom thou hast sent."*

II. Miracles Through Faith and Belief:

- Examples of miraculous interventions: John 11:39-44 – *Jesus said, Take ye away the stone. Martha, the sister of him that was dead, saith unto him, Lord, by this time he stinketh: for he hath been dead four days. 40. Jesus saith unto her, Said I not unto thee, that, if thou wouldest believe, thou shouldest see the glory of God? 41. Then they took away the stone from the place where the dead was laid. And Jesus lifted up his eyes, and said, Father, I thank thee that thou hast heard me. 42. And I knew that thou hearest me always: but because of the people which stand by I said it, that they may believe that thou hast sent me. 43. And when he thus had spoken, he cried with a loud voice, Lazarus, come forth. 44. And he that was dead came forth, bound hand and foot with graveclothes: and his face was bound about with a napkin. Jesus saith unto them, Loose him, and let him go.*

Only Believe.

Text: John 11:40 – *"Jesus saith unto her, Said I not unto thee, that, if thou wouldest believe, thou shouldest see the glory of God?"*

Introduction:

- Encouragement to believe in God's ability to perform miracles.

I. All Things Are Possible with God:

- Overcoming unbelief: Mark 10:27 – *"And Jesus looking upon them saith, With men it is impossible, but not with God: for with God all things are possible."*

  Romans 3:23 *"For all have sinned, and come short of the glory of God."*

- Building faith through hearing God's Word: Romans 10:17 – *"So then faith cometh by hearing, and hearing by the word of God."*

II. Receiving Salvation and Healing Through Faith:

- Examples of faith leading to salvation and healing: John 20:31 – *"But these are written, that ye might believe that Jesus is the Christ, the Son of God; and that believing ye might have life through his name."*

Mark 5:25-28 (KJV) – *"And a certain woman, which had an issue of blood twelve years, 26. And had suffered many things of many physicians, and had spent all that she had, and was nothing bettered, but rather grew worse," 27. When she had heard of Jesus, came in the press behind, and touched his garment." 28. For she said, If I may touch but his clothes, I shall be whole."*

- Acts 16:30-31 (KJV) – *"And brought them out, and said, Sirs, what must I do to be saved? 31. And they said, Believe on the Lord Jesus Christ, and thou shalt be saved, and* *thy* *house.*

Revival of Obedience.

Text: Isaiah 1:19 – *"If ye be willing and obedient, ye shall eat the good of the land."*

Introduction:

- Call for a revival marked by obedience to God's commands.

I. The Necessity of Obedience:

- Obedience as a key to blessings: Luke 9:1-2 – *"Then he called his twelve disciples together, and gave them power and authority over all devils, and to cure diseases. 2. And he sent them to preach the kingdom of God, and to heal the sick."*

- Examples of obedience leading to signs and wonders: Acts 1:13 – *"And when they were come in, they went up into an upper room, where abode both Peter, and James, and John, and Andrew, Philip, and Thomas, Bartholomew, and Matthew, James the son of Alphaeus, and Simon Zelotes, and Judas the brother of James."*

- *Mark 16:15-20 – "And he said unto them, Go ye into all the world, and preach the gospel to every creature. 16. He that believeth and is baptized shall be saved; but he that believeth not shall be damned. 17. And these signs shall follow them that believe; In my name shall they cast out devils; they shall speak with new tongues; 18. They shall take up serpents; and if they drink any deadly thing, it shall not hurt them; they shall lay hands on the sick, and they shall recover. 19. So then after the Lord had spoken unto them, he was received up into heaven, and sat on the right hand of God. 20. And they went forth, and preached every where, the Lord working with them, and confirming the word with signs following. Amen."*

II. Embracing Obedience as a Lifestyle:

- Challenge to walk in obedience to God's Word: Luke 6:46 – *"And why call ye me, Lord, Lord, and do not the things which I say?"*

Power to Heal the Sick.

Text: Matthew 10:8 – *"Heal the sick, cleanse the lepers, raise the dead, cast out devils: freely ye have received, freely give."*

Introduction:

- Emphasis on the command to heal the sick.

I. Christ the Healer:

- Reference to Exodus 15:26b – *"...for I am the Lord that healeth thee."*

  Acts 10:38 (KJV) – *"How God anointed Jesus of Nazareth with the Holy Ghost and with power: who went about doing good, and healing all that were oppressed of the devil; for God was with him."*

- Jesus' ministry of healing as an expression of God's power and presence.

II. Addressing Unbelief:

- Explanation of why many sick people remain in the church.

- Importance of faith and belief for experiencing miracles: Matthew 17:20 – *"And Jesus said unto them, Because of your unbelief: for verily I say unto you, If ye have faith as a grain of mustard seed, ye shall say unto this mountain, Remove hence to yonder place; and it shall remove; and nothing shall be impossible unto you."*

  Mark 16:17-18 (KJV) – *"And these signs shall follow them that believe; In my name shall they cast out devils; they shall speak with new tongues;"* 18. *"They shall take up serpents; and if they drink any deadly thing, it shall not hurt them; they shall lay hands on the sick, and they shall recover."*.

III. The Role of Prayer in Healing:

- Instruction to pray for the sick: James 5:14-15 – *"Is any sick among you? let him call for the elders of the church; and let them pray over him, anointing him with oil in the name of the Lord: 15. And the prayer of faith shall save the sick, and the Lord shall raise him up; and if he have committed sins, they shall be forgiven him."*

- Acknowledgment of the Lord's power to heal: Luke 5:17 – *"And it came to pass on a certain day, as he was teaching, that there were Pharisees and doctors of the law sitting by, which were come out of every town of Galilee, and Judaea, and Jerusalem: and the power of the Lord was present to heal them."*

Conclusion:

- Affirmation of Christ's redemptive work to free humanity from the curse of sickness: Galatians 3:13 – *"Christ hath redeemed us from the curse of the law, being made a curse for us: for it is written, Cursed is every one that hangeth on a tree:"*

- Hebrews 13:8 (KJV) – *"Jesus Christ the same yesterday, and today, and forever."*

Called to Go.

Text: Mark 16:15 – *"And he said unto them, Go ye into all the world, and preach the gospel to every creature."*

Introduction:

- Commissioning believers to go forth and bear fruit.

I. Chosen and Ordained:

- Reference to John 15:16 – *"Ye have not chosen me, but I have chosen you, and ordained you, that ye should go and bring forth fruit, and that your fruit should remain: that whatsoever ye shall ask of the Father in my name, he may give it you."*

  Luke 9:1-2 (KJV) – *"Then he called his twelve disciples together, and gave them power and authority over all devils, and to cure diseases. 2. And he sent them to preach the kingdom of God, and to heal the sick."*

- Obedience leading to salvation and healing: Luke 9:6 – *"And they departed, and went through the towns, preaching the gospel, and healing every where."*

II. Signs Following Obedience:

- Examples of souls saved and healed through obedience: Mark 16:17-18 – • *"And these signs shall follow them that believe; In my name shall they cast out devils; they shall speak with new tongues; 18. They shall take up serpents; and if they drink any deadly thing, it shall not hurt them; they shall lay hands on the sick, and they shall recover."*

- Joy in cities due to the preaching of Christ: Acts 8:5 – *"Then Philip went down to the city of Samaria, and preached Christ unto them."*

  Acts 8:8 (KJV) – *"And there was great joy in that city."*

III. The Necessity of Sending:

- Urgency in sending preachers to proclaim the Gospel.

__Faith to Heal.__

Text: Acts 14:8 – *"And there sat a certain man at Lystra, impotent in his feet, being a cripple from his mother's womb, who had never walked."*

Introduction:

- Recognizing faith as a prerequisite for healing.

I. The Power of Faith:

- Faith in God's Word and promises: Hebrews 11:6 – *"But without faith it is impossible to please him: for he that cometh to God must believe that he is, and that he is a rewarder of them that diligently seek him."*

- Overcoming unbelief: Daniel 3:17 – *"If it be so, our God whom we serve is able to deliver us from the burning fiery furnace, and he will deliver us out of thine hand, O king."*

II. Salvation Plus:

- Linking faith with salvation and healing: Matthew 6:33 – *"But seek ye first the kingdom of God, and his righteousness; and all these things shall be added unto you."*

  Psalm 103:2-3 (KJV) – *"Bless the Lord, O my soul, and forget not all his benefits: 3.Who forgiveth all thine iniquities; who healeth all thy diseases;"*

  1 Peter 2:24 (KJV) – *"Who his own self bare our sins in his own body on the tree, that we, being dead to sins, should live unto righteousness: by whose stripes ye were healed."*

III. Examples of Faith Leading to Healing:

- Stories of individuals healed through faith: Mark 5:28 – *"For she said, If I may touch but his clothes, I shall be whole."*

  Acts 16:30-31 (KJV) – *"And brought them out, and said, Sirs, what must I do to be saved? 31. And they said, Believe on the Lord Jesus Christ, and thou shalt be saved, and thy house.*

God's Royal Telephone.

Text: Psalm 50:15 – *"And call upon me in the day of trouble: I will deliver thee, and thou shalt glorify me."*

Introduction:

- Highlighting prayer as the means of communication with God.

I. The Importance of Prayer:

- Prayer as the key to unlock blessings: Matthew 18:18 – *"Verily I say unto you, Whatsoever ye shall bind on earth shall be bound in heaven: and whatsoever ye shall loose on earth shall be loosed in heaven."*

  Jeremiah 33:3 (KJV) – *"Call unto me, and I will answer thee, and show thee great and mighty things, which thou knowest not."*

- Encouragement to pray without ceasing: Luke 18:7-8 – *"And shall not God avenge his own elect, which cry day and night unto him, though he bear long with them? 8. I tell you that he will avenge them speedily. Nevertheless when the Son of man cometh, shall he find faith on the earth?"*

-

II. God's Promise to Answer Prayer:

- Assurance of God's response to prayer: John 14:13 – *"And whatsoever ye shall ask in my name, that will I do, that the Father may be glorified in the Son."*

  Romans 10:13 (KJV) – *"For whosoever shall call upon the name of the Lord shall be saved."*

III. Power in Prayer:

- Linking prayer with healing and miracles: Matthew 10:8 – *"Heal the sick, cleanse the lepers, raise the dead, cast out devils: freely ye have received, freely give."*

- Matthew 21:22 (KJV) – *"And all things, whatsoever ye shall ask in prayer, believing, ye shall receive."*

Jesus is Lord.

Text: Philippians 2:11 – *"And that every tongue should confess that Jesus Christ is Lord, to the glory of God the Father."*

Introduction:

- Confession of Jesus as Lord and His supremacy.

I. Confession of Faith:

- Acknowledging Jesus' authority over death, Satan, and sickness: Matthew 28:18 – *"And Jesus came and spake unto them, saying, All power is given unto me in heaven and in earth."*

II. The Power of Confession:

- Importance of confessing faith in Jesus for miracles and victory: Proverbs 18:21 – *"Death and life are in the power of the tongue: and they that love it shall eat the fruit thereof."*

  Joel 3:10 – *"Beat your plowshares into swords and your pruninghooks into spears: let the weak say, I am strong."*

III. Living by Faith:

- Call to live by faith and declare Jesus' lordship.

Heal the Sick.

Text: Matthew 10:8 – *"Heal the sick, cleanse the lepers, raise the dead, cast out devils: freely ye have received, freely give."*

Introduction:

- Emphasis on the command to heal the sick.

I. The Two Commissions:

- Preaching the kingdom of God and healing the sick: Luke 9:1-2 – *"Then he called his twelve disciples together, and gave them power and authority over all devils, and to cure diseases. 2. And he sent them to preach the kingdom of God, and to heal the sick."*

II. Faith in Action:

- Linking faith with healing: Mark 11:22 – *"And Jesus answering saith unto them, Have faith in God."*

- Romans 10:17 (KJV) – *"So then faith cometh by hearing, and hearing by the word of God."*

  Hebrews 11:6 (KJV) – *"But without faith it is impossible to please him: for he that cometh to God must believe that he is, and that he is a rewarder of them that diligently seek him."*

III. Miraculous Works of Jesus:

- Examples of Jesus' healing ministry and His power present today.

There Any in the Midst of Them.

Text: Matthew 18:20 – *"For where two or three are gathered together in my name, there am I in the midst of them."*

Introduction:

- Affirmation of Christ's presence among believers.

I. Faith in God:

- Encouragement to have faith in God and His promises: Mark 11:22 –*"And Jesus answering saith unto them, Have faith in God."*

II. All Things Possible:

- Belief in the possibility of miracles: Mark 10:27 – *"And Jesus looking upon them saith, With men it is impossible, but not with God: for with God all things are possible."*

- Mark 16:17-18 (KJV) –*"And these signs shall follow them that believe; In my name shall they cast out devils; they shall speak with new tongues;" 18. They shall take up serpents; and if they drink any deadly thing, it shall not hurt them; they shall lay hands on the sick, and they shall recover."*

III. The Power of Belief:

- Instruction to lay hands on the sick and believe for healing.

Faith in God.

Text: Mark 11:22 – *"And Jesus answering saith unto them, Have faith in God."*

Introduction:

- Emphasis on the importance of faith in God.

I. Examples of Faith Leading to Healing:

- Stories of individuals healed through faith: Mark 5:25-29 – *"And a certain woman, which had an issue of blood twelve years, 26. And had suffered many things of many physicians, and had spent all that she had, and was nothing bettered, but rather grew worse, 27. When she had heard of Jesus, came in the press behind, and touched his garment. 28. For she said, If I may touch but his clothes, I shall be whole. 29. And straightway the fountain of her blood was dried up; and she felt in her body that she was healed of that plague."*

- Luke 17:14 (KJV) – *"And when he saw them, he said unto them, Go shew yourselves unto the priests. And it came to pass, that, as they went, they were cleansed."*

- ## II. Faith Comes by Hearing:

- Encouragement to build faith through hearing God's Word: Romans 10:17 – *"So then faith cometh by hearing, and hearing by the word of God."*

III. Belief in God's Power:

- Affirmation of God's ability to heal and deliver.

Unbelieving Believer.

Text: John 11:39 – *"Jesus said, Take ye away the stone. Martha, the sister of him that was dead, saith unto him, Lord, by this time he stinketh: for he hath been dead four days."*

Introduction:

- Addressing unbelief among believers.

I. Faith to Believe:

- Importance of believing God's Word and acting in faith: Romans 4:3 – *"For what saith the Scripture? Abraham believed God, and it was counted unto him for righteousness."*

- John 14:12-13 (KJV) – *"Verily, verily, I say unto you, He that believeth on me, the works that I do shall he do also; and greater works than these shall he do; because I go unto my Father. 13. And whatsoever ye shall ask in my name, that will I do, that the Father may be glorified in the Son."*

II. The Challenge of Unbelief:

- Exhortation to overcome unbelief and do the works of Jesus: Psalm 50:15 – *"And call upon me in the day of trouble: I will deliver thee, and thou shalt glorify me."*

  Mark 9:23 (KJV) – *"Jesus said unto him, If thou canst believe, all things are possible to him that believeth."*

  III. Time for Believing Believers:

- Urgency in becoming believers who act in faith and obedience.

Doing the Same Work Jesus Did.

Text: John 14:12 – *"Verily, verily, I say unto you, He that believeth on me, the works that I do shall he do also; and greater works than these shall he do; because I go unto my Father."*

Introduction:

- Affirmation of believers' ability to perform the works of Jesus.

I. The Work of Jesus:

- Preaching, teaching, and healing: Matthew 4:23 – *"And Jesus went about all Galilee, teaching in their synagogues, and preaching the gospel of the kingdom, and healing all manner of sickness and all manner of disease among the people."*

  Matthew 10:1 – *"And when he had called unto him his twelve disciples, he gave them power against unclean spirits, to cast them out, and to heal all manner of sickness and all manner of disease."*

II. Signs Following Belief:

- Assurance of signs accompanying those who believe: John 14:12 – *"Verily, verily, I say unto you, He that believeth on me, the works that I do shall he do also; and greater works than these shall he do; because I go unto my Father."*

  Mark 16:17 – *"And these signs shall follow them that believe; In my name shall they cast out devils; they shall speak with new tongues;"*

III. Belief in God's Power:

- Encouragement to believe for healing and deliverance in Jesus' name.

Pouring Out Our Souls: Lessons from Hannah's Prayer.

Text: 1 Samuel 1:15b – *"I have drunk neither wine nor strong drink, but have poured out my soul before the LORD."*

I. Seriousness in Prayer (1 Samuel 1:8-10, 12-13)

"Then said Elkanah her husband to her, Hannah, why weepest thou? and why eatest thou not? and why is thy heart grieved? am not I better to thee than ten sons? So Hannah rose up after they had eaten in Shiloh, and after they had drunk. Now Eli the priest sat upon a seat by a post of the temple of the Lord. And she was in bitterness of soul, and prayed unto the Lord, and wept sore." (1 Samuel 1:8-10)

"And it came to pass, as she continued praying before the Lord, that Eli marked her mouth. Now Hannah, she spake in her heart; only her lips moved, but her voice was not heard: therefore Eli thought she had been drunken." (1 Samuel 1:12-13)

II. Making Vows to God (1 Samuel 1:11)

"And she vowed a vow, and said, O Lord of hosts, if thou wilt indeed look on the affliction of thine handmaid, and remember me, and not forget thine handmaid, but

wilt give unto thine handmaid a man child, then I will give him unto the Lord all the days of his life, and there shall no razor come upon his head." (1 Samuel 1:11)

III. Watchfulness in Prayer (1 Samuel 2:6-7)

"The Lord killeth, and maketh alive: he bringeth down to the grave, and bringeth up. The Lord maketh poor, and maketh rich: he bringeth low, and lifteth up." (1 Samuel 2:6-7)

IV. Humility in Prayer (1 Samuel 1:13-16)

"Now Hannah, she spake in her heart; only her lips moved, but her voice was not heard: therefore Eli thought she had been drunken. And Eli said unto her, How long wilt thou be drunken? put away thy wine from thee. And Hannah answered and said, No, my lord, I am a woman of a sorrowful spirit: I have drunk neither wine nor strong drink, but have poured out my soul before the Lord. Count not thine handmaid for a daughter of Belial: for out of the abundance of my complaint and grief have I spoken hitherto." (1 Samuel 1:13-16)

V. The Answer to Prayer (1 Samuel 1:17-20)

"Then Eli answered and said, Go in peace: and the God of Israel grant thee thy petition that thou hast asked of him. And she said, Let thine handmaid find grace in thy sight. So the woman went her way, and did eat, and her countenance was no more sad." (1 Samuel 1:17-18)

"Wherefore it came to pass, when the time was come about after Hannah had conceived, that she bare a son, and called his name Samuel, saying, Because I have asked him of the Lord." (1 Samuel 1:20)

Prayer from the Heart Brings Fire.

Text: 2 Chronicles 7:1

I. The Need for God's Glory (2 Chronicles 7:1)

"Now when Solomon had made an end of praying, the fire came down from heaven, and consumed the burnt offering and the sacrifices; and the glory of the Lord filled the house." (2 Chronicles 7:1)

II. Identifying Sin as the Barrier (Romans 3:23)

"For all have sinned, and come short of the glory of God;" (Romans 3:23)

III. Elijah's Example (1 Kings 18:36-39)

"And it came to pass at the time of the offering of the evening sacrifice, that Elijah the prophet came near, and said, Lord God of Abraham, Isaac, and of Israel, let it be known this day that thou art God in Israel, and that I am thy servant, and that I have done all these things at thy word. Hear me, O Lord, hear me, that this people may know that thou art the Lord God, and that thou hast turned their heart back again. Then the fire of the Lord fell, and consumed the burnt sacrifice, and the wood, and the stones, and the dust, and licked up the water that was in the trench. And when all the people saw it, they fell on their faces: and they said, The Lord, he is the God; the Lord, he is the God." (1 Kings 18:36-39)

IV. God's Response to Genuine Prayer (2 Chronicles 7:2-3; Exodus 40:34-35)

"And the priests could not enter into the house of the Lord, because the glory of the Lord had filled the Lord's house. And when all the children of Israel saw how the fire came down, and the glory of the Lord upon the house, they bowed themselves with their faces to the ground upon the pavement, and worshipped, and praised the Lord, saying, For he is good; for his mercy endureth for ever." (2 Chronicles 7:2-3)

- *"Then a cloud covered the tent of the congregation, and the glory of the Lord filled the tabernacle."* (Exodus 40:34-35)

Prayer Offered from the Fish Belly.

Text: Jonah 2:1

I. Jonah's Revival (Jonah 1:6)

"So the shipmaster came to him, and said unto him, What meanest thou, O sleeper? arise, call upon thy God, if so be that God will think upon us, that we perish not." (Jonah 1:6)

II. Jonah's Serious Prayer (Jonah 2:2-3)

"And said, I cried by reason of mine affliction unto the Lord, and he heard me; out of the belly of hell cried I, and thou heardest my voice. For thou hadst cast me into the deep, in the midst of the seas; and the floods compassed me about: all thy billows and thy waves passed over me." (Jonah 2:2-3)

As He Did Aforetime.

Text: Daniel 6:10

I. Daniel's Consistent Prayer Life (Daniel 6:10)

"Now when Daniel knew that the writing was signed, he went into his house; and his windows being open in his chamber toward Jerusalem, he kneeled upon his knees three times a day, and prayed, and gave thanks before his God, as he did aforetime." (Daniel 6:10)

II. Jesus' Example of Prayer (Luke 22:39)

"And he came out, and went, as he was wont, to the mount of Olives; and his disciples also followed him." (Luke 22:39)

III. Peter's Devotion to Prayer (Acts 3:1)

"Now Peter and John went up together into the temple at the hour of prayer, being the ninth hour." (Acts 3:1)

Prayer of Faith.

Text: James 5:15a

I. God Still Answers Prayer (1 John 5:14-15)

"And this is the confidence that we have in him, that, if we ask any thing according to his will, he heareth us: And if we know that he hear us, whatsoever we ask, we know that we have the petitions that we desired of him." (1 John 5:14-15)

II. Believing Prayer (Matthew 21:18-22)

- *"And all things, whatsoever ye shall ask in prayer, believing, ye shall receive."* (Matthew 21:22)

Touch of Faith.

Text: Mark 5:28

I. Power in Touching (Mark 5:28)

"For she said, If I may touch but his clothes, I shall be whole." (Mark 5:28)

II. Peter's Shadows (Acts 5:12, 15)

"And by the hands of the apostles were many signs and wonders wrought among the people; (and they were all with one accord in Solomon's porch." (Acts 5:12)

"Insomuch that they brought forth the sick into the streets, and laid them on beds and couches, that at the least the shadow of Peter passing by might overshadow some of them." (Acts 5:15)

III. Paul's Handkerchiefs and Aprons (Acts 19:11-12)

> *"And God wrought special miracles by the hands of Paul: So that from his body were brought unto the sick handkerchiefs or aprons, and the diseases departed from them, and the evil spirits went out of them."* (Acts 19:11-12)

IV. Elijah's Mantle (2 Kings 2:14)

> *"And he took the mantle of Elijah that fell from him, and smote the waters, and said, Where is the Lord God of Elijah? and when he also had smitten the waters, they parted hither and thither: and Elisha went over."* (2 Kings 2:14)

Keep on the Fire of Prayer.

Text: Leviticus 6:13 – *"The fire shall ever be burning upon the altar; it shall never go out."*

I. Continuance in Prayer (Colossians 4:2, Isaiah 62:6-8)

> *"Continue in prayer, and watch in the same with thanksgiving;"* (Colossians 4:2)

> *"I have set watchmen upon thy walls, O Jerusalem, which shall never hold their peace day nor night: ye that make mention of the Lord, keep not silence, And give him no rest, till he establish, and till he make Jerusalem a praise in the earth."* (Isaiah 62:6-7)

II. Giving Yourself to Prayer (Acts 6:4)

> *"But we will give ourselves continually to prayer, and to the ministry of the word."* (Acts 6:4)

III. Bombarding Heaven Until Answer Comes (Genesis 32:24-32, Isaiah 62:7, 1 Thessalonians 5:17)

- *"And Jacob was left alone; and there wrestled a man with him until the breaking of the day."* (Genesis 32:24)

- *"And shall not God avenge his own elect, which cry day and night unto him, though he bear long with them?"* (Luke 18:7)

- *"Pray without ceasing."* (1 Thessalonians 5:17)

IV. Lifting Up the Hand of Prayer (Exodus 17:10-13)

> *"So Joshua did as Moses had said to him, and fought with Amalek: and Moses, Aaron, and Hur went up to the top of the hill. And it came to pass, when Moses held up his*

hand, that Israel prevailed: and when he let down his hand, Amalek prevailed."
(Exodus 17:10-11)

<u>Waiting upon God.</u>

Text: Psalm 27:14

I. Man's Sufficiency in God (2 Corinthians 3:5)

- *"Not that we are sufficient of ourselves to think any thing as of ourselves; but our sufficiency is of God;"* (2 Corinthians 3:5)

II. The Benefits of Waiting upon God (Isaiah 40:31)

- *"But they that wait upon the Lord shall renew their strength; they shall mount up with wings as eagles; they shall run, and not be weary; and they shall walk, and not faint."* (Isaiah 40:31)

III. The Need for Dependence on Him (John 15:4-7)

- *"Abide in me, and I in you. As the branch cannot bear fruit of itself, except it abide in the vine; no more can ye, except ye abide in me."* (John 15:4).

<u>The Sure Promises of God.</u>

Text: Isaiah 43:2

I. Need to Stand in God's Promise (Romans 4:21)

- *"And being fully persuaded that, what he had promised, he was able also to perform."* (Romans 4:21)

II. Application and Fulfillment of God's Promises (Daniel 3:17, 25-27)

- *"If it be so, our God whom we serve is able to deliver us from the burning fiery furnace, and he will deliver us out of thine hand, O king."* (Daniel 3:17)

- *"He answered and said, Lo, I see four men loose, walking in the midst of the fire, and they have no hurt; and the form of the fourth is like the Son of God."* (Daniel 3:25)

- *"And the princes, governors, and captains, and the king's counsellors, being gathered together, saw these men, upon whose bodies the fire had no power, nor was an hair of their head singed, neither were their coats changed, nor the smell of fire had passed on them."* (Daniel 3:27)

<u>The Knowledge of the Truth.</u>

Text: 2 Timothy 3:7 – *"Ever learning, and never able to come to the knowledge of the truth."*

I. God's Word is True (John 8:30)

"As he spake these words, many believed on him." (John 8:30)

"And ye shall know the truth, and the truth shall make you free." (John 8:32)

II. Importance of Studying the Truth (Joshua 1:8, 2 Timothy 2:15)

- *"This book of the law shall not depart out of thy mouth; but thou shalt meditate therein day and night, that thou mayest observe to do according to all that is written therein: for then thou shalt make thy way prosperous, and then thou shalt have good success."* (Joshua 1:8)

- *"Study to shew thyself approved unto God, a workman that needeth not to be ashamed, rightly dividing the word of truth."* (2 Timothy 2:15)

III. The Profit and Wisdom in the Truth (2 Timothy 3:15, 16-17)

- *"And that from a child thou hast known the holy scriptures, which are able to make thee wise unto salvation through faith which is in Christ Jesus."* (2 Timothy 3:15)

- *"All scripture is given by inspiration of God, and is profitable for doctrine, for reproof, for correction, for instruction in righteousness: That the man of God may be perfect, throughly furnished unto all good works."* (2 Timothy 3:16-17)

IV. Biblical Example: King Josiah (2 Kings 22:8-13)

- *"And Hilkiah the high priest said unto Shaphan the scribe, I have found the book of the law in the house of the Lord. And Hilkiah gave the book to Shaphan, and he read it."* (2 Kings 22:8)

- *"And Shaphan the scribe came to the king, and brought the king word again, and said, Thy servants have gathered the money that was found in the house, and have delivered it into the hand of them that do the work, that have the oversight of the house of the Lord."* (2 Kings 22:9-10)

- *"And it came to pass, when the king had heard the words of the book of the law, that he rent his clothes."* (2 Kings 22:11)

- *"Because thine heart was tender, and thou hast humbled thyself before the Lord, when thou heardest what I spake against this place, and against the inhabitants thereof, that they should become a desolation and a curse, and hast rent thy clothes, and wept before me; I also have heard thee, saith the Lord."* (2 Kings 22:19)

The Noble Church.

Text: Acts 17:11 – *"These were more noble than those in Thessalonica, in that they received the word with all readiness of mind, and searched the scriptures daily, whether those things were so."*

Jesus wants His church to be a glorious church. Ephesians 5:27 – *"That he might present it to himself a glorious church, not having spot, or wrinkle, or any such thing; but that it should be holy and without blemish."*

They heard the word. Acts 17:2-3 – *"And Paul, as his manner was, went in unto them, and three sabbath days reasoned with them out of the scriptures, Opening and alleging, that Christ must needs have suffered, and risen again from the dead; and that this Jesus, whom I preach unto you, is Christ."*

They believed the word. Acts 17:4 – *"And some of them believed, and consorted with Paul and Silas; and of the devout Greeks a great multitude, and of the chief women not a few."*

They received the word with readiness. Acts 17:11 – *"These were more noble than those in Thessalonica, in that they received the word with all readiness of mind, and searched the scriptures daily, whether those things were so."*

They searched the scriptures. Joshua 1:8 – *"This book of the law shall not depart out of thy mouth; but thou shalt meditate therein day and night, that thou mayest observe to do according to all that is written therein: for then thou shalt make thy way prosperous, and then thou shalt have good success."*

Faithful in stewardship. 2 Corinthians 8:1-5, Galatians 6:6

- *"Moreover, brethren, we do you to wit of the grace of God bestowed on the churches of Macedonia; How that in a great trial of affliction the abundance of their joy and their deep poverty abounded unto the riches of their liberality."* (2 Corinthians 8:1-2)

- *"Let him that is taught in the word communicate unto him that teacheth in all good things."* (Galatians 6:6)

Studied the word. 2 Timothy 2:15 – *"Study to shew thyself approved unto God, a workman that needeth not to be ashamed, rightly dividing the word of truth."*

Know the scripture. 2 Timothy 3:15 – *"And that from a child thou hast known the holy scriptures, which are able to make thee wise unto salvation through faith which is in Christ Jesus."*

Challenge: Know the truth and stand on it. John 8:31 – *"Then said Jesus to those Jews which believed on him, If ye continue in my word, then are ye my disciples indeed; And ye shall know the truth, and the truth shall make you free."*

The Benefit: Make you grow. 2 Peter 2:2 – *"As newborn babes, desire the sincere milk of the word, that ye may grow thereby:"*

Longsuffering.

Text: Colossians 1:11 – *"Strengthened with all might, according to his glorious power, unto all patience and longsuffering with joyfulness;"*

Longsuffering is one of the fruits of the Spirit. Galatians 5:22 – *"But the fruit of the Spirit is love, joy, peace, longsuffering, gentleness, goodness, faith,"*

The Bible Example: Job. James 5:11 – *"Behold, we count them happy which endure. Ye have heard of the patience of Job, and have seen the end of the Lord; that the Lord is very pitiful, and of tender mercy."* (James 5:11)

Who was Job? Job 1:1-2 – *"There was a man in the land of Uz, whose name was Job; and that man was perfect and upright, and one that feared God, and eschewed evil. And there were born unto him seven sons and three daughters."* (Job 1:1-2)

His suffering. Job 1:18-22 – *"While he was yet speaking, there came also another, and said, Thy sons and thy daughters were eating and drinking wine in their eldest brother's house: And, behold, there came a great wind from the wilderness, and smote the four corners of the house, and it fell upon the young men, and they are dead; and I only am escaped alone to tell thee."*

God's promise. 1 Corinthians 10:13 – *"There hath no temptation taken you but such as is common to man: but God is faithful, who will not suffer you to be tempted above that ye are able; but will with the temptation also make a way to escape, that ye may be able to bear it."* (1 Corinthians 10:13)

The weapon: Purpose. Job 13:15 – *"Though he slay me, yet will I trust in him: but I will maintain mine own ways before him."*

Breakthrough. Job 42:12-13 – *"So the Lord blessed the latter end of Job more than his beginning: for he had fourteen thousand sheep, and six thousand camels, and a thousand yoke of oxen, and a thousand she asses."*

Love.

Text: John 13:34 – *"A new commandment I give unto you, That ye love one another; as I have loved you, that ye also love one another."*

God is love. John 3:16, Romans 5:8

- *"For God so loved the world, that he gave his only begotten Son, that whosoever believeth in him should not perish, but have everlasting life."* (John 3:16)

- *"But God commendeth his love toward us, in that, while we were yet sinners, Christ died for us."* (Romans 5:8)

Jesus is love. John 10:15-18

- *"As the Father knoweth me, even so know I the Father: and I lay down my life for the sheep."*

Believers identification on John 13:35

- *"By this shall all men know that ye are my disciples, if ye have love one to another."*

What is Love? 1 Corinthians 13:4-8, 1 John 3:16-18

- *"Charity suffereth long, and is kind; charity envieth not; charity vaunteth not itself, is not puffed up, Doth not behave itself unseemly, seeketh not her own, is not easily provoked, thinketh no evil;"* (1 Corinthians 13:4-5)

- *"Hereby perceive we the love of God, because he laid down his life for us: and we ought to lay down our lives for the brethren."* (1 John 3:16)

The extension of Love. Matthew 5:43-48, Romans 12:20

- *"But I say unto you, Love your enemies, bless them that curse you, do good to them that hate you, and pray for them which despitefully use you, and persecute you;"* (Matthew 5:44)

- *"Therefore if thine enemy hunger, feed him; if he thirst, give him drink: for in so doing thou shalt heap coals of fire on his head."* (Romans 12:20)

Self Denial.

Text: Mark 8:34 – *"And when he had called the people unto him with his disciples also, he said unto them, Whosoever will come after me, let him deny himself, and take up his cross, and follow me."*

Cost of discipleship. Matthew 16:24-27, Luke 9:23-26, 1 Thessalonians 3:3, 2 Thessalonians 3:12

- *"Then said Jesus unto his disciples, If any man will come after me, let him deny himself, and take up his cross, and follow me."* (Matthew 16:24)

No Self-Denial will not make it. Matthew 10:38

- *"And he that taketh not his cross, and followeth after me, is not worthy of me."* (Matthew 10:38)

Challenge: Sold out for God. Matthew 19:21

- *"Jesus said unto him, If thou wilt be perfect, go and sell that thou hast, and give to the poor, and thou shalt have treasure in heaven: and come and follow me."* (Matthew 19:21)

Rapture.

Text: 1 Thessalonians 4:16-17 – *"For the Lord himself shall descend from heaven with a shout, with the voice of the archangel, and with the trump of God: and the dead in Christ shall rise first: Then we which are alive and remain shall be caught up together with them in the clouds, to meet the Lord in the air: and so shall we ever be with the Lord."* (1 Thessalonians 4:16-17)

How it will happen? In a moment. 1 Corinthians 15:52

"In a moment, in the twinkling of an eye, at the last trump: for the trumpet shall sound, and the dead shall be raised incorruptible, and we shall be changed." (1 Corinthians 15:52)

It is Christian blessed hope. 1 Corinthians 15:19, 1 Thessalonians 4:13-15, 2 Peter 3:13

"If in this life only we have hope in Christ, we are of all men most miserable." (1 Corinthians 15:19)

How? We shall be change. 1 Corinthians 15:51-52

"Behold, I shew you a mystery; We shall not all sleep, but we shall all be changed," (1 Corinthians 15:51)

Celestial body (Heavenly body) 1 Corinthians 15:40

"There are also celestial bodies, and bodies terrestrial: but the glory of the celestial is one, and the glory of the terrestrial is another." (1 Corinthians 15:40)

The rapture: Matthew 24:40-41

"Then shall two be in the field; the one shall be taken, and the other left. 41. Two women shall be grinding at the mill; the one shall be taken, and the other left."

Ye are not of the world.

Text: John 17:14b – *"and the world hath hated them, because they are not of the world, even as I am not of the world."*

- Call out from the world 2 Corinthians 6:17 *"Wherefore come out from among them, and be ye separate, saith the Lord, and touch not the unclean thing; and I will receive you,"*

  Commandment of God to the believers set not your affection on the things of the world. Colossians 3:1-2

  "If ye then be risen with Christ, seek those things which are above, where Christ sitteth on the right hand of God." (Colossians 3:1)

- Love not – 1 John 2:15

  "Love not the world, neither the things that are in the world. If any man love the world, the love of the Father is not in him." (1 John 2:15)

- Be not friend of – James 4:4

  "Ye adulterers and adulteresses, know ye not that the friendship of the world is enmity with God? whosoever therefore will be a friend of the world is the enemy of God."

- Speak not as (sanctification) 1 John 4:5, Ephesians 4:29, Ephesians 5:3-4.

  "They are of the world: therefore speak they of the world, and the world heareth them." (1 John 4:5)

Steadfastness.

Text: Colossians 2:5b – *"For though I be absent in the flesh, yet am I with you in the spirit, joying and beholding your order, and the steadfastness of your faith in Christ."*

- Why does it need to be steadfast?

  "That we henceforth be no more children, tossed to and fro, and carried about with every wind of doctrine, by the sleight of men, and cunning craftiness, whereby they lie in wait to deceive;" (Ephesians 4:14)

- It is the foundation of Christianity – Acts 2:42

  "And they continued stedfastly in the apostles' doctrine and fellowship, and in breaking of bread, and in prayers." (Acts 2:42)

- It make Christian to be overcomers. 1 Peter 5:8-9

- *"Be sober, be vigilant; because your adversary the devil, as a roaring lion, walketh about, seeking whom he may devour: Whom resist stedfast in the faith, knowing that the same afflictions are accomplished in your brethren that are in the world."* (1 Peter 5:8-9)

- It is a key to Christian goal (HEAVEN) 1 Corinthians 15:58, Colossians 4:2-4

  "Therefore, my beloved brethren, be ye stedfast, unmoveable, always abounding in the work of the Lord, forasmuch as ye know that your labour is not in vain in the Lord." (1 Corinthians 15:58)

- *2. "Continue in prayer, and watch in the same with thanksgiving;" 3. "Withal praying also for us, that God would open unto us a door of utterance, to speak the mystery of Christ, for which I am also in bonds:" 4. "That I may make it manifest, as I ought to speak."* Colossians 4:2-4

Do not be slothful.

Text: Hebrews 6:12 – *"That ye be not slothful, but followers of them who through faith and patience inherit the promises."*

Delay in things to be done

  "Slothfulness casteth into a deep sleep; and an idle soul shall suffer hunger." (Proverbs 19:15)

- There will be no success.

  "Not slothful in business; fervent in spirit; serving the Lord;" (Romans 12:11)

- In soul winning

  "After a long time the lord of those servants cometh, and reckoneth with them." (Matthew 25:26)

- Do the right thing at right time.

  "I must work the works of him that sent me, while it is day: the night cometh, when no man can work." (John 9:4).

No Looking back.

Text: Luke 9:62 – *"And Jesus said unto him, No man, having put his hand to the plough, and looking back, is fit for the kingdom of God."*

- Causes of looking back:

  "And it came to pass, that, as they went in the way, a certain man said unto him, Lord, I will follow thee whithersoever thou goest." (Luke 9:57)

- Love of the world

  "Love not the world, neither the things that are in the world. If any man love the world, the love of the Father is not in him." (1 John 2:15)

- Example: Demas

  "For Demas hath forsaken me, having loved this present world, and is departed unto Thessalonica; Crescens to Galatia, Titus unto Dalmatia." (2 Timothy 4:10)

- It is backsliding

  "Now the just shall live by faith: but if any man draw back, my soul shall have no pleasure in him." (Hebrews 10:38)

- The danger

  "For if after they have escaped the pollutions of the world through the knowledge of the Lord and Saviour Jesus Christ, they are again entangled therein, and overcome, the latter end is worse with them than the beginning." (2 Peter 2:20)

Awareness of God's Presence.

Text: Habakkuk 2:20 - *"But the Lord is in his holy temple: let all the earth keep silence before him."*

I. Faith and Belief in God's Presence:

- By faith – Hebrews 11:6 - *"But without faith it is impossible to please him: for he that cometh to God must believe that he is, and that he is a rewarder of them that diligently seek him."*

- Believe God's word – Matthew 18:20 - *"For where two or three are gathered together in my name, there am I in the midst of them."*

- Matthew 28:20 - *"Teaching them to observe all things whatsoever I have commanded you: and, lo, I am with you alway, even unto the end of the world. Amen."*

II. Experiencing the Manifestation of His Presence:

- Martha's testimony: John 11:21 - *"Then said Martha unto Jesus, Lord, if thou hadst been here, my brother had not died."*

III. Conclusion:

- Reflection on the assurance of God's presence in our lives and the blessings and miracles it brings forth.

Coming Back Home.

Text: Luke 15:18 - *"I will arise and go to my father, and will say unto him, Father, I have sinned against heaven, and before thee."*

I. Understanding the Journey Away from God:

- Spirit of ungratefulness: Psalm 103:1-3, Psalm 23:1-3.

  1. "Bless the Lord, O my soul: and all that is within me, bless his holy name. 2. Bless the Lord, O my soul, and forget not all his benefits: 3. Who forgiveth all thine iniquities; who healeth all thy diseases;" Psalm 103:1-3

  Psalm 23:1-3 – *"The Lord is my shepherd; I shall not want. 2. He maketh me to lie down in green pastures: he leadeth me beside the still waters. 3. He restoreth my soul: he leadeth me in the paths of righteousness for his name's sake."*

- Downfall due to evil communication: 1 Corinthians 15:33 – *"Be not deceived: evil communications corrupt good manners."*

- Un-separation from ungodly influences: 2 Corinthians 6:14-17, Luke 15:13-14.

  14. "Be ye not unequally yoked together with unbelievers: for what fellowship hath righteousness with unrighteousness? and what communion hath light with darkness? 15. "And what concord hath Christ with Belial? or what part hath he that believeth with an infidel? 16. And what agreement hath the temple of God with idols? for ye are the temple of the living God; as God hath said, I will dwell in them, and walk in them; and I will be their God, and they shall be my people. 17. Wherefore come out from among them, and be ye separate, saith the Lord, and touch not the unclean thing; and I will receive you,"

  Luke 15:13-14 – *"And not many days after the younger son gathered all together, and took his journey into a far country, and there wasted his substance with riotous living. 14. And when he had spent all, there arose a mighty famine in that land; and he began to be in want."*

II. The Path to Returning Home:

- Making the decision to return: Luke 15:17-20 –

  17. "And when he came to himself, he said, How many hired servants of my father's have bread enough and to spare, and I perish with hunger! 18. I will arise and go to my father, and will say unto him, Father, I have sinned against heaven, and before thee," 19. And am no more worthy to be called thy son: make me as one of thy hired servants. 20. And he arose, and came to his father. But when he was yet a great way off, his father saw him, and had compassion, and ran, and fell on his neck, and kissed him."

- Acknowledging shortcomings and repentance

III. Conclusion:

- Encouragement to make the conscious choice to return to God, acknowledging faults and embracing His forgiveness and love.

Spiritual Deafness.

Text: Isaiah 10:6, Judges 16:5-6.

Isaiah 10:6 – *"I will send him against an hypocritical nation, and against the people of my wrath will I give him a charge, to take the spoil, and to take the prey, and to tread them down like the mire of the streets."*

Judges 16:5-6 –*"And the lords of the Philistines came up unto her, and said unto her, Entice him, and see wherein his great strength lieth, and by what means we may prevail against him, that we may bind him to afflict him: and we will give thee every one of us eleven hundred pieces of silver. 6. And Delilah said to Samson, Tell me, I pray thee, wherein thy great strength lieth, and wherewith thou mightest be bound to afflict thee."*

I. Recognizing the Deception of Spiritual Deafness:

- The weapon of Satan: Isaiah 10:6 – *"I will send him against an hypocritical nation, and against the people of my wrath will I give him a charge, to take the spoil, and to take the prey, and to tread them down like the mire of the streets."*

- The deceiving and lying spirit: Judges 16:5&6, 1 Timothy 4:1, Isaiah 42:18&19

  Judges 16:5-6 – *"And the lords of the Philistines came up unto her, and said unto her, Entice him, and see wherein his great strength lieth, and by what means we may prevail against him, that we may bind him to afflict him: and we will give thee every one of us eleven hundred pieces of silver. 6. And Delilah said to Samson, Tell me, I pray thee, wherein thy great strength lieth, and wherewith thou mightest be bound to afflict thee."*

  1 Timothy 4:1 – *"Now the Spirit speaketh expressly, that in the latter times some shall depart from the faith, giving heed to seducing spirits, and doctrines of devils;"*

Isaiah 42:18-19 – *"Hear, ye deaf; and look, ye blind, that ye may see. 19. Who is blind, but my servant? or deaf, as my messenger that I sent? who is blind as he that is perfect, and blind as the Lord's servant?"*

-

II. The Tragic Consequences of Spiritual Deafness:

- Samson's downfall: Judges 16:7, 11&13, 15-17, 19-25

Judges 16:7 – *"And Samson said unto her, If they bind me with seven green withs that were never dried, then shall I be weak, and be as another man."*

Judges 16:11- *"And he said unto her, If they bind me fast with new ropes that never were occupied, then shall I be weak, and be as another man."*

Judges 16:13 – *"And Delilah said unto Samson, Hitherto thou hast mocked me, and told me lies: tell me wherewith thou mightest be bound. And he said unto her, If thou weavest the seven locks of my head with the web."*

Judges 16:15-17 – *"And she said unto him, How canst thou say, I love thee, when thine heart is not with me? thou hast mocked me these three times, and hast not told me wherein thy great strength lieth. 15. And it came to pass, when she pressed him daily with her words, and urged him, so that his soul was vexed unto death; 16. That he told her all his heart, and said unto her, There hath not come a razor upon mine head; for I have been a Nazarite unto God from my mother's womb: if I be shaven, then my strength will go from me, and I shall become weak, and be like any other man."*

Judges 16:19-25 –*"And she made him sleep upon her knees; and she called for a man, and she caused him to shave off the seven locks of his head; and she began to afflict him, and his strength went from him. 20. And she said, The Philistines be upon thee, Samson. And he awoke out of his sleep, and said, I will go out as at other times before, and shake myself. And he wist not that the Lord was departed from him. 21. But the Philistines took him, and put out his eyes, and brought him down to Gaza, and bound him with fetters of brass; and he did grind in the prison house. 22. Howbeit the hair of his head began to grow again after he was shaven. 23. Then the lords of the Philistines gathered them together for to offer a great sacrifice unto Dagon their god, and to rejoice: for they said, Our god hath delivered Samson our enemy into our hand. 24. And when the people saw him, they praised their god: for they said, Our god hath delivered into our hands our enemy, and the destroyer of our country, which slew many of us. 25. And it came to pass, when their hearts were merry, that they said, Call for Samson, that he may make us sport. And they called for Samson out of the prison house; and he made them sport: and they set him between the pillars."*

III. Conclusion:

- Reflecting on the dangers of spiritual deafness and the importance of discernment and obedience to God's Word.

Ye have not so Learned Christ.

Text: Ephesians 4:20 - *"But ye have not so learned Christ."*

I. Learning Christ's Teachings:

- Repentance: Titus 2:11-12, Acts 3:19

11. *"For the grace of God that bringeth salvation hath appeared to all men,12. Teaching us that, denying ungodliness and worldly lusts, we should live soberly, righteously, and godly, in this present world;"* Titus 2:11-12

"Repent ye therefore, and be converted, that your sins may be blotted out, when the times of refreshing shall come from the presence of the Lord;" Acts 3:19.

- Walking as Gentiles: Ephesians 4:17-19

17. *"This I say therefore, and testify in the Lord, that ye henceforth walk not as other Gentiles walk, in the vanity of their mind, 18. Having the understanding darkened, being alienated from the life of God through the ignorance that is in them, because of the blindness of their heart: 19. Who being past feeling have given themselves over unto lasciviousness, to work all uncleanness with greediness."* Ephesians 4:17-19.

- Transformation: Romans 12:2

"And be not conformed to this world: but be ye transformed by the renewing of your mind, that ye may prove what is that good, and acceptable, and perfect, will of God."

- Embracing Change: Ephesians 4:21-31

21. *"If so be that ye have heard him, and have been taught by him, as the truth is in Jesus: 22. That ye put off concerning the former conversation the old man, which is corrupt according to the deceitful lusts; 23. And be renewed in the spirit of your mind; 24. And that ye put on the new man, which after God is created in righteousness and true holiness. 25. Wherefore putting away lying, speak every man truth with his neighbour: for we are members one of another. 26. Be ye angry, and sin not: let not the sun go down upon your wrath: 27. Neither give place to the devil. 28. Let him that stole steal no more: but rather let him labour, working with his hands the thing which is good, that he may have to give to him that needeth. 29. Let no corrupt communication proceed out of your mouth, but that which is good to the use of edifying, that it may minister grace unto the hearers. 30. And grieve not the holy Spirit of God, whereby ye are sealed unto the day of redemption. 31. Let all bitterness, and wrath, and anger, and clamour, and evil speaking, be put away from you, with all malice."*

- Newness of Life: Romans 6:4, 2 Corinthians 5:17

  Romans 6:4 – *"Therefore we are buried with him by baptism into death: that like as Christ was raised up from the dead by the glory of the Father, even so we also should walk in newness of life."*

  2 Corinthians 5:17 – *"Therefore if any man be in Christ, he is a new creature: old things are passed away; behold, all things are become new."*

II. The Challenge of Judgment:

- Accountability before God: 1 Peter 4:17-18

  17. *"For the time is come that judgment must begin at the house of God: and if it first begin at us, what shall the end be of them that obey not the gospel of God?"*

  18. *"And if the righteous scarcely be saved, where shall the ungodly and the sinner appear?"*

III. Conclusion:

- Encouragement to embrace Christ's teachings, leading to repentance, transformation, and a new life, mindful of the impending judgment.

Do it quickly.

Text: John 13:27b – *"That thou doest, do quickly."*

I. Understanding the Urgency:

- Danger of delay: Hebrews 9:27 – *"And as it is appointed unto men once to die, but after this the judgment."*

- Time is short and death is certain: Ecclesiastes 9:10, John 9:4

  Ecclesiastes 9:10 – *"Whatsoever thy hand findeth to do, do it with thy might; for there is no work, nor device, nor knowledge, nor wisdom, in the grave, whither thou goest."*

  John 9:4 – *"I must work the works of him that sent me, while it is day: the night cometh, when no man can work."*

- The importance of immediate action: John 4:35, 2 Corinthians 6:2

  John 4:35 – *"Say not ye, There are yet four months, and then cometh harvest? behold, I say unto you, Lift up your eyes, and look on the fields; for they are white already to harvest."*

  2 Corinthians 6:2 – *"(For he saith, I have heard thee in a time accepted, and in the day of salvation have I succoured thee: behold, now is the accepted time; behold, now is the day of salvation.)"*

II. The Consequences of Procrastination:

- The parable of the foolish rich man: Luke 12:16-20

  16. *"And he spake a parable unto them, saying, The ground of a certain rich man brought forth plentifully: 17. And he thought within himself, saying, What shall I do, because I have no room where to bestow my fruits? 18. And he said, This will I do: I will pull down my barns, and build greater; and there will I bestow all my fruits and my goods. 19. And I will say to my soul, Soul, thou hast much goods laid up for many years; take thine ease, eat, drink, and be merry. 20. But God said unto him, Thou fool, this night thy soul shall be required of thee: then whose shall those things be, which thou hast provided?"*

III. Conclusion:

- Urging prompt action in response to God's call, as procrastination can lead to missed opportunities and dire consequences.

The Power of Deliverance.

Text: Matthew 27:52, Luke 4:18

Matthew 27:52 – *"And the graves were opened; and many bodies of the saints which slept arose,"*

Luke 4:18 – *"The Spirit of the Lord is upon me, because he hath anointed me to preach the gospel to the poor; he hath sent me to heal the brokenhearted, to preach deliverance to the captives, and recovering of sight to the blind, to set at liberty them that are bruised,"*

I. The Significance of Christ's Death and Resurrection:

- The power of His death and resurrection: John 11:25, 1 Corinthians 15:55, John 5:25-29

  John 11:25 – *"Jesus said unto her, I am the resurrection, and the life: he that believeth in me, though he were dead, yet shall he live:"*

  1 Corinthians 15:55 – *"O death, where is thy sting? O grave, where is thy victory?"*

  John 5:25-29

  25. *"Verily, verily, I say unto you, The hour is coming, and now is, when the dead shall hear the voice of the Son of God: and they that hear shall live. 26. For as the Father hath life in himself; so hath he given to the Son to have life in himself; 27. And hath given him authority to execute judgment also, because he is the Son of man. 28. Marvel not at this: for the hour is coming, in the which all that are in the graves shall hear his voice, 29. And shall come forth; they that have done good, unto the resurrection of life; and they that have done evil, unto the resurrection of damnation."*

- Knowing Him: Philippians 3:10

  "That I may know him, and the power of his resurrection, and the fellowship of his sufferings, being made conformable unto his death;"

II. The Victory Over Satan:

- The empty tomb: Matthew 28:6

  "He is not here: for he is risen, as he said. Come, see the place where the Lord lay."

- The defeat of Satan: Matthew 27:62-66, Matthew 28:1-2, 11-15

Matthew 27:62-66 –*"Now the next day, that followed the day of the preparation, the chief priests and Pharisees came together unto Pilate, 62. Saying, Sir, we remember that that deceiver said, while he was yet alive, After three days I will rise again. 63. Command therefore that the sepulchre be made sure until the third day, lest his disciples come by night, and steal him away, and say unto the people, He is risen from the dead: so the last error shall be worse than the first. 64. Pilate said unto them, Ye have a watch: go your way, make it as sure as ye can. 65. So they went, and made the sepulchre sure, sealing the stone, and setting a watch."*

Matthew 28:1-2 –*"In the end of the sabbath, as it began to dawn toward the first day of the week, came Mary Magdalene and the other Mary to see the sepulchre. 2. And, behold, there was a great earthquake: for the angel of the Lord descended from heaven, and came and rolled back the stone from the door, and sat upon it."*

Matthew 28:11-15 – *"Now when they were going, behold, some of the watch came into the city, and shewed unto the chief priests all the things that were done. 12. And when they were assembled with the elders, and had taken counsel, they gave large money unto the soldiers, 13. Saying, Say ye, His disciples came by night, and stole him away while we slept. 14. And if this come to the governor's ears, we will persuade him, and secure you. 15. So they took the money, and did as they were taught: and this saying is commonly reported among the Jews until this day."*

- The power of resurrection: 1 Corinthians 15:14, 17

  1 Corinthians 15:14 – *"And if Christ be not risen, then is our preaching vain, and your faith is also vain."*

  1 Corinthians 15:17 – *"And if Christ be not raised, your faith is vain; ye are yet in your sins."*

III. Conclusion:

- Celebrating the triumph of the resurrected Christ over sin, death, and Satan, and affirming His eternal reign.

The Empty Tomb.

Text: Matthew 28:6 - *"He is not here: for he is risen, as he said. Come, see the place where the Lord lay."*

I. The Triumph of the Resurrected Christ:

- The defeat of Satan: Matthew 27:62-66, Matthew 28:1-2, 11-15

Matthew 27:62-66 (KJV):

62. *"Now the next day, that followed the day of the preparation, the chief priests and Pharisees came together unto Pilate,"*

63. *"Saying, Sir, we remember that that deceiver said, while he was yet alive, After three days I will rise again."*

64. *"Command therefore that the sepulchre be made sure until the third day, lest his disciples come by night, and steal him away, and say unto the people, He is risen from the dead: so the last error shall be worse than the first."*

65. *"Pilate said unto them, Ye have a watch: go your way, make it as sure as ye can."*

66. *"So they went, and made the sepulchre sure, sealing the stone, and setting a watch."*

Matthew 28:1-2 (KJV):

1. *"In the end of the sabbath, as it began to dawn toward the first day of the week, came Mary Magdalene and the other Mary to see the sepulchre."*

2. *"And, behold, there was a great earthquake: for the angel of the Lord descended from heaven, and came and rolled back the stone from the door, and sat upon it."*

Matthew 28:11-15 (KJV):

11. *"Now when they were going, behold, some of the watch came into the city, and shewed unto the chief priests all the things that were done."*

12. *"And when they were assembled with the elders, and had taken counsel, they gave large money unto the soldiers,"*

13. *"Saying, Say ye, His disciples came by night, and stole him away while we slept."*

14. *"And if this come to the governor's ears, we will persuade him, and secure you."*

15. *"So they took the money, and did as they were taught: and this saying is commonly reported among the Jews until this day."*

- The power of resurrection: 1 Corinthians 15:14, 17

II. Jesus' Eternal Authority:

- His ongoing ministry: Hebrews 7:25, Matthew 28:18-20

III. Conclusion:

- Rejoicing in the reality of the empty tomb, which signifies the victory of Jesus over death, and affirming His everlasting reign and authority.

My Messages

Unpaid Vows.

Text: Ecclesiastes 5:4 – *"When thou vowest a vow unto God, defer not to pay it; for he hath no pleasure in fools: pay that which thou hast vowed."*

I. Warning Against Unpaid Vows:

- Ecclesiastes 4:1-3, 4:5-7

Ecclesiastes 4:1-3

1 So I returned, and considered all the oppressions that are done under the sun: and behold the tears of such as were oppressed, and they had no comforter; and on the side of their oppressors there was power; but they had no comforter.
2 Wherefore I praised the dead which are already dead more than the living which are yet alive.
3 Yea, better is he than both they, which hath not yet been, who hath not seen the evil work that is done under the sun.

Ecclesiastes 4:5-7

5 The fool foldeth his hands together, and eateth his own flesh.
6 Better is a handful with quietness, than both the hands full with travail and vexation of spirit.
7 Then I returned, and I saw vanity under the sun.
8 There is one alone, and there is not a second; yea, he hath neither child nor brother: yet is there no end of all his labour; neither is his eye satisfied with riches; neither saith he, For whom do I labour, and bereave my soul of good? This is also vanity, yea, it is a sore travail.

II. Biblical Examples:

- Jephthah's vow: Judges 11:29-31, 34-4.

29 Then the Spirit of the Lord came upon Jephthah, and he passed over Gilead and Manasseh, and passed over Mizpeh of Gilead, and from Mizpeh of Gilead he passed over unto the children of Ammon.
30 And Jephthah vowed a vow unto the Lord, and said, If thou shalt without fail deliver the children of Ammon into mine hands,
31 Then it shall be, that whatsoever cometh forth of the doors of my house to meet me, when I return in peace from the children of Ammon, shall surely be the Lord's, and I will offer it up for a burnt offering.

Judges 11:34-40

34 And Jephthah came to Mizpeh unto his house, and, behold, his daughter came out to meet him with timbrels and with dances: and she was his only child; beside her he had neither son nor daughter.

35 And it came to pass, when he saw her, that he rent his clothes, and said, Alas, my daughter! thou hast brought me very low, and thou art one of them that trouble me: for I have opened my mouth unto the Lord, and I cannot go back.

36 And she said unto him, My father, if thou hast opened thy mouth unto the Lord, do to me according to that which hath proceeded out of thy mouth; forasmuch as the Lord hath taken vengeance for thee of thine enemies, even of the children of Ammon.

37 And she said unto her father, Let this thing be done for me: let me alone two months, that I may go up and down upon the mountains, and bewail my virginity, I and my fellows.

38 And he said, Go. And he sent her away for two months: and she went with her companions, and bewailed her virginity upon the mountains.

39 And it came to pass at the end of two months, that she returned unto her father, who did with her according to his vow which he had vowed: and she knew no man. And it was a custom in Israel,

40 That the daughters of Israel went yearly to lament the daughter of Jephthah the Gileadite four days in a year.

- Hannah's vow: 1 Samuel 1:11, 22-28

1 Samuel 1:11:

11 And she vowed a vow, and said, O Lord of hosts, if thou wilt indeed look on the affliction of thine handmaid, and remember me, and not forget thine handmaid, but wilt give unto thine handmaid a man child, then I will give him unto the Lord all the days of his life, and there shall no razor come upon his head.

1 Samuel 1:22-28 (KJV):

22 But Hannah went not up; for she said unto her husband, I will not go up until the child be weaned, and then I will bring him, that he may appear before the Lord, and there abide for ever.

23 And Elkanah her husband said unto her, Do what seemeth thee good; tarry until thou have weaned him; only the Lord establish his word. So the woman abode, and gave her son suck until she weaned him.

24 And when she had weaned him, she took him up with her, with three bullocks, and one ephah of flour, and a bottle of wine, and brought him unto the house of the Lord in Shiloh: and the child was young.

25 And they slew a bullock, and brought the child to Eli.

26 And she said, O my lord, as thy soul liveth, my lord, I am the woman that stood by thee here, praying unto the Lord.

27 For this child I prayed; and the Lord hath given me my petition which I asked of him:

28 Therefore also I have lent him to the Lord; as long as he liveth he shall be lent to the Lord. And he worshipped the Lord there.

III. Reflection and Challenge:

- Reflecting on personal vows made

- Encouragement to fulfill vows made to God.

A Man Bearing Pitcher.

Text: Mark 14:13 - *"And he sendeth forth two of his disciples, and saith unto them, Go ye into the city, and there shall meet you a man bearing a pitcher of water: follow him."*

I. The Need for God's Guidance:

Romans 8:14 - *"For as many as are led by the Spirit of God, they are the sons of God."*

Proverb 14:12, Proverb 16:25 - *"There is a way which seemeth right unto a man, but the end thereof are the ways of death."*

Mark 14:12 - *"And the first day of unleavened bread, when they killed the passover, his disciples said unto him, Where wilt thou that we go and prepare that thou mayest eat the passover?"*

II. Following God's Leading:

- Mark 14:13-15 - *"And he sendeth forth two of his disciples, and saith unto them, Go ye into the city, and there shall meet you a man bearing a pitcher of water: follow him."*

III. Obedience:

- Mark 14:16 - *"And his disciples went forth, and came into the city, and found as he had said unto them: and they made ready the passover."*

The Mountain of the Lord.

Text: Psalm 24:3 - *"Who shall ascend into the hill of the Lord? or who shall stand in his holy place?"*

I. The Significance of the Mountain of the Lord:

- The throne of God: Psalm 121:1 - *"I will lift up mine eyes unto the hills, from whence cometh my help."*

II. Conditions for Ascending:

- Psalm 24:4 - *"He that hath clean hands, and a pure heart; who hath not lifted up his soul unto vanity, nor sworn deceitfully."*

- Isaiah 5:11 - *"Woe unto them that rise up early in the morning, that they may follow strong drink; that continue until night, till wine inflame them!"*

Answered Prayer is Prayer.

Text: Psalm 55:17 - *"Evening, and morning, and at noon, will I pray, and cry aloud: and he shall hear my voice." John 16:24 (KJV) - "Hitherto have ye asked nothing in my name: ask, and ye shall receive, that your joy may be full."*

I. Persistence in Prayer:

- Luke 18:1, 28 (KJV) - *"And he spake a parable unto them to this end, that men ought always to pray, and not to faint..."*

II. The Assurance of Answered Prayer:

- Bartimaeus' example: Mark 10:46-52

46 And they came to Jericho: and as he went out of Jericho with his disciples and a great number of people, blind Bartimaeus, the son of Timaeus, sat by the highway side begging.
47 And when he heard that it was Jesus of Nazareth, he began to cry out, and say, Jesus, thou Son of David, have mercy on me.
48 And many charged him that he should hold his peace: but he cried the more a great deal, Thou Son of David, have mercy on me.
49 And Jesus stood still, and commanded him to be called. And they call the blind man, saying unto him, Be of good comfort, rise; he calleth thee.
50 And he, casting away his garment, rose, and came to Jesus.
51 And Jesus answered and said unto him, What wilt thou that I should do unto thee? The blind man said unto him, Lord, that I might receive my sight.
52 And Jesus said unto him, Go thy way; thy faith hath made thee whole. And immediately he received his sight, and followed Jesus in the way.

Effectual Fervent Prayer.

Text: James 5:16b - *"The effectual fervent prayer of a righteous man availeth much."*

I. The Power of Prayer:

- Prayer through the power of the Holy Spirit: Rom. 8:26 - *"Likewise the Spirit also helpeth our infirmities: for we know not what we should pray for as we ought: but the Spirit itself maketh intercession for us with groanings which cannot be uttered."*

- The early Apostles' prayers: Acts 4:31 - *"And when they had prayed, the place was shaken where they were assembled together; and they were all filled with the Holy Ghost, and they spake the word of God with boldness."*

- The early church's prayer for Peter: Acts 12:5, 11-16 - *"Peter therefore was kept in prison: but prayer was made without ceasing of the church unto God for him."*

Acts 12:11-16:

11 And when Peter was come to himself, he said, Now I know of a surety, that the Lord hath sent his angel, and hath delivered me out of the hand of Herod, and from all the expectation of the people of the Jews.
12 And when he had considered the thing, he came to the house of Mary the mother of John, whose surname was Mark; where many were gathered together praying.
13 And as Peter knocked at the door of the gate, a damsel came to hearken, named Rhoda.
14 And when she knew Peter's voice, she opened not the gate for gladness, but ran in, and told how Peter stood before the gate.
15 And they said unto her, Thou art mad. But she constantly affirmed that it was even so. Then said they, It is his angel.
16 But Peter continued knocking: and when they had opened the door, and saw him, they were astonished.

Wrestle in Prayer.

Text: Genesis 32:24 - *"And Jacob was left alone; and there wrestled a man with him until the breaking of the day."*

I. Prayer as a Serious Endeavor:

- Prayer requires effort: Romans 12:11 - *"Not slothful in business; fervent in spirit; serving the Lord."*

- Examples of wrestling in prayer: Genesis 32:24-30, Genesis 27:34-40

Genesis 32:24-30:

24 And Jacob was left alone; and there wrestled a man with him until the breaking of the day.
25 And when he saw that he prevailed not against him, he touched the hollow of his

thigh; and the hollow of Jacob's thigh was out of joint, as he wrestled with him.
26 And he said, Let me go, for the day breaketh. And he said, I will not let thee go, except thou bless me.
27 And he said unto him, What is thy name? And he said, Jacob.
28 And he said, Thy name shall be called no more Jacob, but Israel: for as a prince hast thou power with God and with men, and hast prevailed.
29 And Jacob asked him, and said, Tell me, I pray thee, thy name. And he said, Wherefore is it that thou dost ask after my name? And he blessed him there.
30 And Jacob called the name of the place Peniel: for I have seen God face to face, and my life is preserved.

Genesis 27:34-40:

34 And when Esau heard the words of his father, he cried with a great and exceeding bitter cry, and said unto his father, Bless me, even me also, O my father.
35 And he said, Thy brother came with subtilty, and hath taken away thy blessing.
36 And he said, Is not he rightly named Jacob? for he hath supplanted me these two times: he took away my birthright; and, behold, now he hath taken away my blessing. And he said, Hast thou not reserved a blessing for me?
37 And Isaac answered and said unto Esau, Behold, I have made him thy lord, and all his brethren have I given to him for servants; and with corn and wine have I sustained him: and what shall I do now unto thee, my son?
38 And Esau said unto his father, Hast thou but one blessing, my father? bless me, even me also, O my father. And Esau lifted up his voice, and wept.
39 And Isaac his father answered and said unto him, Behold, thy dwelling shall be the fatness of the earth, and of the dew of heaven from above;
40 And by thy sword shalt thou live, and shalt serve thy brother; and it shall come to pass when thou shalt have the dominion, that thou shalt break his yoke from off thy neck.

II. Conclusion:

- Encouragement to engage in prayer with fervency and persistence, recognizing its significance and effectiveness in the spiritual realm.

The Enemy of Prayer.

Text: Matthew 17:20 - *"And Jesus said unto them, Because of your unbelief: for verily I say unto you, If ye have faith as a grain of mustard seed, ye shall say unto this mountain, Remove hence to yonder place; and it shall remove; and nothing shall be impossible unto you."*

I. The Story of a Hindered Prayer:

- Matthew 17:14-18

14 And when they were come to the multitude, there came to him a certain man, kneeling down to him, and saying,
15 Lord, have mercy on my son: for he is lunatick, and sore vexed: for ofttimes he falleth into the fire, and oft into the water.
16 And I brought him to thy disciples, and they could not cure him.
17 Then Jesus answered and said, O faithless and perverse generation, how long shall I be with you? how long shall I suffer you? bring him hither to me.
18 And Jesus rebuked the devil; and he departed out of him: and the child was cured from that very hour.

II. The Power of Believing Prayer:

- Matthew 17:20-21

20 And Jesus said unto them, Because of your unbelief: for verily I say unto you, If ye have faith as a grain of mustard seed, ye shall say unto this mountain, Remove hence to yonder place; and it shall remove; and nothing shall be impossible unto you.
21 Howbeit this kind goeth not out but by prayer and fasting.

Prayer of Faith When There Is No Hope.

Text: James 5:15a - *"And the prayer of faith shall save the sick, and the Lord shall raise him up..."* Luke 11:24 - *"When the unclean spirit is gone out of a man, he walketh through dry places, seeking rest; and finding none, he saith, I will return unto my house whence I came out."*

I. Facing Challenges with Faith-Filled Prayer:

- Jesus' teaching on the importance of being filled with the Holy Spirit to combat spiritual opposition. –

  Luke 11:22-24

  22 But when a stronger than he shall come upon him, and overcome him, he taketh from him all his armour wherein he trusted, and divideth his spoils.
  23 He that is not with me is against me: and he that gathereth not with me scattereth.

24 When the unclean spirit is gone out of a man, he walketh through dry places, seeking rest; and finding none, he saith, I will return unto my house whence I came out.

- The story of Jonah facing a hopeless situation on the ship – Jonah 1:5-6

5 Then the mariners were afraid, and cried every man unto his god, and cast forth the wares that were in the ship into the sea, to lighten it of them. But Jonah was gone down into the sides of the ship; and he lay, and was fast asleep.
6 So the shipmaster came to him, and said unto him, What meanest thou, O sleeper? arise, call upon thy God, if so be that God will think upon us, that we perish not.

II. Prayer Offered in the Depths of Despair:

- Jonah's prayer from the belly of the fish when all seemed lost – Jonah 2:1-7

1 Then Jonah prayed unto the Lord his God out of the fish's belly,
2 And said, I cried by reason of mine affliction unto the Lord, and he heard me; out of the belly of hell cried I, and thou heardest my voice.
3 For thou hadst cast me into the deep, in the midst of the seas; and the floods compassed me about: all thy billows and thy waves passed over me.
4 Then I said, I am cast out of thy sight; yet I will look again toward thy holy temple.
5 The waters compassed me about, even to the soul: the depth closed me round about, the weeds were wrapped about my head.
6 I went down to the bottoms of the mountains; the earth with her bars was about me for ever: yet hast thou brought up my life from corruption, O Lord my God.
7 When my soul fainted within me I remembered the Lord: and my prayer came in unto thee, into thine holy temple.

- Abraham's example of faith in prayer: Romans 4:18-21

18 Who against hope believed in hope, that he might become the father of many nations, according to that which was spoken, So shall thy seed be.
19 And being not weak in faith, he considered not his own body now dead, when he was about an hundred years old, neither yet the deadness of Sarah's womb:
20 He staggered not at the promise of God through unbelief; but was strong in faith, giving glory to God;
21 And being fully persuaded that, what he had promised, he was able also to perform.

The Church is a Prayer Workshop.

Text: Matthew 21:13 - *"And said unto them, It is written, My house shall be called the house of prayer; but ye have made it a den of thieves."*

Isaiah 56:7 - *"Even them will I bring to my holy mountain, and make them joyful in my house of prayer: their burnt offerings and their sacrifices shall be accepted upon mine altar; for mine house shall be called an house of prayer for all people."*

2 Corinthians 7:11-15 - *"...in all things ye have approved yourselves to be clear in this matter."*

I. The Importance of Prayer in the Church:

- The church as a place of prayer: Acts 6:4, Luke 18:1 & 7 –

Acts 6:4 – *"But we will give ourselves continually to prayer, and to the ministry of the word."*

Luke 18:1 – *"And he spake a parable unto them to this end, that men ought always to pray, and not to faint;"*

Luke 18:7 – *"And shall not God avenge his own elect, which cry day and night unto him, though he bear long with them?"*

- David's commitment to prayer: Psalm 55:16-17 –

16. *"As for me, I will call upon God; and the Lord shall save me."*

17. *"Evening, and morning, and at noon, will I pray, and cry aloud: and he shall hear my voice."*

II. Establishing a Culture of Prayer in the Church:

- The need for dedicated times of prayer: Acts 3:1 –:

"Now Peter and John went up together into the temple at the hour of prayer, being the ninth hour."

<u>The People That Do Know Their God.</u>

Text: Daniel 11:32b - *"But the people that do know their God shall be strong, and do exploits."*

I. Lack of Knowledge of God Today:

- Jesus' conversation with Philip emphasizing the importance of knowing God. John 14:8-12 –

8 *"Philip saith unto him, Lord, show us the Father, and it sufficeth us."*

9 "Jesus saith unto him, Have I been so long time with you, and yet hast thou not known me, Philip? he that hath seen me hath seen the Father; and how sayest thou then, Show us the Father?"

10 "Believest thou not that I am in the Father, and the Father in me? the words that I speak unto you I speak not of myself: but the Father that dwelleth in me, he doeth the works."

11 "Believe me that I am in the Father, and the Father in me: or else believe me for the very works' sake."

12 "Verily, verily, I say unto you, He that believeth on me, the works that I do shall he do also; and greater works than these shall he do; because I go unto my Father."

II. Expectations of Knowing God:

- Paul's desire to know Christ and experience His power. Philippians 3:10

  "That I may know him, and the power of his resurrection, and the fellowship of his sufferings, being made conformable unto his death;"

III. Victors Who Knew Their God:

- The Faith of the Three Hebrews: Daniel 3:16-17

  16 "Shadrach, Meshach, and Abednego, answered and said to the king, O Nebuchadnezzar, we are not careful to answer thee in this matter."

  17 "If it be so, our God whom we serve is able to deliver us from the burning fiery furnace, and he will deliver us out of thine hand, O king."

- Abraham's Faith: Genesis 22:5, 7-8, 10-13, Hebrews 11:17-19

  Genesis 22:5: *"And Abraham said unto his young men, Abide ye here with the ass; and I and the lad will go yonder and worship, and come again to you."*

  Genesis 22:7-8: *7. "And Isaac spake unto Abraham his father, and said, My father: and he said, Here am I, my son. And he said, Behold the fire and the wood: but where is the lamb for a burnt offering?"*

  8. "And Abraham said, My son, God will provide himself a lamb for a burnt offering: so they went both of them together."

  Genesis 22:10-13: *10. "And Abraham stretched forth his hand, and took the knife to slay his son."*

  11. "And the angel of the Lord called unto him out of heaven, and said, Abraham, Abraham: and he said, Here am I."

12. *"And he said, Lay not thine hand upon the lad, neither do thou any thing unto him: for now I know that thou fearest God, seeing thou hast not withheld thy son, thine only son from me."*

13. *"And Abraham lifted up his eyes, and looked, and behold behind him a ram caught in a thicket by his horns: and Abraham went and took the ram, and offered him up for a burnt offering in the stead of his son."*

Hebrews 11:17-19: 17. *"By faith Abraham, when he was tried, offered up Isaac: and he that had received the promises offered up his only begotten son,"*

18. *"Of whom it was said, That in Isaac shall thy seed be called:"*

19. *"Accounting that God was able to raise him up, even from the dead; from whence also he received him in a figure."*

- Daniel's Faithfulness: Daniel 6:11-12, 20-23

11. *"Then these men assembled, and found Daniel praying and making supplication before his God."*

12. *"Then they came near, and spake before the king concerning the king's decree; Hast thou not signed a decree, that every man that shall ask a petition of any god or man within thirty days, save of thee, O king, shall be cast into the den of lions?"*

Daniel 6:20-23 (KJV): 20. *"And when he came to the den, he cried with a lamentable voice unto Daniel: and the king spake and said to Daniel, O Daniel, servant of the living God, is thy God, whom thou servest continually, able to deliver thee from the lions?"*

21. *"Then said Daniel unto the king, O king, live for ever."*

22. *"My God hath sent his angel, and hath shut the lions' mouths, that they have not hurt me: forasmuch as before him innocency was found in me; and also before thee, O king, have I done no hurt."*

23. *"Then was the king exceeding glad for him, and commanded that they should take Daniel up out of the den. So Daniel was taken up out of the den, and no manner of hurt was found upon him, because he believed in his God."*

IV. Prayer for Revelation of God:

- A call for personal prayer for deeper revelation and understanding of God.

The Unrighteous.

Text: 1 Corinthians 6:9 (KJV) - *"Know ye not that the unrighteous shall not inherit the kingdom of God? Be not deceived: neither fornicators, nor idolaters, nor adulterers, nor effeminate, nor abusers of themselves with mankind..."*

I. God's Call to Righteousness:

- The expectation for faithfulness and righteousness in God's servants. 1 Corinthians 4:1-2

  1. "Let a man so account of us, as of the ministers of Christ, and stewards of the mysteries of God."
  2. "Moreover it is required in stewards, that a man be found faithful."

II. The Exaltation of Righteousness:

- Proverbs 14:34 - *"Righteousness exalteth a nation: but sin is a reproach to any people."*

III. Consequences of Unrighteousness:

- The account of Ananias and Sapphira facing judgment for their deceit – Acts 5:1-11

  1. "But a certain man named Ananias, with Sapphira his wife, sold a possession,"

  2. "And kept back part of the price, his wife also being privy to it, and brought a certain part, and laid it at the apostles' feet."

  3. "But Peter said, Ananias, why hath Satan filled thine heart to lie to the Holy Ghost, and to keep back part of the price of the land?"

  4 "Whiles it remained, was it not thine own? and after it was sold, was it not in thine own power? why hast thou conceived this thing in thine heart? thou hast not lied unto men, but unto God."

  5. "And Ananias hearing these words fell down, and gave up the ghost: and great fear came on all them that heard these things."

  6. "And the young men arose, wound him up, and carried him out, and buried him."

  7. "And it was about the space of three hours after, when his wife, not knowing what was done, came in."

  8. "And Peter answered unto her, Tell me whether ye sold the land for so much? And she said, Yea, for so much."

  9. "Then Peter said unto her, How is it that ye have agreed together to tempt the Spirit of the Lord? behold, the feet of them which have buried thy husband are at the door, and shall carry thee out."

10. *"Then fell she down straightway at his feet, and yielded up the ghost: and the young men came in, and found her dead, and, carrying her forth, buried her by her husband."*

11. *"And great fear came upon all the church, and upon as many as heard these things."*

- Luke 6:9-10 (KJV) - Jesus' teaching on righteousness and its rewards.

9. *"Then said Jesus unto them, I will ask you one thing; Is it lawful on the sabbath days to do good, or to do evil? to save life, or to destroy it?"*

10. *"And looking round about upon them all, he said unto the man, Stretch forth thy hand. And he did so: and his hand was restored whole as the other."*

IV. Challenge and Warning:

- A final warning against unrighteousness and a call to righteousness before the Lord's return. Revelation 22:11-12

11. *"He that is unjust, let him be unjust still: and he which is filthy, let him be filthy still: and he that is righteous, let him be righteous still: and he that is holy, let him be holy still."*

12. *"And, behold, I come quickly; and my reward is with me, to give every man according as his work shall be."*

To Be Like Jesus.

Text: Acts 11:26b - *"...And the disciples were called Christians first in Antioch."*

I. What Makes Them Like Jesus?

- Embracing the Word of God as their guide.

II. Following God, Not Man:

- Following the example of Paul as he follows Christ. 1 Corinthians 11:1

"Be ye followers of me, even as I also am of Christ."

III. Disciples Emulating Their Master:

- The challenge to reflect the image of God in our lives as disciples of Christ.

Abounding in Christ.

Text: 1 Corinthians 15:58 - *"Therefore, my beloved brethren, be ye stedfast, unmoveable, always abounding in the work of the Lord, forasmuch as ye know that your labour is not in vain in the Lord." John 15:7 (KJV) - "If ye abide in me, and my words abide in you, ye shall ask what ye will, and it shall be done unto you."*

I. Pursuing Perfection in Faith:

- Encouragement to grow in faith and spiritual maturity.

II. Abounding in Love:

- Exhortations to love one another and let the word of Christ dwell in us richly. 1 Thessalonians 3:12 (KJV), Colossians 3:16 (KJV) -

  1 Thessalonians 3:12 –

  "And the Lord make you to increase and abound in love one toward another, and toward all men, even as we do toward you;"

  Colossians 3:16 –

  "Let the word of Christ dwell in you richly in all wisdom; teaching and admonishing one another in psalms and hymns and spiritual songs, singing with grace in your hearts to the Lord."

III. Grounded in the Word:

- Being rooted and built up in Christ and established in the faith. Colossians 2:7 (KJV) –

  "Rooted and built up in him, and stablished in the faith, as ye have been taught, abounding therein with thanksgiving."

IV. Upholding the Believer:

- The importance of virtues and fruitfulness in the Christian life according to 2 Peter 1:8-10 –

  8."For if these things be in you, and abound, they make you that ye shall neither be barren nor unfruitful in the knowledge of our Lord Jesus Christ."

9. *"But he that lacketh these things is blind, and cannot see afar off, and hath forgotten that he was purged from his old sins."*

10. *"Wherefore the rather, brethren, give diligence to make your calling and election sure: for if ye do these things, ye shall never fall:"*

We Are His Witnesses.

Text: Acts 5:32a - *"And we are his witnesses of these things..."*

I. The Purpose of Pentecost:

- Jesus' commission to His disciples to be witnesses in Jerusalem, Judea, Samaria, and to the ends of the earth. Acts 1:8 –

  "But ye shall receive power, after that the Holy Ghost is come upon you: and ye shall be witnesses unto me both in Jerusalem, and in all Judaea, and in Samaria, and unto the uttermost part of the earth."

II. Examples of Witnesses:

- Andrew bringing Simon Peter to Jesus. John 1:40-41-

  40. *"One of the two which heard John speak, and followed him, was Andrew, Simon Peter's brother."*

  41. *"He first findeth his own brother Simon, and saith unto him, We have found the Messiah, which is, being interpreted, the Christ."*

- Philip bringing Nathanael to Jesus. John 1:43-46

  43. *"The day following Jesus would go forth into Galilee, and findeth Philip, and saith unto him, Follow me."*

  44. *"Now Philip was of Bethsaida, the city of Andrew and Peter."*

  45. *"Philip findeth Nathanael, and saith unto him, We have found him, of whom Moses in the law, and the prophets, did write, Jesus of Nazareth, the son of Joseph."*

  46. *"And Nathanael said unto him, Can there any good thing come out of Nazareth? Philip saith unto him, Come and see."*

- The Samaritan Woman: Her testimony leading many Samaritans to believe in Jesus. – John 4:28-30, 40-42.

  John 4:28-30:

28. *"The woman then left her waterpot, and went her way into the city, and saith to the men,"*

29. *"Come, see a man, which told me all things that ever I did: is not this the Christ?"*

30. *"Then they went out of the city, and came unto him."*

John 4:40-42:

40. *"So when the Samaritans were come unto him, they besought him that he would tarry with them: and he abode there two days."*

41. *"And many more believed because of his own word;"*

42. *"And said unto the woman, Now we believe, not because of thy saying: for we have heard him ourselves, and know that this is indeed the Christ, the Saviour of the world."*

- The Gadarene Man: The demoniac's witness to his own people. Mark 5:18-20.

18. *"And when he was come into the ship, he that had been possessed with the devil prayed him that he might be with him."*

19. *"Howbeit Jesus suffered him not, but saith unto him, Go home to thy friends, and tell them how great things the Lord hath done for thee, and hath had compassion on thee."*

20. *"And he departed, and began to publish in Decapolis how great things Jesus had done for him: and all men did marvel."*

- Philip's Evangelism: Philip's preaching in Samaria and to the Ethiopian eunuch. Acts 8:5-8, 26

Acts 8:5-8:

5. *"Then Philip went down to the city of Samaria, and preached Christ unto them."*

6. *"And the people with one accord gave heed unto those things which Philip spake, hearing and seeing the miracles which he did."*

7. *"For unclean spirits, crying with loud voice, came out of many that were possessed with them: and many taken with palsies, and that were lame, were healed."*

8. *"And there was great joy in that city."*

Acts 8:26:

26. *"And the angel of the Lord spake unto Philip, saying, Arise, and go toward the south unto the way that goeth down from Jerusalem unto Gaza, which is desert."*

- The Apostles' Boldness: Their refusal to stop preaching despite opposition from the council. Acts 5:29-32, 40-42

  Acts 5:29-32:

29. *"Then Peter and the other apostles answered and said, We ought to obey God rather than men."*

30. *"The God of our fathers raised up Jesus, whom ye slew and hanged on a tree."*

31. *"Him hath God exalted with his right hand to be a Prince and a Saviour, for to give repentance to Israel, and forgiveness of sins."*

32. *"And we are his witnesses of these things; and so is also the Holy Ghost, whom God hath given to them that obey him."*

  Acts 5:40-42:

40. *"And to him they agreed: and when they had called the apostles, and beaten them, they commanded that they should not speak in the name of Jesus, and let them go."*

41. *"And they departed from the presence of the council, rejoicing that they were counted worthy to suffer shame for his name."*

42. *"And daily in the temple, and in every house, they ceased not to teach and preach Jesus Christ."*

III. Challenge:

- We are debtors to share the gospel: The call to shine as witnesses for Christ – : Romans 8:12 (KJV), Daniel 12:3

Romans 8:12:

"Therefore, brethren, we are debtors, not to the flesh, to live after the flesh."

Daniel 12:3:

"And they that be wise shall shine as the brightness of the firmament; and they that turn many to righteousness as the stars for ever and ever."

Big Faith.

Text: Matthew 8:10 - *"When Jesus heard it, he marvelled, and said to them that followed, Verily I say unto you, I have not found so great faith, no, not in Israel."*

I. Faith Firmly Rooted in the Word:

- Little Faith vs. Great Faith: Jesus' teaching on the power of faith. Matthew 17:20

  "And Jesus said unto them, Because of your unbelief: for verily I say unto you, If ye have faith as a grain of mustard seed, ye shall say unto this mountain, Remove hence to yonder place; and it shall remove; and nothing shall be impossible unto you."

II. The Significance of Great Faith:

- Great faith brings heaven to the soul, expecting from God what is beyond human expectation.

III. Examples of Great Faith:

- Abraham's Obedience: Abraham's unwavering faith in offering Isaac. Genesis 22:5, 7.

  "And Abraham said unto his young men, Abide ye here with the ass; and I and the lad will go yonder and worship, and come again to you."

  Genesis 22:7:

  "And Isaac spake unto Abraham his father, and said, My father: and he said, Here am I, my son. And he said, Behold the fire and the wood: but where is the lamb for a burnt offering?"

IV. Encouragement to Grow in Faith:

- The call to emulate the examples of great faith in Scripture and to trust in God's promises beyond all doubt.

<u>The Ministry of Prayer.</u>

Text: Acts 6:4 - *"But we will give ourselves continually to prayer, and to the ministry of the word."*

I. The Vital Role of Prayer:

- Acknowledging the indispensable nature of prayer for accomplishing God's work. Matthew 17:21

  "Howbeit this kind goeth not out but by prayer and fasting."

II. The Power of Faith:

- Exploring the reasons behind our ability to perform miracles through faith. Matthew 17:19.

"Then came the disciples to Jesus apart, and said, Why could not we cast him out?"

III. Examples of Prayer Warriors:

- Hannah's Ministry of Prayer: Hannah's devout prayer life and dedication to God's service. Luke 2:36-38

  36. "And there was one Anna, a prophetess, the daughter of Phanuel, of the tribe of Asher: she was of a great age, and had lived with a husband seven years from her virginity;"

  37. "And she was a widow of about fourscore and four years, which departed not from the temple, but served God with fastings and prayers night and day."

  38. "And she coming in that instant gave thanks likewise unto the Lord, and spake of him to all them that looked for redemption in Jerusalem."

IV. Victorious Praying Churches:

- The victorious prayers of the early church in times of persecution and adversity. Acts 4:23-31, Acts 12:4-5 -

Acts 4:23-31:

  23. "And being let go, they went to their own company, and reported all that the chief priests and elders had said unto them."

  24. "And when they heard that, they lifted up their voice to God with one accord, and said, Lord, thou art God, which hast made heaven, and earth, and the sea, and all that in them is:"

  25. "Who by the mouth of thy servant David hast said, Why did the heathen rage, and the people imagine vain things?"

  26. "The kings of the earth stood up, and the rulers were gathered together against the Lord, and against his Christ."

  27. "For of a truth against thy holy child Jesus, whom thou hast anointed, both Herod, and Pontius Pilate, with the Gentiles, and the people of Israel, were gathered together,"

  28. "For to do whatsoever thy hand and thy counsel determined before to be done."

  29. "And now, Lord, behold their threatenings: and grant unto thy servants, that with all boldness they may speak thy word,"

  30. "By stretching forth thine hand to heal; and that signs and wonders may be done by the name of thy holy child Jesus."

31. *"And when they had prayed, the place was shaken where they were assembled together; and they were all filled with the Holy Ghost, and they spake the word of God with boldness."*

Acts 12:4-5:

4. *"And when he had apprehended him, he put him in prison, and delivered him to four quaternions of soldiers to keep him; intending after Easter to bring him forth to the people."*

5. *"Peter therefore was kept in prison: but prayer was made without ceasing of the church unto God for him."*

This Book of the Law.

Text: Joshua 1:8 - *"This book of the law shall not depart out of thy mouth; but thou shalt meditate therein day and night, that thou mayest observe to do according to all that is written therein: for then thou shalt make thy way prosperous, and then thou shalt have good success."*

I. Devotion to God's Word:

- The command to meditate on God's law day and night for success.

II. Characteristics of a Man of God:

- Seeking, doing, and teaching the law of God. *"For Ezra had prepared his heart to seek the law of the LORD, and to do it, and to teach in Israel statutes and judgments."* - Ezra 7:10

III. The Impact of God's Word:

- Building Happy Homes: Deuteronomy 6:1-9 - *1 "Now these are the commandments, the statutes, and the judgments, which the LORD your God commanded to teach you, that ye might do them in the land whither ye go to possess it:*

  2 That thou mightest fear the LORD thy God, to keep all his statutes and his commandments, which I command thee, thou, and thy son, and thy son's son, all the days of thy life; and that thy days may be prolonged.

  3 Hear therefore, O Israel, and observe to do it; that it may be well with thee, and that ye may increase mightily, as the LORD God of thy fathers hath promised thee, in the land that floweth with milk and honey.

4 Hear, O Israel: The LORD our God is one LORD:

5 And thou shalt love the LORD thy God with all thine heart, and with all thy soul, and with all thy might.

6 And these words, which I command thee this day, shall be in thine heart:

7 And thou shalt teach them diligently unto thy children, and shalt talk of them when thou sittest in thine house, and when thou walkest by the way, and when thou liest down, and when thou risest up.

8 And thou shalt bind them for a sign upon thine hand, and they shall be as frontlets between thine eyes.

9 And thou shalt write them upon the posts of thy house, and on thy gates."

- Noble Churches: Acts 17:10-14 - *10 "And the brethren immediately sent away Paul and Silas by night unto Berea: who coming thither went into the synagogue of the Jews.*

  11 These were more noble than those in Thessalonica, in that they received the word with all readiness of mind, and searched the scriptures daily, whether those things were so.

  12 Therefore many of them believed; also of honourable women which were Greeks, and of men, not a few.

  13 But when the Jews of Thessalonica had knowledge that the word of God was preached of Paul at Berea, they came thither also, and stirred up the people.

  14 And then immediately the brethren sent away Paul to go as it were to the sea: but Silas and Timotheus abode there still."

- Personal Growth: 2 Timothy 3:15-17 (KJV) -

  15 "And that from a child thou hast known the holy scriptures, which are able to make thee wise unto salvation through faith which is in Christ Jesus.

  16 All scripture is given by inspiration of God, and is profitable for doctrine, for reproof, for correction, for instruction in righteousness:

  17 That the man of God may be perfect, thoroughly furnished unto all good works."

  1 Peter 2:2

  2 "As newborn babes, desire the sincere milk of the word, that ye may grow thereby."

Be Vigilant.

Text: 1 Peter 5:8 - *"Be sober, be vigilant; because your adversary the devil, as a roaring lion, walketh about, seeking whom he may devour."*

I. The Adversary:

- Satan, the Adversary: Highlighting the existence and tactics of the enemy.

II. Jesus' Warning:

- Luke 22:40 - . 40 *"And when he was at the place, he said unto them, Pray that ye enter not into temptation."*

III. Peter's Lesson:

- Luke 22:31-34, Matthew 26:69-75, Matthew 26:34-35 (KJV) –

31 "And the Lord said, Simon, Simon, behold, Satan hath desired to have you, that he may sift you as wheat:"

32 "But I have prayed for thee, that thy faith fail not: and when thou art converted, strengthen thy brethren."

33 "And he said unto him, Lord, I am ready to go with thee, both into prison, and to death."

34 "And he said, I tell thee, Peter, the cock shall not crow this day, before that thou shalt thrice deny that thou knowest me."

Matthew 26:69-75:

69 "Now Peter sat without in the palace: and a damsel came unto him, saying, Thou also wast with Jesus of Galilee."

70 "But he denied before them all, saying, I know not what thou sayest."

71 "And when he was gone out into the porch, another maid saw him, and said unto them that were there, This fellow was also with Jesus of Nazareth."

72 "And again he denied with an oath, I do not know the man."

73 "And after a while came unto him they that stood by, and said to Peter, Surely thou also art one of them; for thy speech betrayeth thee."

74 "Then began he to curse and to swear, saying, I know not the man. And immediately the cock crew."

75 "And Peter remembered the word of Jesus, which said unto him, Before the cock crow, thou shalt deny me thrice. And he went out, and wept bitterly."

Matthew 26:34-35:

34 "Jesus said unto him, Verily I say unto thee, That this night, before the cock crow, thou shalt deny me thrice."

35 "Peter said unto him, Though I should die with thee, yet will I not deny thee. Likewise also said all the disciples."

IV. The Need for God's Power:

- Ephesians 6:10-12 (KJV) –

10 "And he said unto them, Behold, when ye are entered into the city, there shall a man meet you, bearing a pitcher of water; follow him into the house where he entereth in."

11 "And ye shall say unto the goodman of the house, The Master saith unto thee, Where is the guestchamber, where I shall eat the passover with my disciples?"

12 "And he shall shew you a large upper room furnished: there make ready."

<u>Leaving All.</u>

Text: Luke 14:33 - *"So likewise, whosoever he be of you that forsaketh not all that he hath, he cannot be my disciple."*

I. Renouncing Worldly Attachments:

1 Timothy 6:7 - *"For we brought nothing into this world, and it is certain we can carry nothing out."*

Mark 10:28 - *"Then Peter began to say unto him, Lo, we have left all, and have followed thee.".*

Luke 5:27-28 – *"27 And after these things he went forth, and saw a publican, named Levi, sitting at the receipt of custom: and he said unto him, Follow me. 28 And he left all, rose up, and followed him."*

II. Hindrances to Following Christ:

2 Timothy 2:4 -
No man that warreth entangleth himself with the affairs of this life; that he may please him who hath chosen him to be a soldier.

Philippians 3:8
Yea doubtless, and I count all things but loss for the excellency of the knowledge of Christ Jesus my Lord: for whom I have suffered the loss of all things, and do count them but dung, that I may win Christ.

III. Promised Rewards:

- Matthew 19:27-29 –

27. Then answered Peter and said unto him, Behold, we have forsaken all, and followed thee; what shall we have therefore?
28. And Jesus said unto them, Verily I say unto you, That ye which have followed me, in the regeneration when the Son of man shall sit in the throne of his glory, ye also shall sit upon twelve thrones, judging the twelve tribes of Israel.
29. And every one that hath forsaken houses, or brethren, or sisters, or father, or mother, or wife, or children, or lands, for my name's sake, shall receive an hundredfold, and shall inherit everlasting life.

Luke 18:29-30:
29. And he said unto them, Verily I say unto you, There is no man that hath left house, or parents, or brethren, or wife, or children, for the kingdom of God's sake,
30. Who shall not receive manifold more in this present time, and in the world to come life everlasting.

IV. The Challenge:

- Matthew 19:21-22 (KJV) -

  21. Jesus said unto him, If thou wilt be perfect, go and sell that thou hast, and give to the poor, and thou shalt have treasure in heaven: and come and follow me.

  22. But when the young man heard that saying, he went away sorrowful: for he had great possessions.

You Need Not to be Bound.

Text: Luke 4:18 - *"The Spirit of the Lord is upon me, because he hath anointed me to preach the gospel to the poor; he hath sent me to heal the brokenhearted, to preach deliverance to the captives, and recovering of sight to the blind, to set at liberty them that are bruised."*

I. The Purpose of Jesus' Ministry:

- Luke 4:18 (KJV) - Jesus' mission to bring freedom and deliverance.

II. Knowing Jesus for Freedom:

- John 8:32 (KJV), Luke 13:11-17 (KJV) - The transformative power of knowing Jesus for liberation from bondage.

Thanksgiving.

Text: Psalm 103:2 - *"Bless the Lord, O my soul, and forget not all his benefits."*

I. Remembering His Benefits:

- Psalm 103:3 (KJV) - Acknowledging and remembering the goodness of God.

II. Gratitude for His Blessings:

- Psalm 124:1-8 (KJV) - Reflecting on God's deliverance and protection.

III. Jesus' Approval of Thanksgiving:

- Luke 17:12-14 (KJV) - Jesus' validation of gratitude through the healing of ten lepers.

Message to the Church.

Text: Psalm 84:11b - *"No good thing will he withhold from them that walk uprightly."*

I. Walking Uprightly:

- Hebrews 10:25 (KJV) - Encouraging steadfastness in fellowship and worship.

- Seeking God's Law: Ezra 7:10, Joshua 1:8 (KJV) - Emphasizing the importance of seeking and following God's Word.

II. Resolution for the Year:

- To Read the Bible Through: Acts 17:11 (KJV) - Committing to the diligent study and reading of Scripture throughout the year.

For the Zeal of Thine House.

Text: Psalm 69:9 - *"For the zeal of thine house hath eaten me up; and the reproaches of them that reproached thee are fallen upon me."*

I. Godly Zeal:

- Hebrews 6:12 (KJV) - Encouraging diligence and fervor in serving God.

- Jesus' Example: John 2:17, John 4:8, 31-34, Luke 19:10 (KJV) - Illustrating Jesus' zeal for God's house and His mission.

II. Zeal in Unbelievers and Believers:

- Romans 10:2 (KJV) - Noting the zeal of unbelievers.

- Examples from Scripture: 2 Corinthians 9:2b, Philippians 3:6 (KJV) - Highlighting instances of zeal in both believers and non-believers.

III. Zeal Empowered by the Holy Spirit:

- 1 Corinthians 14:12 (KJV) - Emphasizing the importance of zeal inspired by the Holy Ghost.

- Zealous for Good Deeds: Titus 2:14b (KJV) - Encouraging zeal in pursuing righteousness and good works.

The Unrighteous.

Text: *1 Corinthians 6:9 (KJV) - "Know ye not that the unrighteous shall not inherit the kingdom of God? Be not deceived: neither fornicators, nor idolaters, nor adulterers, nor effeminate, nor abusers of themselves with mankind..."*

I. The Exaltation of Righteousness:

- Proverbs 14:34 (KJV) - Recognizing the elevation of righteousness.

- God's Desire for Righteousness: Matthew 5:48 (KJV) - God's expectation for His children to pursue righteousness.

II. Divine Justice and Reward:

- Hebrews 6:10 (KJV) - Assurance of God's righteousness in rewarding His servants.

- The Judgment of the Unrighteous: Revelation 22:11-12 (KJV) - Warning of the fate of the unrighteous.

III. Addressing Unrighteousness in the Church:

- Acts 5:1-11 (KJV) - An example of unrighteousness confronted within the early Church.

Be Ye Also Ready.

Text: Matthew 24:44 - *"Therefore be ye also ready: for in such an hour as ye think not the Son of man cometh."*

I. The Imperative of Readiness:

- Reason for Readiness: Matthew 24:42, Matthew 25:13 (KJV) - Emphasizing the unpredictability of Christ's return.

- Preparedness for the Second Coming: Hebrews 10:27 (KJV) - Highlighting the importance of readiness for Christ's return.

- The Danger of Drawing Back: Hebrews 10:38-39 (KJV) - Warning against the consequences of falling away from faith.

II. Parable of the Ten Virgins:

- Matthew 25:1-13 (KJV) - Illustrating the importance of being spiritually prepared for Christ's return.

III. Signs of Christ's Coming:

- Matthew 24:5-14, 37-39 (KJV) - Examining the signs preceding the second coming of Christ.

Growing in Grace.

Text: 2 Peter 3:18 (KJV) - *"But grow in grace, and in the knowledge of our Lord and Saviour Jesus Christ. To him be glory both now and for ever. Amen."*

I. Maturing in Faith:

- Ephesians 4:14 (KJV) - God's desire for Christians to mature and grow in faith.

- Means of Growth: Knowing the Scriptures - 1 Peter 2:2, John 7:17, 2 Timothy 3:15-17 (KJV) - Emphasizing the importance of scripture in spiritual growth.

- Standing Firm in the Word: John 8:31, James 1:22, Acts 2:42 (KJV) - Encouraging steadfastness in the teachings of Christ.

II. Growth in Faith:

- 2 Thessalonians 1:3 (KJV) - The necessity of faith to grow and develop.

- Challenge to the Berea Church: Acts 17:11 (KJV) - Commending the Bereans for their diligent study of the scriptures.

One Thing Remaineth of Thee.

Text: Luke 18:22a - *"Now when Jesus heard these things, he said unto him, Yet lackest thou one thing: sell all that thou hast, and distribute unto the poor, and thou shalt have treasure in heaven: and come, follow me."*

I. The Quest for Eternal Life:

The Rich Young Ruler's Inquiry: Luke 18:18 (KJV) - Introducing the rich young ruler's question about attaining eternal life.

Keeping the Commandments: Matthew 19:20 (KJV) - The young man's claim to have kept the commandments from his youth.

The Call to Perfection: Genesis 17:1, Matthew 5:48, 2 Corinthians 7:1 (KJV) - God's standard of perfection and wholeness.

II. The Challenge to Sell Out for God:

The Call to Sacrifice: Matthew 19:21 (KJV) - Jesus' instruction to the rich young ruler to sell his possessions and follow Him.

Hindrances to Perfection: Luke 18:23-25 (KJV) - Worldly possessions and affairs as obstacles to spiritual perfection.

III. What Remaineth of You?:

Reflecting on one's commitment and dedication to God in light of worldly attachments.

The Friendship of the World.

Text: James 4:4 - *"Ye adulterers and adulteresses, know ye not that the friendship of the world is enmity with God? whosoever therefore will be a friend of the world is the enemy of God."*

I. Separation from the World:

The Called Out People: 2 Corinthians 6:17 (KJV) - God's call for His people to separate themselves from the ways of the world.

Not of the World: John 15:19 (KJV) - Jesus' teaching that His followers are not of this world.

The Commandment Not to Love the World: 1 John 2:15-17 (KJV) - Warning against loving the world and its ways.

II. Reasons for Separation:

Our Identity as Children of God: 1 John 4:4-6 (KJV) - Because we belong to God, we should not befriend the world and its ways.

Ephesians 5:11, 2 Corinthians 6:14-16 (KJV) - Additional scriptures emphasizing the importance of separation from worldly influences.

<u>Where Art Thou?</u>

Text: Genesis 3:9 - "And the Lord God called unto Adam, and said unto him, Where art thou?"

I. The Consequence of Disobedience:

Adam and Eve's Disobedience: Genesis 3:9 (KJV) - The question posed by God after Adam and Eve's disobedience in the garden.

Warning to the Children of Israel: Deuteronomy 6:12 (KJV) - Cautioning against forgetting the Lord after receiving blessings.

Refusal to Heed Warning: Psalm 137:1-4 (KJV) - The consequences of ignoring God's warnings.

II. Pertinent Question for Today's Church:

Galatians 5:1 (KJV) - Calling the church to stand firm in freedom and not be entangled again in the yoke of bondage.

Examination of Spiritual State: 2 Corinthians 13:5, 1 Timothy 4:1 (KJV) - Urging self-examination and vigilance against deception.

Christ Our Captain.

Text: Matthew 28:20b - *"...lo, I am with you alway, even unto the end of the world. Amen."*

I. The Sovereignty and Unchangeableness of Christ:

All Power Belongs to Him: Matthew 28:18 (KJV) - Christ's declaration of His authority before His ascension.

His Unchangeable Nature: Hebrews 13:8 (KJV) - The assurance that Christ remains the same throughout time.

His Authority and Influence: Matthew 8:8 (KJV) - Demonstrating His power even from a distance.

II. Challenges Faced by the Church:

Lack of Obedience: John 8:31, Luke 6:46 (KJV) - Highlighting the importance of obedience to Christ's teachings.

Lack of Intimate Knowledge of Him: John 14:9, Matthew 16:13-18, Daniel 11:32b, Philippians 3:10 (KJV) - Emphasizing the need for a deep, personal relationship with Christ.

III. Overcoming Hindrances:

Unbelief and Doubt: Matthew 17:19-21 (KJV) - Addressing the obstacles of unbelief and doubt that hinder miracles.

Confronting Sin: John 9:31, Psalm 66:18, Romans 6:1-2, Proverbs 28:13 (KJV) - The importance of repentance and turning away from sin.

IV. The Unchangeable Promises of Our Captain:

Matthew 28:20, Mark 16:17-20, Isaiah 54:17 (KJV) - Assurance of Christ's presence, power, and protection for His followers.

Son of Perdition.

Text: John 17:12b - *"Those that thou gavest me I have kept, and none of them is lost, but the son of perdition; that the scripture might be fulfilled."*

I. Characteristics of the Son of Perdition:

Rejection of Truth and Word of God: John 8:31, James 1:22 (KJV) - The refusal to abide in the truth and teachings of God's Word.

God's Desire for Salvation: John 3:16, 2 Peter 3:9 (KJV) - Christ's mission to save humanity from perishing.

II. The Tragic Example of Judas:

Chosen but Chose Satan: Matthew 10:4, John 6:70, Acts 1:16-18 (KJV) - Judas' betrayal despite being selected as one of the disciples.

Rejection of Christ's Counsel: Matthew 26:21-25 (KJV) - Judas' refusal to heed Jesus' warnings.

Fulfillment of Secret Mission: Matthew 26:14-16, John 12:3-6 (KJV) - Judas' clandestine agreement to betray Jesus.

Repentance Came Too Late: Matthew 27:3-5 (KJV) - Judas' remorse and subsequent tragic end.

III. Lessons from Lot's Wife:

Ignoring God's Warning: Genesis 19:17, Genesis 19:26 (KJV) - Lot's wife's disobedience and resulting fate.

Provocation of God's Judgment: Proverbs 29:1 (KJV) - The consequences of persistent rebellion.

IV. The Challenge of Identity:

Son of Perdition or Son of the Kingdom?: Examining one's allegiance and obedience to God's will.

Blessing Through Giving.

Text: Luke 6:38 (KJV) - *"Give, and it shall be given unto you; good measure, pressed down, and shaken together, and running over, shall men give into your bosom. For with the same measure that ye mete withal it shall be measured to you again."*

I. The Principle of Giving:

Priority of Self-Giving: 2 Corinthians 8:5 (KJV) - Emphasizing the significance of offering oneself first to God.

God's Generosity: John 3:16 (KJV) - Illustrating God's ultimate act of giving through the sacrifice of His Son.

Greater Blessing in Giving: Acts 20:35b (KJV) - Highlighting the spiritual abundance found in generosity.

II. The Gateway to Prosperity:

Prosperity through Generosity: 2 Corinthians 8:1-4, Proverbs 11:25 (KJV) - The correlation between giving and receiving blessings.

Exemplary Giving of Abraham: Genesis 22:16-18 (KJV) - Abraham's obedience and subsequent blessing.

III. What to Give and to Whom:

Giving Everything: Luke 21:1-4 (KJV) - The value of sacrificial giving, regardless of the amount.

Beneficiaries of Giving: Galatians 6:6, 1 Timothy 5:8, Galatians 6:10 (KJV) - Supporting gospel ministers, family, and others in need.

IV. The Transformative Power of Giving:

Personal and Spiritual Enrichment: Romans 12:1, Proverbs 11:25 (KJV) - The spiritual growth and enrichment that come from selfless giving.

The Challenge to Give: Acts 4:34-35 (KJV) - Encouragement to embrace generosity as a life-changing practice.

Complete Salvation.

Text: Psalm 103:3 (KJV) - *"Who forgiveth all thine iniquities; who healeth all thy diseases."*

I. Understanding Complete Salvation:

Holistic Redemption: Salvation encompassing spirit, soul, and body.

Incomplete Salvation: Merely being saved from sin without addressing sickness.

Christ's Atonement for Sin and Sickness: Isaiah 53:5, Matthew 8:17, 1 Peter 2:24 (KJV) - Jesus' sacrifice covering both sin and physical ailments.

Biblical Examples of Complete Deliverance: Exodus 15:26, Psalm 105:37 (KJV) - The Israelites' experience of comprehensive healing and redemption.

II. Embracing Complete Salvation Today:

Freedom from Adamic Sickness and Curse: Galatians 3:13, 3 John 2, 1 Timothy 5:23, Matthew 3:11-12 (KJV) - Liberation from the consequences of Adam's fall, including illness and spiritual bondage.

Empty Barrel.

Text: Judges 16-20

I. The Cold and Sick Church:

Lukewarmness and Spiritual Apathy: Revelation 3:15-16, Acts 19:13-16 (KJV) - The peril of spiritual indifference.

Lack of Signs: Psalm 74:9-12 (KJV) - Absence of God's miraculous interventions and manifestations in the church.

A Call to Rekindle the Fire: Judges 16:28-30 (KJV) - Urging the church to seek restoration and revival.

II. Restoring Lost Glory:

Recognizing Spiritual Bankruptcy: Acknowledging the emptiness and need for revival.

Seeking God's Power: Pursuing divine intervention to revive the church and restore its former glory.

Oh Sleeper, Arise.

Text: Jonah 1:6 (KJV) - *"So the shipmaster came to him, and said unto him, What meanest thou, O sleeper? arise, call upon thy God, if so be that God will think upon us, that we perish not."*

I. The Great Challenge:

Unbelievers Seeking Their Gods: Jonah 1:5 (KJV) - Contrast between the urgency of pagan sailors and spiritual lethargy.

Church Out of Position: Psalm 74:9-10, Luke 18:8, 1 Timothy 4:1 (KJV) - The church's need to awaken from spiritual slumber and confront the adversary.

II. Accepting the Challenge:

Jonah's Response: Jonah 2:1 (KJV) - Jonah's acknowledgment of the need to call upon God amidst crisis.

Early Disciples' Example: Acts 4:24-31 (KJV) - Apostolic fervor in seeking God's intervention through prayer and revival.

\

Revive Thy Work.

Text: Habakkuk 3:2 - *"O Lord, I have heard thy speech, and was afraid: O Lord, revive thy work in the midst of the years, in the midst of the years make known; in wrath remember mercy."*

I. The Urgent Need for Revival:

- Inadequate Spiritual State:
- Lack of Complete Salvation.
- Spiritual Emptiness and Apathy.
- Joyless Church Environment.
- Absence of God's Fire and Holiness.
- Dormant Prayer Life.

II. Hindrances to Revival:

- Sins and Iniquities.
- Love of Money.
- Worldliness and Hypocrisy.

III. Prerequisites for Revival:

Repentance: 2 Chronicles 7:14, Acts 3:19 (KJV) - Turning away from sins and returning to God.

Humble Seeking of God: Embracing prayer, righteousness, and a genuine desire for spiritual renewal.

The Creative Power.

Text: Genesis 2:7 - *"And the LORD God formed man of the dust of the ground, and breathed into his nostrils the breath of life, and man became a living soul."*

I. Christ's Role in Creation:

Co-Creator with God: Proverbs 8:22-30 (KJV) - Jesus involved in the creation process.

Counteracting Satan's Destruction: John 10:10 (KJV) - Jesus' mission to counteract Satan's destructive influence and offer salvation.

II. Demonstrating Creative Power:

Healing the Blind: John 9:6 (KJV) - Jesus' miraculous act of restoring sight to the blind, showcasing His creative authority.

Empowering Believers: Ephesians 3:20 (KJV) - The transformative power of Christ at work within believers.

The Power of God.

Text: 2 Chronicles 16:9 - *"For the eyes of the LORD run to and fro throughout the whole earth, to shew himself strong in the behalf of them whose heart is perfect toward him..."*

I. Understanding the Need for God's Power:

Confronting Spiritual Forces: Ephesians 6:10-11 (KJV) - The necessity of God's power to withstand spiritual adversaries.

Overcoming Sin: John 16:8 (KJV) - The Holy Spirit's role in convicting and empowering believers to overcome sin.

Fulfillment of Promises: Luke 24:49 (KJV) - The assurance of God's power to fulfill His promises, including the outpouring of the Holy Spirit.

II. The Promise of the Holy Spirit:

Prophesied Outpouring: Joel 2:28 (KJV) - The prophecy of the Holy Spirit's coming.

Reasons for Unbelief:

Ignorance: Acts 19:2-3 (KJV) - Lack of understanding among some regarding the Holy Spirit's role.

III. Receiving the Promise Today:

Conditions for Receiving:

Repentance: Acts 2:38 (KJV) - Turning away from sin and seeking forgiveness.

Seeking: Luke 13:11 (KJV) - Asking God to bestow His power and blessings upon believers.

Ye Must Be Born Again.

Text: John 3:7 - *"Marvel not that I said unto thee, Ye must be born again."*

I. The Eternity Question: The Kingdom of God

Significance of Being Born Again: i. Spiritual Perception: John 3:3 (KJV) - Without being born again, one cannot perceive the kingdom of God. ii. Access to God's Kingdom: John 3:5 (KJV) - Only those born again can enter into God's kingdom.

What Salvation Is Not.

I. Salvation Is Not Achieved Through Works

Ephesians 2:8-9 (KJV) - Emphasizes salvation by grace through faith, not by human works.

II. Salvation Is Not Attained Through Human Names

Acts 4:12 (KJV) - Salvation is found only through Jesus Christ, not through any other name.

III. Salvation Is Not Obtained Through Baptism Alone

Mark 16:16 (KJV) - Baptism is important but not sufficient for salvation; faith is essential.

IV. Salvation Is Not Mere Religious Observance

John 3:4-6 (KJV) - Nicodemus' misunderstanding highlights that salvation requires a spiritual rebirth, not merely adherence to religious rituals.

Salvation Is a Radical Transformation of Heart

Genuine Confession: Romans 10:9-10 (KJV) - True salvation involves confessing Jesus as Lord and believing in His resurrection.

Evidenced by Faith: Matthew 7:20 (KJV) - True conversion is reflected in one's actions, demonstrating their faith.

Deliverance from Sin: 1 John 3:19 (KJV) - Salvation involves being freed from the bondage of sin.

Becoming a New Creation: 2 Corinthians 5:17 (KJV) - Salvation results in becoming a new person in Christ, with renewed thoughts and attitudes.

Salvation Call – Come Out.

Text: Abraham's Call - Genesis 12:1-3 – *1. Now the LORD had said unto Abram, Get thee out of thy country, and from thy kindred, and from thy father's house, unto a land that I will shew thee:*

2. And I will make of thee a great nation, and I will bless thee, and make thy name great; and thou shalt be a blessing:

3.And I will bless them that bless thee, and curse him that curseth thee: and in thee shall all families of the earth be blessed.

- Abraham's Call - Abraham's call to leave his country and kindred signifies a separation from worldly ties for God's purpose.

Today's Believers Called Out - 2 Corinthians 6:17-18

- Believers are urged to come out from among unbelievers and be separate, touching not the unclean, to receive God's promises.

Salvation Precedes Service to God

- Importance of Salvation: Matthew 19:27-28, Matthew 7:22-23
  - Jesus emphasized the necessity of salvation before engaging in ministry or good works.

Steps to Salvation:

i. **Belief**: Acts 16:30-31 - Salvation begins with faith in Jesus Christ as the Savior.
ii. **Repentance**: Acts 3:19 - Genuine repentance is essential for receiving salvation.

They Disappointed God.

Text: Genesis 6:6

- God was grieved by the wickedness of humanity, leading to His judgment in the days of Noah.

  "And it repented the LORD that he had made man on the earth, and it grieved him at his heart." Genesis 6:6

Reasons for Disappointment:

- Fellowship with the Ungodly: Genesis 6:4-5 - People's association with the ungodly led to moral corruption and displeased God.

- Consequences of Disobedience: Genesis 6:7 - God's judgment followed due to humanity's disobedience and wickedness.

Judas' Betrayal of Jesus: Matthew 26:21-25 (14-16)

- Judas' betrayal of Jesus exemplifies disappointment in one who was close to Him, choosing greed and betrayal over loyalty.

Modern Church's Disappointment:

- Lack of Obedience: Luke 6:46 - Jesus rebuked those who called Him "Lord" but didn't obey Him.

- Embracing Worldliness: 1 Timothy 4:1, 2 Peter 2:20-22 - The church's compromise with worldly desires and false teachings leads to disappointment in God's sight.

Passion for the Lost Souls.

Text: Matthew 9:36

- Jesus' compassion for the lost is evident throughout His ministry, reflecting His mission to seek and save the lost.

  "But when he saw the multitudes, he was moved with compassion on them, because they fainted, and were scattered abroad, as sheep having no shepherd." - Matthew 9:36

Christ's Mission to Save Souls:

- Zacchaeus: Luke 19:1-11 - Jesus sought to save Zacchaeus, demonstrating His mission to seek and save the lost.

- Samaritan Woman: John 4:31-42 - Jesus' encounter with the Samaritan woman reveals His passion for saving souls.

- Healing the Blind Man: John 9:1-7 - Jesus' healing of the blind man highlights His mission to bring spiritual sight to the lost.

- Healing the Leper: Matthew 8:1-4 - Jesus' compassion extends to the outcast, illustrating His desire to save souls.

The Early Disciples' Mission:

- Commissioned by Jesus: Luke 9:1-5, Mark 16:15-20 - The disciples were sent out to preach the Gospel, emphasizing the urgency of reaching the lost.

The Compulsion to Preach:

- Paul's Compulsion: 1 Corinthians 9:16-17 - Paul felt compelled to preach the Gospel, underscoring the necessity of sharing the Good News.

Challenge and Purpose of the Holy Spirit:

- Elisha's Challenge: 2 Kings 7:10-11 - Elisha's servants recognized the urgency of sharing good news, prompting action.

- Purpose of the Holy Spirit: Acts 1:8 - The Holy Spirit empowers believers to be witnesses, fulfilling Christ's mission to save souls.

Be Ye Doers of the Word.

Text: James 1:22, Romans 2:13b

- True faith is evidenced by obedience to God's Word, not just hearing it.

  James 1:22:

  "Be ye doers of the word, and not hearers only, deceiving your own selves."

  Romans 2:13b:

  "for not the hearers of the law are just before God, but the doers of the law shall be justified."

The Power in Obedience to God's Word:

- Matthew 8:8b - The centurion's faith in Jesus' authority demonstrates the power in obedience to God's Word.

- Love as Obedience: John 14:15 - Jesus connects love for Him with obedience to His commands.

Avoiding Hypocrisy:

- Matthew 7:26-27, Luke 6:46 - Jesus warns against mere lip service, urging genuine obedience to His teachings.

Setting Goals in Spiritual Growth:

- Ezra's Example: Ezra 7:10 - Ezra's commitment to study, observe, and teach God's law serves as a model for spiritual growth and obedience.

For Thy God.

Text: Job 5:27

What are the goods or benefits of serving God?

Job 5:27:

"Lo this, we have searched it, so it is; hear it, and know thou it for thy good."

1. Eternal Life and Good Things:

Salvation: John 3:16 - Believers receive eternal life through Christ.

Goodness: Psalm 84:11b - God provides good things for His children.

2. Free Salvation:

John 1:12 - Those who receive Christ are given the right to become children of God.

3. Good Success and the Word of God:

Joshua 1:8 - Meditating on God's Word leads to success and prosperity.

4. Wisdom and New Birth:

2 Timothy 3:15 - The Scriptures make one wise for salvation through faith in Christ.

5. Prayer and Receiving from God:

John 14:13 - Believers can ask anything in Jesus' name, and it will be done for them.

6. Gateway to God's Blessing and Holiness:

Psalm 1:1-4 - Those who delight in the law of the Lord are blessed and fruitful.

7. Reasonable Service and Separation:

Romans 12:1-2 - Believers are called to offer their bodies as living sacrifices, holy and pleasing to God.

8. Gateway to Heaven and Holiness:

Hebrews 12:14 - Pursuing holiness is essential for seeing the Lord.

The Affliction of the Righteous.

Text: Psalm 34:19
- Afflictions are inevitable for believers but ultimately work for their good.

"Many are the afflictions of the righteous: but the Lord delivereth him out of them all."

Assurance and Strength in Affliction:
- John 16:33, Philippians 1:29 - Believers can find peace and joy even in tribulation.
- Romans 8:28 - God works all things for the good of those who love Him.

Examples of Endurance:
- Various biblical figures such as Sarah, Hannah, Abraham, Isaac, Joseph, Daniel, and the three Hebrew children endured afflictions with courage and faith.

Encouragement and Divine Intervention:
- Job 13:15 - Believers are urged to maintain their integrity and trust in God during trials.
- 1 Corinthians 10:13 - God provides a way of escape in every temptation.
- Psalm 50:15 - Believers are encouraged to call upon God in times of trouble.

God's People.

Text: 1 John 3:9 - *"Whosoever is born of God doth not commit sin; for his seed remaineth in him: and he cannot sin, because he is born of God."*

Recognition of God's People:

- **By Their Fruits:** Matthew 7:16 - Known by their actions and character.

- **By Their Wise Preparation:** Matthew 25 - Prepared for the kingdom of heaven.

Characteristics of God's People:

- **Followers of God:** Ephesians 5:1 - Imitators of God, walking in love.

- **Striving for Perfection:** Matthew 5:48 - Called to be perfect as God is perfect.

- **Pursuing Holiness:** 1 Peter 1:15-16 - Commanded to be holy as God is holy.

Identification and Qualities:

- **A Peculiar People:** Exodus 19:5 - Set apart for God's own possession.

- **A Holy People:** Deuteronomy 7:6 - Set apart to the Lord as a treasured possession.

- **Chosen by Jehovah:** Deuteronomy 14:2 - Called by God as His own people.

- **Exalted Above All Nations:** Deuteronomy 26:19 - Lifted high by God among all peoples.

- **Guided and Protected:** Psalm 29:11, Psalm 78:52, Psalm 100:3 - Led and cared for like a flock.

- **Prepared for Service:** Luke 1:17b, Acts 15:14 - Equipped and appointed for God's work.

- **Characterized by Zeal:** Titus 2:14b - Eager for good works and the glory of God.

- **Law Written Upon Their Hearts:** Hebrews 8:10 - God's law internalized and lived out by His people.

Open Thou Mine Eyes.

Text: Psalm 119:18 -

Open thou mine eyes, that I may behold wondrous things out of thy law.

Need for Spiritual Enlightenment:

- Because of Spiritual Blindness: 2 Corinthians 4:4 - Blinded by the god of this world.

- Because of Veils of the Heart: 2 Corinthians 3:14 - Veiled minds hindering understanding.

Examples of Spiritual Awakening:

- Balaam: Numbers 22:31-35 - Eyes opened to God's truth and presence.

- The Prophet Elisha: 2 Kings 6:15-17 - Eyes opened to see the reality of God's protection.

- Saul's Conversion: Acts 9:1-2, Acts 9:17-18 - Eyes opened to the truth of Christ, leading to repentance and conversion.

- Repentance Leading to Spiritual Illumination: 2 Corinthians 3:16 - Turning to Christ removes the veil and brings understanding.

- The Work of the Spirit: 2 Corinthians 3:17 - The Spirit of God brings freedom and insight to believers.

The Deceitful Heart.

Text: Jer. 17:9 – *"The heart is deceitful above all things, and desperately wicked: who can know it?"*

Understanding the Deceitful Heart:
- God's Knowledge of the Heart: Jer. 17:10 - God comprehensively understands every heart.
- Hypocrisy and Deception: Mark 7:6-7, Luke 6:46 - Warning against hypocritical hearts that honor with lips but not with actions.
- Attempts to Hide from God: Isaiah 28:15, 29:15 - Fruitless efforts to conceal intentions from God's sight.
- Example of Deceit: Joseph's Brothers - Gen. 42:8-14 - Deceptive hearts causing harm and distress to others.
- Wholeness of Heart Desired: Jer. 2:13-14, Joel 2:12-13 - Urging for genuine repentance and return to God.
- Consequences of Deception: Gal. 6:7-8, Rev. 22:11-12 - Reaping what is sown, facing divine judgment.

Danger of Apathy.

Text: Mark 3:24 – *"And if a kingdom be divided against itself, that kingdom cannot stand."*
Genesis 11:7: *"Go to, let us go down, and there confound their language, that they may not understand one another's speech."*

Understanding Apathy:
- Indifference and Inaction: Luke 9:49-50 - Apathy leading to societal and spiritual decline.
- Apathy in the Church: 1 Tim. 4:12 - Neglect of doctrine, truth, and holiness standards.
- Contrast with the Early Church: Acts 2:41-47 - The fervor and commitment of the early believers.
- Effects of Apathy: Acts 2:1-4, Acts 4:31-35 - Diminished power and vitality in the church.

Identifying Apathetic Attitudes:
1. Unconcerned Individuals: Acts 5:1-10 - Lack of concern and dishonesty.
2. Slothful Individuals: John 4:35, Jer. 48:10 - Laziness and indifference to spiritual matters.

Challenge Against Apathy:
- Recognizing the Dangers: Heb. 6:12 - Urging believers to fight against apathy, be involved, and serve God wholeheartedly.

Love of Money.

Text: 1Tim. 6:10 – *"For the love of money is the root of all evil: which while some coveted after, they have erred from the faith, and pierced themselves through with many sorrows."*

Understanding the Love of Money:
1. Root of Evil: 1Tim. 6:10 - Described as the root of all evil, leading to various forms of wrongdoing.
2. Diversion from Spiritual Pursuits: 1Tim. 6:6-11 - Hinders the pursuit of godliness and righteousness.
3. Contentment in Godliness: 1Tim. 6:6-8, Heb. 13:5-7 - Encouragement to find satisfaction in godliness and truth, rather than material wealth.

Dangers of the Love of Money:
- It leads individuals astray from the path of righteousness and faithfulness.

Examples from Scripture:
- Achan: Joshua 7:21 - Achan's greed led to disobedience and disastrous consequences for Israel.
- Gehazi: 2Kings 5:26-27 - Gehazi's desire for wealth resulted in punishment and disgrace.
- Judas Iscariot: Mat. 26:14-16, Mat. 27:3-5 - Judas's betrayal of Jesus for thirty pieces of silver highlights the tragic outcome of greed.

God's People.

Text: 1Peter. 2:9 – *"But ye are a chosen generation, a royal priesthood, an holy nation, a peculiar people; that ye should shew forth the praises of him who hath called you out of darkness into his marvellous light.*
Zechariah 2:8b:
For he that toucheth you toucheth the apple of his eye.

Characteristics of God's People:
- Chosen by God: Deut. 14:2 - Selected as a special people by Jehovah.
- Peculiar Treasure: Exodus 19:5 - Regarded as a treasured possession.
- Exalted Above All Nations: Deut. 26:19, 1Sam. 12:22, Psalm 29:11 - Elevated and guided by God.
- Guided Like a Flock: Psalm 78:52 - Carefully shepherded and guided by God's hand.
- Characterized by Zeal: Titus 2:14 - Displaying fervor and passion in their faith.
- Law Written on Their Hearts: Heb. 8:10, 1Pet. 2:9b - Guided by the principles of God's law within their hearts.
- Prepared for Service: Luke 1:17, Acts 15:14b - Equipped and appointed for service in God's kingdom.

Challenge:
- Are You Among God's People? Encouragement to examine one's life and faith to ensure alignment with God's chosen people.

Armor of God.

Text: Ephesians 6:11: *"Put on the whole armour of God, that ye may be able to stand against the wiles of the devil."*

Purpose of the Armor:
- To Stand Against: Eph. 6:11b - Equips believers to withstand the schemes of the devil.

Understanding the Armor:
- Protector and Defender: Prov. 18:10 - Acts as a shield and refuge, providing protection from spiritual attacks.
- Identifying the True Enemy: Eph. 6:12-13 - Recognizes that the ultimate adversary is Satan, not fellow humans.

Christian Weapons:
- Spiritual Warfare: 2Cor. 10:3-4 - Engaging in spiritual battles with weapons empowered by God.
- Spiritual Armor: Eph. 6:17 - Equipped with the full armor of God to defend against spiritual attacks.
- Power of Testimony: Rev. 12:11 - Overcoming the enemy by the blood of the Lamb and the word of testimony.

Shield of Faith.

Text: Eph. 6:16

Understanding the Shield of Faith:
- **Foundation in Christ:** Mat. 16:18 - The church is built upon Christ, the solid Rock.
- **Rock of Salvation:** 1Cor. 10:4b - Jesus is likened to a rock, providing stability and protection.
- **The Word of Testimony:** Rev. 12:11 - The shield of faith is reinforced by the word of one's testimony.
- **Readily Available:** Psalm 3:3, Psalm 5:12, 33:20, 115:9, 119:114 - The shield of faith is ever-present, offering refuge and protection.

Challenge:
- **Come Right Now Unto Him:** Prov. 18:10 - Encouragement to seek refuge and protection in the Lord, relying on the shield of faith.

Misuse of Tongue.

Text: James 3:2: *"For in many things we offend all. If any man offend not in word, the same is a perfect man, and able also to bridle the whole body."*

Understanding the Danger:

- Tongue's Power: James 3:5-6 - Acknowledges the immense power of the tongue to cause harm.

- Watch What You Say: Eph. 4:29 - Encourages sanctification in speech, avoiding words that can cause harm.

- Confession Over Life: Rom. 10:8-10 - Emphasizes the significance of one's confession in shaping their life.

- Power of Words: Rom. 18:21, Phil. 2:11 - Highlights the importance of being mindful of the words spoken, as they have the power to impact oneself and others.

Wait Upon the Lord.

Text: Psalm 27:14: *"Wait on the LORD: be of good courage, and he shall strengthen thine heart: wait, I say, on the LORD."*

Reasons for Waiting Upon God:

1. **He is Our Help:** Isa. 40:31 - God is the ultimate source of strength and assistance for those who wait upon Him.

2. **Goodness to Those Who Wait:** Lame. 3:25 - God shows favor and goodness to those who patiently wait for Him.

Example:

- **Impotent Man:** John 5:3-9 - Illustrates the importance of waiting upon the Lord for healing and restoration.

Challenge:

- **Patience in Waiting:** Hab. 2:3b - Despite delays, it's essential to maintain patience and trust in God's timing.

Last Minute Miracle.

Text: Gen. 22:13:"*And Abraham lifted up his eyes, and looked, and behold behind him a ram caught in a thicket by his horns: and Abraham went and took the ram, and offered him up for a burnt offering in the stead of his son.*"

Key Points:
- **Word of Faith:** Gen. 22:5, 7 - Abraham's faith and obedience are evident in his willingness to follow God's instructions, even when it seemed impossible.
- **Obedience to the Last Minute:** Gen. 22:9-10 - Abraham's obedience was unwavering, even when faced with sacrificing his son, Isaac.
- **God Desires Perfect Obedience:** 2Cor. 10:6 - God values and rewards complete obedience from His followers.
- **Miracle Follows Obedience:** Gen. 22:11-13 - Abraham's obedience led to the provision of a ram for sacrifice, showcasing how miracles often follow obedience to God's commands. Similar instances are seen in Jonah 1:15-17 and 2:1.

Debt-Free Life.

Text: Romans 13:8: "*Owe no man any thing, but to love one another: for he that loveth another hath fulfilled the law.*"

Key Points:
- **God's Promises:** Psalm 34:10, Psalm 37:25 - God promises to provide for His people and ensure they lack nothing.
- **God as the Provider:** 2King 4:1-7 - The story of Elisha and the widow illustrates God's ability to miraculously pay off debts and provide for His people's needs.

The Lost Thing in the Church.

Text: Psalm 74:9: "*We see not our signs: there is no more any prophet: neither is there among us any that knoweth how long.*"

Key Points:
- **The Church's Great Need:** The absence of prophets and a decline in spiritual vitality leave the church in a vulnerable state (Psalm 74:10).
- **The Gospel of Power:** Despite the challenges, the church must reclaim the gospel's power, as seen in Luke 9:2-6, Luke 10:17, and Mark 16:17-18.

Change Your Garment.

Text: Gen. 35:2b: *"Put away the strange gods that are among you, and be clean, and change your garments."*

Key Points:
- Returning to Bethel: Just as Jacob returned to Bethel in obedience to God (Gen. 35:1), the church must also return to its place of spiritual encounter and renewal.
- Obedience: Gen. 35:4 highlights the importance of obedience in the process of spiritual transformation.
- The Rebellious Church: Drawing from Jer. 6:16, the sermon highlights the tendency of the church to rebel against God's standards and seek worldly friendships (James 4:4).
- God's Standard vs. Man's Standard: Contrasting Gen. 3:7 with Gen. 3:21, Jer. 10:1-2, and 1John 2:15-17, the sermon emphasizes the importance of adhering to God's standards rather than worldly fashions.
- Christian Adorning: The sermon concludes by referencing 1Pet. 3:3-6, which emphasizes inner beauty and a heart aligned with God over external appearances.

Repentance is Compulsory.

Text: Acts 17:30 – *"And the times of this ignorance God winked at; but now commandeth all men every where to repent."*

Key Points:
- **Mission Given to the Church:** The mission to preach repentance and forgiveness of sins was given to the Church (Luke 24:47).
- **Purpose of Christ's Coming:** Jesus came into the world not for the righteous, but to call sinners to repentance (Mat. 9:13).
- **God's Command:** Mark 1:15 emphasizes God's command for all to repent.
- **Understanding Repentance:** Repentance is defined in Acts 3:19, Prov. 28:13, and Mat. 3:8 as turning away from sin and turning towards God.
- **Genuine Repentance:** Genuine repentance is seen in the story of Zacchaeus (Luke 19:8-10) and results in a new creation (2Cor. 5:17, Rom. 6:4).
- **Warning of Judgment:** Luke 13:3 highlights the urgency of repentance by warning of impending judgment.

Have Faith in God.

Text: Mark 11:22 – *"And Jesus answering saith unto them, Have faith in God."*
Key Points:
- Faith in God's Word: Faith in God stands on His Word and does not accept defeat (Gen. 1:1-2).
- The Power of Spoken Word: Throughout Scripture, God's spoken word brings about creation and change (Gen. 1:3, Gen. 6:7).
- Human Response in Faith: Individuals like Hezekiah (Isa. 38:1, 38:2-3) and the centurion (Mat. 8:8) responded in faith by speaking out and believing in God's power.

Men of Action.

Text: Mark 16:20a – *"And they went forth, and preached every where, the Lord working with them, and confirming the word with signs following."*
Key Points:
- God's Work with Prophets and Apostles: The effectiveness of God's work was evident through the actions of old prophets, Apostles, and disciples (Luke 9:1-6, Acts 1:12-14, Acts. 2:1-2, Acts 4:19-20, 2Kings 2:12-15).
- The Importance of Action: Many are not saved, healed, or blessed today because they lack the proactive nature demonstrated by these men of action.

The Urgency of the Gospel.

Text: John 13:27b – *"And they went forth, and preached every where, the Lord working with them."*
Key Points:
- God's Command: The urgency of the gospel stems from God's command to go and preach it (Mark 16:15, Mat. 28:19).
- Necessity of Preaching: Preaching the gospel is a necessity, as expressed by Paul in 1Corinthians 9:16.
- Perishing Souls: The urgency is heightened by the reality of souls perishing without the gospel (John 3:18, Rom. 10:14).
- Example of the Four Lepers: The urgency of action is illustrated through the story of the four lepers in 2Kings 7:9-12.

Abiding in the Light.

Text: John 14:6 – *"Jesus saith unto him, I am the way, the truth, and the life: no man cometh unto the Father, but by me."*

What is Light? What does light do? Who is the **light in this lesson?**

- **Defining Light:** Light symbolizes truth, guidance, and revelation.
- **Function of Light:** Light illuminates darkness, provides direction, and reveals truth.
- **Jesus as the Light:** Jesus is identified as the light (John 12:4b, John 8:12, John 9:4-5), signifying His role in providing spiritual enlightenment and guidance.
- **Abiding in the Light:** Abiding in the light means abiding in Christ (John 14:6, John 15:4-10), emphasizing the necessity of remaining connected to Jesus for spiritual growth and understanding.
- **Importance of Abiding:** Abiding in the light ensures fellowship with God (1John 1:7) and reflects the transformative nature of Christianity, where believers become lights themselves (Mat. 5:14-16, Col. 1:13).

The Mark of True Believers.

Text: 1John 3:9 – *"Whosoever is born of God doth not commit sin; for his seed remaineth in him: and he cannot sin, because he is born of God."*

Key Points:

- **Purpose of the Message:** The message is delivered in light of the signs of the last days (Mat. 24:12), emphasizing the necessity of being born again (John 3:3-5) to avoid spiritual perdition.
- **Identification with Satan:** Those who continue in sin are identified as being of Satan (John 8:41), underlining the contrast between righteousness and sin.
- **The Liberating Truth:** The truth sets believers free (John 8:32 & 36, Eph. 4:21-24), enabling them to live in accordance with God's will.
- **Opposition to Truth:** Some may resist the truth (2Tim. 3:7), highlighting the challenges faced in conveying spiritual truths.
- **Challenge:** The audience is urged to pay heed to the message and avoid neglecting salvation (Heb. 2:3).

Change Your Garment.

Text: Gen. 35:2b – *"Put away the strange gods that are among you, and be clean, and change your garments.*

Key Points:

- **Back to Bethel:** Returning to Bethel signifies a return to a place of spiritual significance and connection with God (Gen. 35:1).
- **Understanding Bethel:** Bethel, meaning "House of God," holds symbolic importance as a place of encounter with God (Gen. 28:19).
- **Call to Obedience:** The call to change one's garment (symbolizing a change in lifestyle) is accompanied by obedience (Gen. 35:3-4), reflecting a commitment to align with God's will.
- **Church Rebellion:** Drawing parallels with Jeremiah 6:16, the message highlights the dangers of rebellion and worldliness in the church (James 4:4).
- **Sinful Fashion:** Worldly fashion is condemned as sin (Jer. 10:1-2, 1John 2:15), contrasting with the Christian call to adornment in 1Peter 3:3-6.
- **Example of Healing:** Referencing the Gadarene demoniac's healing (Mark 5:15), the sermon emphasizes the transformative power of holiness.
- **Challenge:** The audience is challenged to align their lives with God's will, symbolized by setting their houses in order (Isaiah 38:1b).

God's Provision.

Text: Psalm 121:1 – *"I will lift up mine eyes unto the hills, from whence cometh my help."*

Key Points:

- **Faith in God's Provision:** Encouragement to trust in God's provision, as stated in Philippians 4:19.
- **Biblical Examples:** Several instances from Scripture illustrate God's provision:
  - **The Ram:** Referencing Genesis 22:13, highlighting the importance of obedience and reverence for God.
  - **Provision for Elijah:** Drawing from 1 Kings 17:6, emphasizing obedience as a prerequisite for God's provision.
  - **Money in the Fish:** Matthew 17:27 serves as an example of God's miraculous provision in response to obedience.
  - **Miracle of Wine:** The narrative in John 2:10b illustrates God's provision in response to faith and obedience.

Do Not Give Up.

Text: Luke 1:18 - *"And Zacharias said unto the angel, Whereby shall I know this? for I am an old man, and my wife well stricken in years."*

I. Zacharias' Struggle with Unbelief:

Who was Zacharias – Luke 1:5-7 - *"There was in the days of Herod, the king of Judaea, a certain priest named Zacharias, of the course of Abia: and his wife was of the daughters of Aaron, and her name was Elisabeth. And they were both righteous before God, walking in all the commandments and ordinances of the Lord blameless. And they had no child, because that Elisabeth was barren, and they both were now well stricken in years."*

God's promises to him – Luke 1:6-17 – *"And they were both righteous before God, walking in all the commandments and ordinances of the Lord blameless. And they had no child, because that Elisabeth was barren, and they both were now well stricken in years. And the angel answering said unto him, I am Gabriel, that stand in the presence of God; and am sent to speak unto thee, and to shew thee these glad tidings. And, behold, thou shalt be dumb, and not able to speak, until the day that these things shall be performed, because thou believest not my words, which shall be fulfilled in their season. And the people waited for Zacharias, and marvelled that he tarried so long in the temple. And when he came out, he could not speak unto them: and they perceived that he had seen a vision in the temple: for he beckoned unto them, and remained speechless. And it came to pass, that, as soon as the days of his ministration were accomplished, he departed to his own house. And after those days his wife Elisabeth conceived, and hid herself five months, saying, Thus hath the Lord dealt with me in the days wherein he looked on me, to take away my reproach among men. And in the sixth month the angel Gabriel was sent from God unto a city of Galilee, named Nazareth, To a virgin espoused to a man whose name was Joseph, of the house of David; and the virgin's name was Mary. And the angel came in unto her, and said, Hail, thou that art highly favoured, the Lord is with thee: blessed art thou among women. And when she saw him, she was troubled at his saying, and cast in her mind what manner of salutation this should be."*

Because of unbelief looking unto his problem – Luke 1:18 - *"And Zacharias said unto the angel, Whereby shall I know this? for I am an old man, and my wife well stricken in years."*

Believe what God says – Mark 10:27 - *"And Jesus looking upon them saith, With men it is impossible, but not with God: for with God all things are possible."*

As Mary: God's Promises – Luke 1:27-33 - *"To a virgin espoused to a man whose name was Joseph, of the house of David; and the virgin's name was Mary. And the angel came in unto her, and said, Hail, thou that art highly favoured, the Lord is with thee: blessed art thou among women. And when she saw him, she was troubled at his saying, and cast in her mind what manner of salutation this should be. And the angel said unto her, Fear not, Mary: for* *thou hast found favour with God. And, behold, thou shalt conceive in thy womb, and bring forth a son, and shalt call his name Jesus. He shall be great, and shall be called the Son of the Highest: and the Lord God shall give unto him the throne of his father David: And he shall reign over the house of Jacob for ever; and of his kingdom there shall be no end."*

Mary wants to know – Luke 1:34-35 - *"Then said Mary unto the angel, How shall this be, seeing I know not a man? And the angel answered and said unto her, The Holy Ghost shall come upon thee, and the power of the Highest shall overshadow thee: therefore also that holy thing which shall be born of thee shall be called the Son of God."*

God's Plan for Mankind.

Text**:** Luke 1:71 - *"That we should be saved from our enemies, and from the hand of all that hate us;"*

I. To Have Freedom to Serve God:

- Text: Luke 1:74-75 - *"That he would grant unto us, that we being delivered out of the hand of our enemies might serve him without fear, In holiness and righteousness before him, all the days of our life."*

- John 5:1-9 - *"After this there was a feast of the Jews; and Jesus went up to Jerusalem. Now there is at Jerusalem by the sheep market a pool, which is called in the Hebrew tongue Bethesda, having five porches. In these lay a great multitude of impotent folk, of blind, halt, withered, waiting for the moving of the water. For an angel went down at a certain season into the pool, and troubled the water: whosoever then first after the troubling of the water stepped in was made whole of whatsoever disease he had. And a certain man was there, which had an infirmity thirty and eight years. When Jesus saw him lie, and knew that he had been now a long time in that case, he saith unto him, Wilt thou be made whole? The impotent man answered him, Sir, I have no man, when the water is troubled, to put me into the pool:"*

II. Salvation and Intercession:

- Hebrews 7:25 - *"Wherefore he is able also to save them to the uttermost that come unto God by him, seeing he ever liveth to make intercession for them."*

Christ Our Substitute.

Text: Isaiah 53:5 - *"But he was wounded for our transgressions, he was bruised for our iniquities: the chastisement of our peace was upon him; and with his stripes we are healed."*

I. The Sacrificial Atonement:

- Isaiah 53:4-7 - *"Surely he hath borne our griefs, and carried our sorrows: yet we did esteem him stricken, smitten of God, and afflicted. But he was wounded for our transgressions, he was bruised for our iniquities: the chastisement of our peace was upon him; and with his stripes we are healed. All we like sheep have gone astray; we have turned every one to his own way; and the Lord hath laid on him the iniquity of us all. He was oppressed, and he was afflicted, yet he opened not his mouth: he is brought as a lamb to the slaughter, and as a sheep before her shearers is dumb, so he openeth not his mouth."*

- John 18:4-7 - *"Jesus therefore, knowing all things that should come upon him, went forth, and said unto them, Whom seek ye? They answered him, Jesus of Nazareth. Jesus saith unto them, I am he. And Judas also, which betrayed him, stood with them. As soon then as he had said unto them, I am he, they went backward, and fell to the ground."*

- John 19:19-22 - *"And Pilate wrote a title, and put it on the cross. And the writing was, Jesus Of Nazareth The King Of The Jews. This title then read many of the Jews: for the place where Jesus was crucified was nigh to the city: and it was written in Hebrew, and Greek, and Latin. Then said the chief priests of the Jews to Pilate, Write not, The King of the Jews; but that he said, I am King of the Jews. Pilate answered, What I have written I have written."*

- Matthew 27:50-53 - *"Jesus, when he had cried again with a loud voice, yielded up the ghost. And, behold, the veil of the temple was rent in twain from the top to the bottom; and the earth did quake, and the rocks rent; And the graves were opened; and many bodies of the saints which slept arose, And came out of the graves after his resurrection, and went into the holy city, and appeared unto many."*

Jesus, the Miracle Worker.

Text: John 20:30 - *"And many other signs truly did Jesus in the presence of his disciples, which are not written in this book:"*

I. His Name is Wonderful:

Isaiah 9:6 - *"For unto us a child is born, unto us a son is given: and the government shall be upon his shoulder: and his name shall be called Wonderful, Counsellor, The mighty God, The everlasting Father, The Prince of Peace."*

II. Believe and Receive Miracles:

John 20:31 - *"But these are written, that ye might believe that Jesus is the Christ, the Son of God; and that believing ye might have life through his name."*

John 21:1-8 - *"After these things Jesus shewed himself again to the disciples at the sea of Tiberias; and on this wise shewed he himself. There were together Simon Peter, and Thomas called Didymus, and Nathanael of Cana in Galilee, and the sons of Zebedee, and two other of his disciples. Simon Peter saith unto them, I go a fishing. They say unto him, We also go with thee. They went forth, and entered into a ship immediately; and that night they caught nothing. But when the morning was now come, Jesus stood on the shore: but the disciples knew not that it was Jesus. Then Jesus saith unto them, Children, have ye any meat? They answered him, No. And he said unto them, Cast the net on the right side of the ship, and ye shall find. They cast therefore, and now they were not able to draw it for the multitude of fishes. Therefore that disciple whom Jesus loved saith unto Peter, It is the Lord. Now when Simon Peter heard that it was the Lord, he girt his fisher's coat unto him, (for he was naked,) and did cast himself into the sea. And the other disciples came in a little ship; (for they* were not far from land, but as it were two hundred cubits,) dragging the net with fishes."

John 1:9 - *"That was the true Light, which lighteth every man that cometh into the world."*

III. Feasting on His Miracles:

Feast with Jesus - John 21:12-14 - *"Jesus saith unto them, Come and dine. And none of the disciples durst ask him, Who art thou? knowing that it was the Lord. Jesus then cometh, and taketh bread, and giveth them, and fish likewise. This is now the third time that Jesus shewed himself to his disciples, after that he was risen from the dead."*

More Miracles - John 21:25 - *"And there are also many other things which Jesus did, the which, if they should be written every one, I suppose that even the world itself could not contain the books that should be written. Amen."*

<u>Wonders Happened.</u>

Text: Matthew 27:54 - *"Now when the centurion, and they that were with him, watching Jesus, saw the earthquake, and those things that were done, they feared greatly, saying, Truly this was the Son of God."*

I. Miracles Witnessed:

Matthew 27:51-53 - *"And, behold, the veil of the temple was rent in twain from the top to the bottom; and the earth did quake, and the rocks rent; And the graves were opened; and many bodies of the saints which slept arose, And came out of the graves after his resurrection, and went into the holy city, and appeared unto many."*

II. Jesus is Alive Forever:

Matthew 28:6 - *"He is not here: for he is risen, as he said. Come, see the place where the Lord lay."*

III. Eternal Power to Save, Deliver, and Heal:

Hebrews 7:25 - *"Wherefore he is able also to save them to the uttermost that come unto God by him, seeing he ever liveth to make intercession for them."*

<u>Automatic Blessing.</u>

Text: **Psalm 1:3b** - *"And whatsoever he doeth shall prosper."*

- **Joshua 1:7-9 -** *"Only be thou strong and very courageous, that thou mayest observe to do according to all the law, which Moses my servant commanded thee: turn not from it to the right hand or to the left, that thou mayest prosper whithersoever thou goest. This book of the law shall not depart out of thy mouth; but thou shalt meditate therein day and night, that thou mayest observe to do according to all that is written therein: for then thou shalt make thy way prosperous, and then thou shalt have good success. Have not I commanded thee? Be strong and of a good courage; be not afraid, neither be thou dismayed: for the Lord thy God is with thee whithersoever thou goest."*

- **Proverbs 16:7 -** *"When a man's ways please the Lord, he maketh even his enemies to be at peace with him."*

- **Psalm 34:19 -** *"Many are the afflictions of the righteous: but the Lord delivereth him out of them all."*

- **Jeremiah 17:7-8** - *"Blessed is the man that trusteth in the Lord, and whose hope the Lord is. For he shall be as a tree planted by the waters, and that spreadeth out her roots by the river, and shall not see when heat cometh, but her leaf shall be green; and shall not be careful in the year of drought, neither shall cease from yielding fruit."*

Don't Give Up.

Text: Job 13:15 - *"Though he slay me, yet will I trust in him: but I will maintain mine own ways before him."*

- **James 5:11** - *"Behold, we count them happy which endure. Ye have heard of the patience of Job, and have seen the end of the Lord; that the Lord is very pitiful, and of tender mercy."*

I. The Example of Abraham:

- **Genesis 11:29-30** - *"And Abram and Nahor took them wives: the name of Abram's wife was Sarai; and the name of Nahor's wife, Milcah, the daughter of Haran, the father of Milcah, and the father of Iscah. But Sarai was barren; she had no child."*

- **Genesis 12:4** - *"So Abram departed, as the Lord had spoken unto him; and Lot went with him: and Abram was seventy and five years old when he departed out of Haran."*

- **Genesis 21:5** - *"And Abraham was an hundred years old, when his son Isaac was born unto him."*

- **Genesis 15:1-5** - *"After these things the word of the Lord came unto Abram in a vision, saying, Fear not, Abram: I am thy shield, and thy exceeding great reward."*

II. After the Death of Sarah:

- **Genesis 25:1-7** - *"Then again Abraham took a wife, and her name was Keturah. And she bare him Zimran, and Jokshan, and Medan, and Midian, and Ishbak, and Shuah. And Jokshan begat Sheba, and Dedan. And the sons of Dedan were Asshurim, and Letushim, and Leummim. And the sons of Midian; Ephah, and Epher, and Hanoch, and Abidah, and Eldaah. All these were the children of Keturah. And Abraham gave all that he had unto Isaac. But unto the sons of the concubines, which Abraham had, Abraham gave gifts, and sent them away from Isaac his son, while he yet lived, eastward, unto the east country. And these are the days of the years of Abraham's life which he lived, an hundred threescore and fifteen years."*

III. The Secret of Abraham's Faith:

- **Romans 4:17-22** - *"(As it is written, I have made thee a father of many nations,) before him whom he believed, even God, who quickeneth the dead, and calleth those things which be not as though they were. Who against hope believed in hope, that he might become the father of many nations, according to that which was spoken, So shall thy seed be. And being not weak in faith, he considered not his own body now dead, when he was about an hundred years old, neither yet the deadness of Sarah's womb: He staggered not at the promise of God through unbelief; but was strong in faith, giving glory to God; And being fully persuaded that, what he had promised, he was able also to perform. And therefore it was imputed to him for righteousness."*

Not Withstanding, in This Rejoice Not.

Text: Luke 10:20a - *"Notwithstanding in this rejoice not, that the spirits are subject unto you; but rather rejoice, because your names are written in heaven."*

I. Rejoicing in Eternal Matters:

- **Luke 10:20b** - *"But rather rejoice, because your names are written in heaven."*

- **Dan. 11:32b** - *"but the people that do know their God shall be strong, and do exploits."*

- **1 Timothy 6:7** - *"For we brought nothing into this world, and it is certain we can carry nothing out."*

- **1 John 2:15-17** - *"Love not the world, neither the things that are in the world. If any man love the world, the love of the Father is not in him. For all that is in the world, the lust of the flesh, and the lust of the eyes, and the pride of life, is not of the Father, but is of the world. And the world passeth away, and the lust thereof: but he that doeth the will of God abideth for ever."*

- **John 6:26-27** - *"Jesus answered them and said, Verily, verily, I say unto you, Ye seek me, not because ye saw the miracles, but because ye did eat of the loaves, and were filled. Labour not for the meat which perisheth, but for that meat which endureth unto everlasting life, which the Son of man shall give unto you: for him hath God the Father sealed."*

- **Romans 14:17-20** - *"For the kingdom of God is not meat and drink; but righteousness, and peace, and joy in the Holy Ghost. For he that in these things serveth Christ is acceptable to God, and approved of men. Let us therefore follow after the things which make for peace, and things wherewith one may edify another. For meat destroy not the work of God. All things indeed are pure; but it is evil for that man who eateth with offence."*

II. Pursuing Eternal Salvation:

- **Luke 4:5-9** - *"And the devil, taking him up into an high mountain, shewed unto him all the kingdoms of the world in a moment of time. And the devil said unto him, All this power will I give thee, and the glory of them: for that is delivered unto me; and to whomsoever I will I give it. If thou therefore wilt worship me, all shall be thine. And Jesus answered and said unto him, Get thee behind me, Satan: for it is written, Thou shalt worship the Lord thy God, and him only shalt thou serve. And he brought him to Jerusalem, and set him on a pinnacle of the temple, and said unto him, If thou be the Son of God, cast thyself down from hence."*

- **Matthew 16:26** - *"For what is a man profited, if he shall gain the whole world, and lose his own soul? or what shall a man give in exchange for his soul?"*

III. How to Ensure Your Name is Written in Heaven:

- **Repent and Accept Jesus as Lord and Savior - Acts 3:19** - *"Repent ye therefore, and be converted, that your sins may be blotted out, when the times of refreshing shall come from the presence of the Lord;"*

- **Mark 1:15** - *"And saying, The time is fulfilled, and the kingdom of God is at hand: repent ye, and believe the gospel."*

- **Acts 17:30** - *"And the times of this ignorance God winked at; but now commandeth all men every where to repent:"*

Challenge:

- **Revelation 20:15** - *"And whosoever was not found written in the book of life was cast into the lake of fire."*

Followers of God.

Text: Ephesians 5:1 - *"Be ye therefore followers of God, as dear children."*

I. Characteristics of God:

1. God is Holy: 1 Peter 1:15-16 - *"But as he which hath called you is holy, so be ye holy in all manner of conversation; Because it is written, Be ye holy; for I am holy."*

2. God is Perfect: Matthew 5:48 - *"Be ye therefore perfect, even as your Father which is in heaven is perfect."*

   2 Corinthians 7:1 - *"Having therefore these promises, dearly beloved, let us cleanse ourselves from all filthiness of the flesh and spirit, perfecting holiness in the fear of God."*

3. God is Love: John 13:35 - *"By this shall all men know that ye are my disciples, if ye have love one to another."*

II. Characteristics of Followers of God:

- Most Followers are Born of God: 1 John 3:9 - *"Whosoever is born of God doth not commit sin; for his seed remaineth in him: and he cannot sin, because he is born of God."*

a. Studying the Word: John 7:17 - *"If any man will do his will, he shall know of the doctrine, whether it be of God, or whether I speak of myself."*

b. Doing the Word: 2 Timothy 2:16 - *"But shun profane and vain babblings: for they will increase unto more ungodliness."*

Joshua 1:8 - *"This book of the law shall not depart out of thy mouth; but thou shalt meditate therein day and night, that thou mayest observe to do according to all that is written therein: for then thou shalt make thy way prosperous, and then thou shalt have good success."*

James 1:22 - *"But be ye doers of the word, and not hearers only, deceiving your own selves."*

c. Separation from the World:

2 Corinthians 6:17 - *"Wherefore come out from among them, and be ye separate, saith the Lord, and touch not the unclean thing; and I will receive you."*

d. Not Loving the World:

1 John 2:15-17 - *"Love not the world, neither the things that are in the world. If any man love the world, the love of the Father is not in him. For all that is in the world, the lust of the flesh, and the lust of the eyes, and the pride of life, is not of the Father, but is of the world. And the world passeth away, and the lust thereof: but he that doeth the will of God abideth for ever."*

e. No Compromise:

James 4:4 - *"Ye adulterers and adulteresses, know ye not that the friendship of the world is enmity with God? whosoever therefore will be a friend of the world is the enemy of God."*

Challenge:

- Are You a Follower of God or Man?

1 Corinthians 11:1 - *"Be ye followers of me, even as I also am of Christ."*

Lose Not Heavenly Vision.

Text: Acts 26:19b - "I was not disobedient unto the heavenly vision."

- Romans 8:35-39 - *"Who shall separate us from the love of Christ? shall tribulation, or distress, or persecution, or famine, or nakedness, or peril, or sword? As it is written, For thy sake we are killed all the day long; we are accounted as sheep for the slaughter. Nay, in all these things we are more than conquerors through him that loved us. For I am persuaded, that neither death, nor life, nor angels, nor principalities, nor powers, nor things present, nor things to come, Nor height, nor depth, nor any other creature, shall be able to separate us from the love of God, which is in Christ Jesus our Lord."*

I. The Importance of Heavenly Vision:

- Nothing to Exchange with Heaven:

Mark 8:36-37 - *"For what shall it profit a man, if he shall gain the whole world, and lose his own soul? Or what shall a man give in exchange for his soul?"*

Daniel 3:16-18 - *"Shadrach, Meshach, and Abednego, answered and said to the king, O Nebuchadnezzar, we are not careful to answer thee in this matter. If it be so, our God whom we serve is able to deliver us from the burning fiery furnace, and he will deliver us out of thine hand, O king. But if not, be it known unto thee, O king, that we will not serve thy gods, nor worship the golden image which thou hast set up."*

II. Examples of Those Who Maintained Heavenly Vision:

- The Three Hebrew Children: Job 13:15 - *"Though he slay me, yet will I trust in him: but I will maintain mine own ways before him."*

III. Examples of Those Who Lost Their Heavenly Vision:

- Judas: Matthew 26:14 - *"Then one of the twelve, called Judas Iscariot, went unto the chief priests,"*

- Demas: 2 Timothy 4:10 - *"For Demas hath forsaken me, having loved this present world, and is departed unto Thessalonica; Crescens to Galatia, Titus unto Dalmatia."*

IV. Men of Heavenly Vision (Men of Faith):

Hebrews 11:13-16 - *"These all died in faith, not having received the promises, but having seen them afar off, and were persuaded of them, and embraced them, and confessed that they were strangers and pilgrims on the earth."*

V. What Gave Them Victory?

- Embracing and Confessing Their Faith:

  - Hebrews 11:13b - *"...and were persuaded of them, and embraced them, and confessed that they were strangers and pilgrims on the earth."*

He that Committed Sin.

Text: 1 John 3:8 (KJV) - *"He that committeth sin is of the devil; for the devil sinneth from the beginning. For this purpose the Son of God was manifested, that he might destroy the works of the devil."*

I. Understanding Sin:

- Sin Defined:

1 John 3:4-7 - *"Whosoever committeth sin transgresseth also the law: for sin is the transgression of the law. And ye know that he was manifested to take away our sins; and in him is no sin. Whosoever abideth in him sinneth not: whosoever sinneth hath not seen him, neither known him. Little children, let no man deceive you: he that doeth righteousness is righteous, even as he is righteous."*

- All Unrighteousness is Sin.

II. The Necessity of Being Born Again:

- To See and Enter the Kingdom of God:

  John 3:3&5 - *"Jesus answered and said unto him, Verily, verily, I say unto thee, Except a man be born again, he cannot see the kingdom of God... Except a man be born of water and of the Spirit, he cannot enter into the kingdom of God."*

- Repentance is Compulsory:

  Acts 2:37-38 - *"Now when they heard this, they were pricked in their heart, and said unto Peter and to the rest of the apostles, Men and brethren, what shall we do? Then Peter said unto them, Repent, and be baptized every one of you in the name of Jesus Christ for the remission of sins, and ye shall receive the gift of the Holy Ghost."*

  Acts 3:19 - *"Repent ye therefore, and be converted, that your sins may be blotted out, when the times of refreshing shall come from the presence of the Lord."*

III. Signs of Being Born Again:

- Sin Not:

1 John 3:9-10 - *"Whosoever is born of God doth not commit sin; for his seed remaineth in him: and he cannot sin, because he is born of God. In this the children of God are manifest, and the children of the devil: whosoever doeth not righteousness is not of God, neither he that loveth not his brother."*

- Newness of Life:

  Romans 6:4 - *"Therefore we are buried with him by baptism into death: that like as Christ was raised up from the dead by the glory of the Father, even so we also should walk in newness of life."*

- Everything Becomes New:

  2 Corinthians 5:17 - *"Therefore if any man be in Christ, he is a new creature: old things are passed away; behold, all things are become new."*

God Commanded Repentance.

Text: Acts 17:30 - *"And the times of this ignorance God winked at; but now commandeth all men every where to repent."*

I. Purpose of Jesus to the World:

   Mark 2:17 - *"When Jesus heard it, he saith unto them, They that are whole have no need of the physician, but they that are sick: I came not to call the righteous, but sinners to repentance."*

II. Commandment to Preach Repentance:

- Jesus Commanded Believers to Preach It:

  Luke 24:47 - *"And that repentance and remission of sins should be preached in his name among all nations, beginning at Jerusalem."*

III. Why Repentance?

- God's Desire for Salvation:

  2 Peter 3:9 - *"The Lord is not slack concerning his promise, as some men count slackness; but is longsuffering to us-ward, not willing that any should perish, but that all should come to repentance."*

- Jesus Preached It:

  Matthew 4:17 - *"From that time Jesus began to preach, and to say, Repent: for the kingdom of heaven is at hand."*

Mark 1:15 - *"And saying, The time is fulfilled, and the kingdom of God is at hand: repent ye, and believe the gospel."*

- The Heaven Rejoices Over Repentance:

Luke 15:7 - *"I say unto you, that likewise joy shall be in heaven over one sinner that repenteth, more than over ninety and nine just persons, which need no repentance."*

- No Shortcut to Salvation:

Luke 13:3&5 - *"I tell you, Nay: but, except ye repent, ye shall all likewise perish."*

IV. True Repentance:

- Conversion from Sin:

Matthew 3:6 - *"And were baptized of him in Jordan, confessing their sins."*

Faith.

Text: Mark 11:22 - *"And Jesus answering saith unto them, Have faith in God."*

I. Understanding Faith:

- Faith is Believing the Word of God:

Hebrews 11:1 - *"Now faith is the substance of things hoped for, the evidence of things not seen."*

Romans 10:17 - *"So then faith cometh by hearing, and hearing by the word of God."*

II. The Necessity to Preach Faith:

- Faith Must Be Preached:

Romans 10:8 - *"But what saith it? The word is nigh thee, even in thy mouth, and in thy heart: that is, the word of faith, which we preach."*

Acts 20:21 - *"Testifying both to the Jews, and also to the Greeks, repentance toward God, and faith toward our Lord Jesus Christ."*

III. Challenging Faith:

- Examples of Challenging Faith:

Matthew 8:10 - *"When Jesus heard it, he marvelled, and said to them that followed, Verily I say unto you, I have not found so great faith, no, not in Israel."*

- Examples of Prayers of Faith: Matthew 6:6-13, Matthew 15:28, Matthew 21:27

Challenge:

- The Bible as the Testimonies of God:

  John 20:31 - *"But these are written, that ye might believe that Jesus is the Christ, the Son of God; and that believing ye might have life through his name."*

  1 John 5:9 - *"If we receive the witness of men, the witness of God is greater: for this is the witness of God which he hath testified of his Son."*

Faith in Jesus' Name:

- Acts 3:16 - *"And his name through faith in his name hath made this man strong, whom ye see and know: yea, the faith which is by him hath given him this perfect soundness in the presence of you all."*

Chastening.

Text: Revelation 3:19 - *"As many as I love, I rebuke and chasten: be zealous therefore, and repent."*

I. Understanding Chastening:

- Reasons for Chastening:

- God's Desire for Salvation:

2 Peter 3:9 (KJV) - "The Lord is not slack concerning his promise, as some men count slackness; but is longsuffering to us-ward, not willing that any should perish, but that all should come to repentance."

- God's Love:

  Revelation 3:19 - *"As many as I love, I rebuke and chasten: be zealous therefore, and repent."*

  Hebrews 12:5-8 - *"And ye have forgotten the exhortation which speaketh unto you as unto children, My son, despise not thou the chastening of the Lord, nor faint when thou art rebuked of him: For whom the Lord loveth he chasteneth, and scourgeth every son whom he receiveth. If ye endure chastening, God dealeth with you as with sons; for what son is he whom the father chasteneth not? But if ye be without chastisement, whereof all are partakers, then are ye bastards, and not sons."*

II. Benefits of Chastening:

- For Man's Blessing:

Job 5:17 - *"Behold, happy is the man whom God correcteth: therefore despise not thou the chastening of the Almighty."*

Must Be Accepted:

Proverbs 3:11 - *"My son, despise not the chastening of the LORD; neither be weary of his correction:"*

III. The Danger of Not Accepting Chastening:

Proverbs 29:1 - *"He, that being often reproved hardeneth his neck, shall suddenly be destroyed, and that without remedy."*

Hebrews 12:11 - *"Now no chastening for the present seemeth to be joyous, but grievous: nevertheless afterward it yieldeth the peaceable fruit of righteousness unto them which are exercised thereby."*

IV. Examples of Consequences:

- Example of Judas:

Matthew 26:21-25 - *"And as they did eat, he said, Verily I say unto you, that one of you shall betray me. And they were exceeding sorrowful, and began every one of them to say unto him, Lord, is it I? And he answered and said, He that dippeth his hand with me in the dish, the same shall betray me. The Son of man goeth as it is written of him: but woe unto that man by whom the Son of man is betrayed! it had been good for that man if he had not been born. Then Judas, which betrayed him, answered and said, Master, is it I? He said unto him, Thou hast said."*

Matthew 27:3-4 - *"Then Judas, which had betrayed him, when he saw that he was condemned, repented himself, and brought again the thirty pieces of silver to the chief priests and elders, Saying, I have sinned in that I have betrayed the innocent blood. And they said, What is that to us? see thou to that."*

God's Presence.

Text: Psalm 16:11b - *"In thy presence is fulness of joy; at thy right hand there are pleasures for evermore."*

I. The Fullness of Joy in God's Presence:

2 Chronicles 7:1-3 - *"Now when Solomon had made an end of praying, the fire came down from heaven, and consumed the burnt offering and the sacrifices; and the glory of the LORD filled the house. And the priests could not enter into the house of the LORD, because the glory of the LORD had filled the LORD'S house. And when all the children of Israel saw how the fire came down, and the glory of the LORD upon the house, they bowed themselves with their faces to the ground upon the pavement, and worshipped, and praised the LORD, saying, For he is good; for his mercy endureth for ever."*

Acts 2:1-3 - *"And when the day of Pentecost was fully come, they were all with one accord in one place. And suddenly there came a sound from heaven as of a rushing mighty wind, and it filled all the house where they were sitting. And there appeared unto them cloven tongues like as of fire, and it sat upon each of them."*

Luke 1:35 - *"And the angel answered and said unto her, The Holy Ghost shall come upon thee, and the power of the Highest shall overshadow thee: therefore also that holy thing which shall be born of thee shall be called the Son of God."*

- Acts 4:31 - *"And when they had prayed, the place was shaken where they were assembled together; and they were all filled with the Holy Ghost, and they spake the word of God with boldness."*

- Acts 8:5-8 - *"Then Philip went down to the city of Samaria, and preached Christ unto them. And the people with one accord gave heed unto those things which Philip spake, hearing and seeing the miracles which he did. For unclean spirits, crying with loud voice, came out of many that were possessed with them: and many taken with palsies, and that were lame, were healed. And there was great joy in that city."*

Evidence of Knowing God.

Text: 1 John 2:6 - *"He that saith he abideth in him ought himself also so to walk, even as he walked."*

I. Christ's Example of Knowing God:

- Christ's Obedience to God's Word:

John 14:31 - *"But that the world may know that I love the Father; and as the Father gave me commandment, even so I do. Arise, let us go hence."*

John 14:15 - *"If ye love me, keep my commandments."*

II. Proofs of Knowing God:

Keeping His Commandments:

John 8:31 - *"Then said Jesus to those Jews which believed on him, If ye continue in my word, then are ye my disciples indeed;"*

1 John 2:4-5 - *"He that saith, I know him, and keepeth not his commandments, is a liar, and the truth is not in him. But whoso keepeth his word, in him verily is the love of God perfected: hereby know we that we are in him."*

ii. Walking as Him:

Acts 11:26 - *"And when he had found him, he brought him unto Antioch. And it came to pass, that a whole year they assembled themselves with the church, and taught much people. And the disciples were called Christians first in Antioch."*

1 John 2:6 - *"He that saith he abideth in him ought himself also so to walk, even as he walked."*

iii. Walking in the Light of God:

1 John 1:5-7 - *"This then is the message which we have heard of him, and declare unto you, that God is light, and in him is no darkness at all. If we say that we have fellowship with him, and walk in darkness, we lie, and do not the truth: But if we walk in the light, as he is in the light, we have fellowship one with another, and the blood of Jesus Christ his Son cleanseth us from all sin."*

iv. Followers of God:

Ephesians 5:1 - *"Be ye therefore followers of God, as dear children;"*

1 Corinthians 11:1 - *"Be ye followers of me, even as I also am of Christ."*

v. Deliverance from Sin:

1 John 3:6, 8-9 - *"Whosoever abideth in him sinneth not: whosoever sinneth hath not seen him, neither known him... He that committeth sin is of the devil; for the devil sinneth from the beginning. For this purpose the Son of God was manifested, that he might destroy the works of the devil. Whosoever is born of God doth not commit sin; for his seed remaineth in him: and he cannot sin, because he is born of God."*

Sell Not Your Birthright.

Text: Genesis 25:33 - *"And Jacob said, Swear to me this day; and he sware unto him: and he sold his birthright unto Jacob."*

I. Understanding Birthright:

- Heritage of God to His Children:

  Holiness as the Heritage of God's Children:

  John 3:36 - *"He that believeth on the Son hath everlasting life: and he that believeth not the Son shall not see life; but the wrath of God abideth on him."*

  Hebrews 12:14 - *"Follow peace with all men, and holiness, without which no man shall see the Lord:"*

  1 Peter 1:15-16 - *"But as he which hath called you is holy, so be ye holy in all manner of conversation; Because it is written, Be ye holy; for I am holy."*

II. God's Warning Against Selling One's Birthright:

- No Exchange Worth It:

  Mark 8:36-38 - *"For what shall it profit a man, if he shall gain the whole world, and lose his own soul? Or what shall a man give in exchange for his soul? Whosoever therefore shall be ashamed of me and of my words in this adulterous and sinful generation; of him also shall the Son of man be ashamed, when he cometh in the glory of his Father with the holy angels."*

III. Examples of Those Who Sold Their Birthright:

- Esau:

  Genesis 25:29-33 (KJV) - *"And Jacob sod pottage: and Esau came from the field, and he was faint: And Esau said to Jacob, Feed me, I pray thee, with that same red pottage; for I am faint: therefore was his name called Edom. And Jacob said, Sell me this day thy birthright. And Esau said, Behold, I am at the point to die: and what profit shall this birthright do to me? And Jacob said, Swear to me this day; and he sware unto him: and he sold his birthright unto Jacob."*

  Genesis 27:34-38, 40 - *"And when Esau heard the words of his father, he cried with a great and exceeding bitter cry, and said unto his father, Bless me, even me also, O my father. And he said, Thy brother came with subtilty, and hath taken away thy blessing. And he said, Is not he rightly named Jacob? for he hath supplanted me these two times: he took away my birthright; and, behold, now he hath taken away my blessing. And he said, Hast thou not reserved a blessing for me? And Isaac answered and said unto Esau, Behold, I have made him thy lord, and all his brethren have I given to him for servants; and with corn and wine have I sustained him: and what shall I do now unto thee, my son? And Esau said unto his father, Hast thou but one blessing, my father? bless me, even me also, O my father. And Esau lifted up his voice, and wept."*

- Judas:

Matthew 26:14-16 - *"Then one of the twelve, called Judas Iscariot, went unto the chief priests, And said unto them, What will ye give me, and I will deliver him unto you? And they covenanted with him for thirty pieces of silver. And from that time he sought opportunity to betray him."*

Matthew 27:3-5 - *"Then Judas, which had betrayed him, when he saw that he was condemned, repented himself, and brought again the thirty pieces of silver to the chief priests and elders, Saying, I have sinned in that I have betrayed the innocent blood. And they said, What is that to us? see thou to that. And he cast down the pieces of silver in the temple, and departed, and went and hanged himself."*

Walking Uprightly.

Text: Psalm 84:11b - *"...no good thing will he withhold from them that walk uprightly."*

I. Importance of Walking Uprightly:

- Commanded by God:

Hebrews 10:25 - *"Not forsaking the assembling of ourselves together, as the manner of some is; but exhorting one another: and so much the more, as ye see the day approaching."*

- Ensures Lack of Good Things:

Psalm 84:11b - *"...no good thing will he withhold from them that walk uprightly."*

- Example of the Early Church:

Acts 2:46-47 - *"And they, continuing daily with one accord in the temple, and breaking bread from house to house, did eat their meat with gladness and singleness of heart, Praising God, and having favour with all the people. And the Lord added to the church daily such as should be saved."*

II. Benefits of Walking Uprightly:

i. Key to Making Heaven:

Psalm 15:1-2 - *"Lord, who shall abide in thy tabernacle? who shall dwell in thy holy hill? He that walketh uprightly, and worketh righteousness, and speaketh the truth in his heart."*

ii. Sure Walks:

Proverbs 10:9 - *"He that walketh uprightly walketh surely: but he that perverteth his ways shall be known."*

iii. Access to God's Power:

Proverbs 2:7 - *"He layeth up sound wisdom for the righteous: he is a buckler to them that walk uprightly."*

- Example of Hezekiah:

Isaiah 38:1-5 - *"In those days was Hezekiah sick unto death. And Isaiah the prophet the son of Amoz came unto him, and said unto him, Thus saith the Lord, Set thine house in order: for thou shalt die, and not live. Then Hezekiah turned his face toward the wall, and prayed unto the Lord, And said, Remember now, O Lord, I beseech thee, how I have walked before thee in truth and with a perfect heart, and have done that which is good in thy sight. And Hezekiah wept sore. Then came the word of the Lord to Isaiah, saying, Go, and say to Hezekiah, Thus saith the Lord, the God of David thy father, I have heard thy prayer, I have seen thy tears: behold, I will add unto thy days fifteen years."*

iv. Receiving Good Things:

Psalm 84:11 - *"For the Lord God is a sun and shield: the Lord will give grace and glory: no good thing will he withhold from them that walk uprightly."*

Proverbs 28:10b - *"...but the upright shall have good things in possession."* v. Salvation and Riches:

Proverbs 28:18 - *"Whoso walketh uprightly shall be saved: but he that is perverse in his ways shall fall at once."*

III. The Secret of Early Church's Power and Blessings:

- Continual Prayer and Fellowship:

Acts 4:31-33 - *"And when they had prayed, the place was shaken where they were assembled together; and they were all filled with the Holy Ghost, and they spake the word of God with boldness. And the multitude of them that believed were of one heart and of one soul: neither said any of them that ought of the things which he possessed was his own; but they had all things common. And with great power gave the apostles witness of the resurrection of the Lord Jesus: and great grace was upon them all."*

Challenge: Are you walking uprightly? Are you actively participating in church services, fellowship, and prayer meetings?

Add Virtue to Your Faith.

Text: 2 Peter 1:5b/9- *"Add to your faith virtue... But he that lacketh these things is blind, and cannot see afar off, and hath forgotten that he was purged from his old sins."*

I. Importance of Virtue:

- Having a Good Name:

  Proverbs 22:1 - *"A good name is rather to be chosen than great riches, and loving favour rather than silver and gold."*

  Ecclesiastes 7:1 - *"A good name is better than precious ointment; and the day of death than the day of one's birth."*

- Exemplifying Virtue:

  Christian Character Virtue:

  Proverbs 31:10 & 30 (KJV) - *"Who can find a virtuous woman? for her price is far above rubies... Favour is deceitful, and beauty is vain: but a woman that feareth the Lord, she shall be praised."*

II. Examples of Virtuous Individuals:

i. Hezekiah:

  Isaiah 38:3

ii. Job: Job 1:1 & 8 –

  "There was a man in the land of Uz, whose name was Job; and that man was perfect and upright, and one that feared God, and eschewed evil... And the Lord said unto Satan, Hast thou considered my servant Job, that there is none like him in the earth, a perfect and an upright man, one that feareth God, and escheweth evil?"

iii. Early Church:

  Acts 6:3 - *"Wherefore, brethren, look ye out among you seven men of honest report, full of the Holy Ghost and wisdom, whom we may appoint over this business."*

iv. Cornelius:

Acts 10:2 & 22 - *"A devout man, and one that feared God with all his house, which gave much alms to the people, and prayed to God alway... And they said, Cornelius the centurion, a just man, and one that feareth God, and of good report among all the nation of the Jews, was warned from God by an holy angel to send for thee into his house, and to hear words of thee."*

v. Timothy:

Acts 16:1 & 2 (KJV) - *"Then came he to Derbe and Lystra: and, behold, a certain disciple was there, named Timotheus, the son of a certain woman, which was a Jewess, and believed; but his father was a Greek: Which was well reported of by the brethren that were at Lystra and Iconium."*

vi. Ananias:

Acts 22:12, 9:10 (KJV)

vii. Demetrius:

3 John 12 (KJV) - *"Demetrius hath good report of all men, and of the truth itself: yea, and we also bear record; and ye know that our record is true."*

Unrighteous Mammon.

Text: Luke 16:11 (KJV) - *"If therefore ye have not been faithful in the unrighteous mammon, who will commit to your trust the true riches?"*

I. Understanding Unrighteous Mammon:

The Unrighteous Bring Bad Report:

Luke 16:1-2 - *"And he said also unto his disciples, There was a certain rich man, which had a steward; and the same was accused unto him that he had wasted his goods. And he called him, and said unto him, How is it that I hear this of thee? give an account of thy stewardship; for thou mayest be no longer steward."*

True Riches Defined:

Eternal Things:

John 17:23 (KJV) - *"I in them, and thou in me, that they may be made perfect in one; and that the world may know that thou hast sent me, and hast loved them, as thou hast loved me."*

Consequences of the Love of Money:

1 Timothy 6:10 (KJV) - *"For the love of money is the root of all evil: which while some coveted after, they have erred from the faith, and pierced themselves through with many sorrows."*

II. Examples of Those Who Fell Due to Unrighteous Mammon:

a. Gehazi: 2 Kings 5:20-22 & 27

b. Achan: Joshua 7:20-26

c. Judas: Matthew 26:14-16, Matthew 27:3-5

d. Ananias and His Wife: Acts 5:1-(5 & 10)

III. Warning and Christian Goals:

Warning Against Pursuing Mammon: 1 Timothy 6:6-10

- Christian Goal:

1 Timothy 6:11-12 - *"But thou, O man of God, flee these things; and follow after righteousness, godliness, faith, love, patience, meekness. Fight the good fight of faith, lay hold on eternal life, whereunto thou art also called, and hast professed a good profession before many witnesses."*

- The Impossibility of Serving Both God and Money:

Luke 16:13 - *"No servant can serve two masters: for either he will hate the one, and love the other; or else he will hold to the one, and despise the other. Ye cannot serve God and mammon."*

The Beauty of Salvation.

Text: Psalm 149:4 - *"For the Lord taketh pleasure in his people: he will beautify the meek with salvation."*

I. Understanding the Beauty of Salvation:

- Holiness as Beauty: Galatians 5:22-23 - *"But the fruit of the Spirit is love, joy, peace, longsuffering, gentleness, goodness, faith, Meekness, temperance: against such there is no law."*

- The Importance of Scripture:

- 2 Timothy 3:15 - *"And that from a child thou hast known the holy scriptures, which are able to make thee wise unto salvation through faith which is in Christ Jesus."*

- Worshiping God in the Beauty of Holiness:

  Psalm 96:9 - *"O worship the Lord in the beauty of holiness: fear before him, all the earth."*

- Necessity for Salvation for Seeing the Lord:

  Hebrews 12:14 - *"Follow peace with all men, and holiness, without which no man shall see the Lord:"*

- Having a Goal in Salvation:

  Ezra 7:10 - *"For Ezra had prepared his heart to seek the law of the Lord, and to do it, and to teach in Israel statutes and judgments."*

Faithfulness of God.

Text: Psalm 119:90 - *"Thy faithfulness is unto all generations: thou hast established the earth, and it abideth."*

I. The Eternal Faithfulness of God:

- Throughout Generations:

  Psalm 89:1 - *"I will sing of the mercies of the Lord for ever: with my mouth will I make known thy faithfulness to all generations."*

- God's Inherent Faithfulness:

  1 Thessalonians 5:24 - *"Faithful is he that calleth you, who also will do it."*

- Desire for Human Faithfulness:

  1 Corinthians 4:2 - *"Moreover it is required in stewards, that a man be found faithful."*

- Avoiding Corrupt Practices:

  2 Corinthians 2:17 - *"For we are not as many, which corrupt the word of God: but as of sincerity, but as of God, in the sight of God speak we in Christ."*

- Faith as Demonstrated by Abraham:

Romans 4:17 - *"(As it is written, I have made thee a father of many nations,) before him whom he believed, even God, who quickeneth the dead, and calleth those things which be not as though they were."*

- Obedience to God's Commands:
  a. Genesis 12:1-4
  b. Genesis 17:1-3
  c. Genesis 22:1-3, 16

- God's Faithfulness in Keeping His Promises:

  2 Thessalonians 3:3 - *"But the Lord is faithful, who shall stablish you, and keep you from evil."*

We See Not Our Sign.

Text: Psalm 74:9 (KJV) - *"We see not our signs: there is no more any prophet: neither is there among us any that knoweth how long."*

I. Reasons for the Lack of Signs:

- Sins, Disobedience, and Unbelief:

  Proverbs 1:24-25 - *"Because I have called, and ye refused; I have stretched out my hand, and no man regarded; But ye have set at nought all my counsel, and would none of my reproof:"*

  Mark 16:17 - *"And these signs shall follow them that believe; In my name shall they cast out devils; they shall speak with new tongues;"*

- Steps to Take:

  Repentance:

  2 Chronicles 7:14 - *"If my people, which are called by my name, shall humble themselves, and pray, and seek my face, and turn from their wicked ways; then will I hear from heaven, and will forgive their sin, and will heal their land."*

  Proverbs 28:13 - *"He that covereth his sins shall not prosper: but whoso confesseth and forsaketh them shall have mercy."*

  Acts 3:19 - *"Repent ye therefore, and be converted, that your sins may be blotted out, when the times of refreshing shall come from the presence of the Lord;"*

God in Need of Women.

Text: Genesis 2:18 - *"And the Lord God said, It is not good that the man should be alone; I will make him an help meet for him."*

I. God's Plan Involving Women:

- God's Recognition of Need:

2 Chronicles 16:9 - *"For the eyes of the Lord run to and fro throughout the whole earth, to shew himself strong in the behalf of them whose heart is perfect toward him..."*

- Women Standing Firm in Doctrine:

John 8:31 - *"Then said Jesus to those Jews which believed on him, If ye continue in my word, then are ye my disciples indeed;"*

Acts 2:41 - *"Then they that gladly received his word were baptized: and the same day there were added unto them about three thousand souls."*

- Chosen Ones of Good Name:

John 15:16 - *"Ye have not chosen me, but I have chosen you, and ordained you, that ye should go and bring forth fruit, and that your fruit should remain: that whatsoever ye shall ask of the Father in my name, he may give it you."*

Acts 6:3 - *"Wherefore, brethren, look ye out among you seven men of honest report, full of the Holy Ghost and wisdom, whom we may appoint over this business."*

- Examples of Exemplary Women:

John 13:15 - *"For I have given you an example, that ye should do as I have done to you."*

1 Timothy 4:12 - *"Let no man despise thy youth; but be thou an example of the believers, in word, in conversation, in charity, in spirit, in faith, in purity."*

Titus 2:7 - *"In all things shewing thyself a pattern of good works: in doctrine shewing uncorruptness, gravity, sincerity,"*

2 Thessalonians 3:9 - *"Not because we have not power, but to make ourselves an ensample unto you to follow us."*

James 5:10 - *"Take, my brethren, the prophets, who have spoken in the name of the Lord, for an example of suffering affliction, and of patience."*

II. Women of Biblical Example:

- Deborah:

    A Dedicated Woman:

    Joined Hands with Judge Barak - Judges 4:4

    Summoned Barak to Deliver Israel - Judges 4:6

    Agreed to Accompany Barak - Judges 4:9

    Inspired Him to Action - Judges 4:14

- Leadership and Victory:

    Sang a Psalm of Victory and Stood as a Mother Figure - Judges 5:1-6

    Rebuked the Indifference of the Tribes - Judges 5:16-17, 23

Like Deborah and other biblical women, they can inspire and lead others to victory. Let us all take our stand for God and continue in His word, following the examples set before us.

The True Provider.

Text: Genesis 22:8 - *"And Abraham said, My son, God will provide himself a lamb for a burnt offering: so they went both of them together."*

I. The Provider Revealed:

- Need to know him:

    Philippians 3:10 (KJV) - *"That I may know him, and the power of his resurrection, and the fellowship of his sufferings, being made conformable unto his death;"*

    Mat. 3:33 - *"But seek ye first the kingdom of God, and his righteousness; and all these things shall be added unto you."*

    Psalm 34:10 - *"The young lions do lack, and suffer hunger: but they that seek the Lord shall not want any good thing."*

II. The Provider for the Righteous:

   Psalm 37:25 - *"I have been young, and now am old; yet have I not seen the righteous forsaken, nor his seed begging bread."*

III. Those Who Trust in God:

147

- Abraham: Genesis 22:8-13 - *"And Abraham said, My son, God will provide himself a lamb for a burnt offering: so they went both of them together."*

- Elijah: 1 Kings 17:2-9 - *"And the word of the Lord came unto him, saying, Get thee hence, and turn thee eastward, and hide thyself by the brook Cherith, that is before Jordan."*

- David: Psalm 23:1, 5-6 - *"The Lord is my shepherd; I shall not want... Thou preparest a table before me in the presence of mine enemies: thou anointest my head with oil; my cup runneth over. Surely goodness and mercy shall follow me all the days of my life: and I will dwell in the house of the Lord forever."*

- Paul: Philippians 4:19 - *"But my God shall supply all your need according to his riches in glory by Christ Jesus."*

IV. Conclusion:

- In every generation, God has revealed Himself as the true provider for those who trust in Him. From Abraham to Paul, countless individuals have experienced His provision and faithfulness. Let us follow their example and place our complete trust in God, knowing that He will always provide for our needs.

Passion for Souls.

Text: Matthew 9:36 (KJV) - *"But when he saw the multitudes, he was moved with compassion on them, because they fainted, and were scattered abroad, as sheep having no shepherd."*

I. Jesus' Mission to Seek and Save:

Luke 19:10 - *"For the Son of man is come to seek and to save that which was lost."*

John 4:34 - *"Jesus saith unto them, My meat is to do the will of him that sent me, and to finish his work."*

II. Jesus' Goal to Finish Evangelism:

John 9:4 - *"I must work the works of him that sent me, while it is day: the night cometh, when no man can work."*

III. Evangelism: A Task That Must Be Done:

1 Corinthians 9:16 (KJV) - "For though I preach the gospel, I have nothing to glory of: for necessity is laid upon me; yea, woe is unto me, if I preach not the gospel!"

IV. The Disciples Must Obey the Commission: Mark 16:15-20 (KJV) - *"And he said unto them, Go ye into all the world, and preach the gospel to every creature."*

Satan is After You.

Text: Luke 22:31 (KJV) - *"And the Lord said, Simon, Simon, behold, Satan hath desired to have you, that he may sift you as wheat."*

I. Satan's Target:

Satan is always after the church: Revelation 12:17 - *"And the dragon was wroth with the woman, and went to make war with the remnant of her seed, which keep the commandments of God, and have the testimony of Jesus Christ."*

Peter's Experience: Luke 22:56-62 - *"But he denied, saying, Woman, I know him not."*

God's Protection for the Church: Matthew 16:18 - *"And I say also unto thee, That thou art Peter, and upon this rock I will build my church; and the gates of hell shall not prevail against it."*

II. Satan's Opposition to Heaven-Bound Christians:

Job's Test: Job 1:8-12 - *"Then Satan answered the Lord, and said, Doth Job fear God for nought?"*

Jeremiah's Struggle: Jeremiah 15:10a - *"Woe is me, my mother, that thou hast borne me a man of strife and a man of contention to the whole earth!"*

Vigilance Against Satan, Sin, and the World: 1 Peter 5:8-11 - *"Be sober, be vigilant; because your adversary the devil, as a roaring lion, walketh about, seeking whom he may devour: Whom resist stedfast in the faith, knowing that the same afflictions are accomplished in your brethren that are in the world."*

III. Conclusion:

Your problem is a spiritual battle that must be fought with spiritual weapons. Stay vigilant, grounded in faith, and equipped with the armor of God, for Satan seeks to undermine your faith and lead you astray. But remember, greater is He that is in you than he that is in the world.

Do What God Says First.

Text: 1 Kings 17:12b & 5 (KJV) - *"As the Lord thy God liveth, I have not a cake, but an handful of meal in a barrel, and a little oil in a cruse: and, behold, I am gathering two sticks, that I may go in and dress it for me and my son, that we may eat it, and die."*

I. God's Call to Obedience:

God's Instruction to Elijah: 1 Kings 17:9 - *"Arise, get thee to Zarephath, which belongeth to Zidon, and dwell there: behold, I have commanded a widow woman there to sustain thee."*

God's Promise: 1 Kings 17:14 - *"For thus saith the Lord God of Israel, The barrel of meal shall not waste, neither shall the cruse of oil fail, until the day that the Lord sendeth rain upon the earth."*

II. Obedience Leads to Blessing:

- Conditionality of Blessing: 1 Kings 17:15 - *"And she went and did according to the saying of Elijah: and she, and he, and her house, did eat many days."*

- The Secret of Abraham's Blessings:

  Total Separation: Genesis 12:1-7 - *"Now the Lord had said unto Abram, Get thee out of thy country, and from thy kindred, and from thy father's house, unto a land that I will shew thee."*

  Giving Preeminence to God: Genesis 22:16-18 - *"And said, By myself have I sworn, saith the Lord, for because thou hast done this thing, and hast not withheld thy son, thine only son: That in blessing I will bless thee, and in multiplying I will multiply thy seed as the stars of the heaven, and as the sand which is upon the sea shore; and thy seed shall possess the gate of his enemies;"*

  Living a Generous Life: Genesis 13:1-2 - *"And Abram went up out of Egypt, he, and his wife, and all that he had, and Lot with him, into the south."*

III. Conclusion:

Obedience to God's commands is the pathway to His blessings. Just as the widow obeyed Elijah and experienced God's miraculous provision, so too can we experience God's blessings when we prioritize obedience to His word above all else. Let us learn from the example of faithful servants like Abraham and diligently obey what God says first, trusting in His promises and provisions.

The New Testament.

The First: The Only Foundation of the Kingdom and Righteousness:

Acts 3:19 - *"Repent ye therefore, and be converted, that your sins may be blotted out, when the times of refreshing shall come from the presence of the Lord."*

The First: The Church

Acts 2:42 - *"And they continued stedfastly in the apostles' doctrine and fellowship, and in breaking of bread, and in prayers."*

Acts 4:32-34 - *"And the multitude of them that believed were of one heart and of one soul: neither said any of them that ought of the things which he possessed was his own; but they had all things common."*

The Church of Macedonia

2 Corinthians 8:1-5 - *"Moreover, brethren, we do you to wit of the grace of God bestowed on the churches of Macedonia;"*

Repentance

Proverbs 28:13 - *"He that covereth his sins shall not prosper: but whoso confesseth and forsaketh them shall have mercy."*

Spirit of Fear.

Text: 2 Timothy 1:7 (KJV) - *"For God hath not given us the spirit of fear; but of power, and of love, and of a sound mind." Luke 1:74 (KJV) - "That he would grant unto us, that we being delivered out of the hand of our enemies might serve him without fear,"*

- It is the Devil's Spirit.
- It has to be mentored: 1 John 4:18b - *"There is no fear in love; but perfect love casteth out fear: because fear hath torment. He that feareth is not made perfect in love."*
- It is for sinners: Proverbs 28:1a - *"The wicked flee when no man pursueth: but the righteous are bold as a lion."*
- God's Power to Those Who Believe in Him: Matthew 28:18-20 - *"And Jesus came and spake unto them, saying, All power is given unto me in heaven and in earth."*
- Christian Need Not Fear the Devil. Why? Because God has Enveloped Christians with His Power: Isaiah 54:17 - *"No weapon that is formed against thee shall prosper; and every tongue that shall rise against thee in judgment thou shalt condemn. This is*

the heritage of the servants of the Lord, and their righteousness is of me, saith the Lord."

- Boldness in Him: Proverbs 28:1 - *"The wicked flee when no man pursueth: but the righteous are bold as a lion."*

- Examples: Daniel 3:17-18 - *"If it be so, our God whom we serve is able to deliver us from the burning fiery furnace, and he will deliver us out of thine hand, O king."*

- Acts 4:33 - *"And with great power gave the apostles witness of the resurrection of the Lord Jesus: and great grace was upon them all."*

<u>Achan in the Camp</u>.

Text: Joshua 7:1 - *"But the children of Israel committed a trespass in the accursed thing: for Achan, the son of Carmi, the son of Zabdi, the son of Zerah, of the tribe of Judah, took of the accursed thing: and the anger of the Lord was kindled against the children of Israel."*

I. God's Command to Israel:

- Joshua 3:5 - *"And Joshua said unto the people, Sanctify yourselves: for tomorrow the Lord will do wonders among you."*

To the Church:

- 2 Corinthians 6:17-18 - *"Wherefore come out from among them, and be ye separate, saith the Lord, and touch not the unclean thing; and I will receive you, And will be a Father unto you, and ye shall be my sons and daughters, saith the Lord Almighty."*

- Problem in the Camp: 2 Corinthians 7:4-8 - *"Great is my boldness of speech toward you, great is my glorying of you: I am filled with comfort, I am exceeding joyful in all our tribulation."*

Why?:

- The Camp Supposed to Be Holy: Joshua 7:13 - *"Up, sanctify the people, and say, Sanctify yourselves against tomorrow: for thus saith the Lord God of Israel, There is an accursed thing in the midst of thee, O Israel: thou canst not stand before thine enemies, until ye take away the accursed thing from among you."*

God Revealed the Secret:

- Joshua 7:18-19 - *"And he brought his household man by man; and Achan, the son of Carmi, the son of Zabdi, the son of Zerah, of the tribe of Judah, was taken. And Joshua said unto Achan, My son, give, I pray thee, glory to the Lord God of Israel, and make confession unto him; and tell me now what thou hast done; hide it not from me."*

Achan's Confession:

- Joshua 7:20-21 - *"And Achan answered Joshua, and said, Indeed I have sinned against the Lord God of Israel, and thus and thus have I done: When I saw among the spoils a goodly Babylonish garment, and two hundred shekels of silver, and a wedge of gold of fifty shekels weight, then I coveted them, and took them; and, behold, they are hid in the earth in the midst of my tent, and the silver under it."*

Judgment:

- Joshua 7:22-26 - *"So Joshua sent messengers, and they ran unto the tent; and, behold, it was hid in his tent, and the silver under it."*

- The Achan in the Early Church: Acts 5:1-11

Achan in the Church Today: The Apathy

Repack Your Load.

Text: Isaiah 38:1b - *"Thus saith the Lord, Set thine house in order: for thou shalt die, and not live."*

I. Why?: Because Death is Sure

- Hebrews 9:27 - *"And as it is appointed unto men once to die, but after this the judgment:"*

Examine Yourself:

- Lamentations 3:40 - *"Let us search and try our ways, and turn again to the Lord."*

- 2 Corinthians 13:5 - *"Examine yourselves, whether ye be in the faith; prove your own selves. Know ye not your own selves, how that Jesus Christ is in you, except ye be reprobates?"*

The Hindrance to Go:

- Hebrews 12:1 - *"Wherefore seeing we also are compassed about with so great a cloud of witnesses, let us lay aside every weight, and the sin which doth so easily beset us, and let us run with patience the race that is set before us,"*

It is the Narrow Way to Heaven:

- Matthew 7:13-14 - *"Enter ye in at the strait gate: for wide is the gate, and broad is the way, that leadeth to destruction, and many there be which go in thereat: Because strait is the gate, and narrow is the way, which leadeth unto life, and few there be that find it."*

Remove the Vanity:

- Ecclesiastes 2:11 - *"Then I looked on all the works that my hands had wrought, and on the labour that I had laboured to do: and, behold, all was vanity and vexation of spirit, and there was no profit under the sun."*

- 1 Timothy 6:9 - *"But they that will be rich fall into temptation and a snare, and into many foolish and hurtful lusts, which drown men in destruction and perdition."*

What Lack I Yet?

Text: Matthew 19:20b (KJV) - *"What lack I yet?"*

I. Eternity Question:

- Eternity Question: Matthew 19:16 - *"And, behold, one came and said unto him, Good Master, what good thing shall I do, that I may have eternal life?"*

He Was a Religious Man:

- Matthew 19:18-20 - *"He saith unto him, Which? Jesus said, Thou shalt do no murder, Thou shalt not commit adultery, Thou shalt not steal, Thou shalt not bear false witness, Honour thy father and thy mother: and, Thou shalt love thy neighbour as thyself. The young man saith unto him, All these things have I kept from my youth up: what lack I yet?"*

Sell Out for God:

- Sell Out for God: Mark 8:34 - *"And when he had called the people unto him with his disciples also, he said unto them, Whosoever will come after me, let him deny himself, and take up his cross, and follow me."*

- Matthew 19:21 - *"Jesus said unto him, If thou wilt be perfect, go and sell that thou hast, and give to the poor, and thou shalt have treasure in heaven: and come and follow me."*

- Luke 18:4-10 - *"And he would not for a while: but afterward he said within himself, Though I fear not God, nor regard man;"*

No Go Area of His Life:

- Matthew 19:22 - *"But when the young man heard that saying, he went away sorrowful: for he had great possessions."*

God's Call:

- Romans 12:1-2 - *"I beseech you therefore, brethren, by the mercies of God, that ye present your bodies a living sacrifice, holy, acceptable unto God, which is your reasonable service. And be not conformed to this world: but be ye transformed by the renewing of your mind, that ye may prove what is that good, and acceptable, and perfect, will of God."*

Visit Us, O Lord.

Text: Jeremiah 29:10 (KJV) - *"For thus saith the Lord, That after seventy years be accomplished at Babylon I will visit you, and perform my good word toward you, in causing you to return to this place."*

I. Children of Israel:

- *Warning:* Deuteronomy 6:12 - *"Then beware lest thou forget the Lord, which brought thee forth out of the land of Egypt, from the house of bondage."*

- *But:* Psalm 137:1-4 - *"By the rivers of Babylon, there we sat down, yea, we wept, when we remembered Zion."*

Church Today:

- John 8:31 - *"Then said Jesus to those Jews which believed on him, If ye continue in my word, then are ye my disciples indeed;"*

- Galatians 5:1 - *"Stand fast therefore in the liberty wherewith Christ hath made us free, and be not entangled again with the yoke of bondage."*

Why Do We Need God's Visitation?

i. Iniquity Abound: Matthew 24:12a - *"And because iniquity shall abound, the love of many shall wax cold."*

ii. Love Wax Cold and Deadness in the Church: Matthew 24:12b (KJV) - *"But he that shall endure unto the end, the same shall be saved."*

iii. Refusal to Walk in Old Paths: Proverbs 22:28 - *"Remove not the ancient landmark, which thy fathers have set."*

iv. No More Fire and Signs in the Church: Psalm 74:9-10 - *"We see not our signs: there is no more any prophet: neither is there among us any that knoweth how long."*

v. God's Promises: Sarah: Genesis 21:1-2 - *"And the Lord visited Sarah as he had said, and the Lord did unto Sarah as he had spoken."*

vi. Church: Jeremiah 29:10-14 - *"For thus saith the Lord, That after seventy years be accomplished at Babylon I will visit you, and perform my good word toward you, in causing you to return to this place."*

The Church in the Prison.

Text: Luke 4:18 (KJV) - *"The Spirit of the Lord is upon me, because he hath anointed me to preach the gospel to the poor; he hath sent me to heal the brokenhearted, to preach deliverance to the captives, and recovering of sight to the blind, to set at liberty them that are bruised,"*

I. The Meaning of Church:

- The Called Out One Set Free: John 8:32 - *"And ye shall know the truth, and the truth shall make you free."*

In Prison for Failure to Stand in the Truth:

- **In the Prison of What?**

1. Prison of Bondage of Sin: Matthew 24:12 - *"And because iniquity shall abound, the love of many shall wax cold."*

   1 John 3:8-9 - *"He that committeth sin is of the devil; for the devil sinneth from the beginning. For this purpose the Son of God was manifested, that he might destroy the works of the devil. Whosoever is born of God doth not commit sin; for his seed remaineth in him: and he cannot sin, because he is born of God."*

- Prison of Fear: Luke 1:71, 74 - *"That we should be saved from our enemies, and from the hand of all that hate us;" "That he would grant unto us, that we being delivered out of the hand of our enemies might serve him without fear,"*

- 2 Timothy 1:7 - *"For God hath not given us the spirit of fear; but of power, and of love, and of a sound mind."*

- Prison of Unbelief: Matthew 17:17-21 - *"Then Jesus answered and said, O faithless and perverse generation, how long shall I be with you? how long shall I suffer you? bring him hither to me."*

- Mark 16:17-18 (KJV) - *"And these signs shall follow them that believe; In my name shall they cast out devils; they shall speak with new tongues; They shall take up serpents; and if they drink any deadly thing, it shall not hurt them; they shall lay hands on the sick, and they shall recover."*

- *Prison of Poverty and Wants:* Psalm 34:9-10 (KJV) - *"O fear the Lord, ye his saints: for there is no want to them that fear him. The young lions do lack, and suffer hunger: but they that seek the Lord shall not want any good thing."*

- Psalm 37:25 - *"I have been young, and now am old; yet have I not seen the righteous forsaken, nor his seed begging bread."*

The Way Out Of:

- Matthew 27:51-54 - *"And, behold, the veil of the temple was rent in twain from the top to the bottom; and the earth did quake, and the rocks rent;"*

Old Time Faith.

Text: Jude 3b (KJV) - *"It was needful for me to write unto you, and exhort you that ye should earnestly contend for the faith which was once delivered unto the saints."*

The Need to Fight for It:

- Why? Jesus Died for It Prophecy: Luke 18:8b - *"...Nevertheless when the Son of man cometh, shall he find faith on the earth?"*

- 1 Timothy 4:1 - *"Now the Spirit speaketh expressly, that in the latter times some shall depart from the faith, giving heed to seducing spirits, and doctrines of devils;"*

- Matthew 24:24 - *"For there shall arise false Christs, and false prophets, and shall shew great signs and wonders; insomuch that, if it were possible, they shall deceive the very elect."*

Old Time Faith = HARD:

- Saying From Time: Matthew 11:12- *"And from the days of John the Baptist until now the kingdom of heaven suffereth violence, and the violent take it by force."*

- John Baptist: John 6:60, 63, 66 - *"Many therefore of his disciples, when they had heard this, said, This is an hard saying; who can hear it?" "It is the spirit that quickeneth; the flesh profiteth nothing: the words that I speak unto you, they are spirit, and they are life." "From that time many of his disciples went back, and walked no more with him."*

- John Baptist: Matthew 3:7 - *"But when he saw many of the Pharisees and Sadducees come to his baptism, he said unto them, O generation of vipers, who hath warned you to flee from the wrath to come?"*

i. Faith That Will Never...: Genesis 6:5-8 - *"And God saw that the wickedness of man was great in the earth, and that every imagination of the thoughts of his heart was only evil continually."*

ii. Stand for the Truth

iii. Walk on Narrow Way

iv. Walk in Old Time Faith: Proverbs 22:28 - *"Remove not the ancient landmark, which thy fathers have set."*

- Jeremiah 6:16 - *"Thus saith the Lord, Stand ye in the ways, and see, and ask for the old paths, where is the good way, and walk therein, and ye shall find rest for your souls. But they said, We will not walk therein."*

How Shall Ye Escape?

Text: Hebrews 2:3 (KJV) - *"How shall we escape, if we neglect so great salvation; which at the first began to be spoken by the Lord, and was confirmed unto us by them that heard him;"*

I. Jesus is God's Gift to Mankind:

- God Did Not Want Anyone to Perish: 2 Peter 3:9b - *"but is longsuffering to us-ward, not willing that any should perish, but that all should come to repentance."*

- Why He Came: Matthew 1:21 - *"And she shall bring forth a son, and thou shalt call his name JESUS: for he shall save his people from their sins."*

- The Good News: Luke 2:9-11 - *"And, lo, the angel of the Lord came upon them, and the glory of the Lord shone round about them: and they were sore afraid. And the angel said unto them, Fear not: for, behold, I bring you good tidings of great joy, which shall be to all people. For unto you is born this day in the city of David a Saviour, which is Christ the Lord."*

Repentance is Compulsory:

- Repentance is Compulsory: Mark 1:15 - *"And saying, The time is fulfilled, and the kingdom of God is at hand: repent ye, and believe the gospel."*

- Acts 3:19 - *"Repent ye therefore, and be converted, that your sins may be blotted out, when the times of refreshing shall come from the presence of the Lord;"*

Hope for the Lost:

- Hope for the Lost: Hebrews 7:25 - *"Wherefore he is able also to save them to the uttermost that come unto God by him, seeing he ever liveth to make intercession for them."*

- Isaiah 42:22 - *"But this is a people robbed and spoiled; they are all of them snared in holes, and they are hid in prison houses: they are for a prey, and none delivereth; for a spoil, and none saith, Restore."*

Showing Forth the Praise of Jesus.

Text: 1 Peter 2:9b (KJV) - *"that ye should shew forth the praises of him who hath called you out of darkness into his marvellous light:"*

Why? Because We Are of God:

- What We Are: 1 Peter 2:9b - *"a chosen generation, a royal priesthood, an holy nation, a peculiar people; that ye should shew forth the praises of him who hath called you out of darkness into his marvellous light:"*

- We Are: Deuteronomy 6-7 - *"And thou shalt teach them diligently unto thy children, and shalt talk of them when thou sittest in thine house, and when thou walkest by the way, and when thou liest down, and when thou risest up."*

Year of: Dedication, Seriousness, Holy Living:

- Year of: Ephesians 4:21-24 - *"If so be that ye have heard him, and have been taught by him, as the truth is in Jesus: That ye put off concerning the former conversation the old man, which is corrupt according to the deceitful lusts; And be renewed in the spirit of your mind; And that ye put on the new man, which after God is created in righteousness and true holiness."*

- Ephesians 4:29-31 - *"Let no corrupt communication proceed out of your mouth, but that which is good to the use of edifying, that it may minister grace unto the hearers. And grieve not the holy Spirit of God, whereby ye are sealed unto the day of redemption. Let all bitterness, and wrath, and anger, and clamour, and evil speaking, be put away from you, with all malice:"*

What Is Expected:

- What Is Expected: Matthew 5:13-16 - *"Ye are the salt of the earth: but if the salt have lost his savour, wherewith shall it be salted? it is thenceforth good for nothing, but to be cast out, and to be trodden under foot of men. Ye are the light of the world. A city that is set on an hill cannot be hid. Neither do men light a candle, and put it under a bushel, but on a candlestick; and it giveth light unto all that are in the house. Let your light so shine before men, that they may see your good works, and glorify your Father which is in heaven."*

Fear of God.

Text: Proverbs 1:7 (KJV) - *"The fear of the Lord is the beginning of knowledge: but fools despise wisdom and instruction."*

Fear of God Will Make You Keep God's Command and Hate Evil and Live a Holy Life:

- *Prov. 8:13 (KJV) - "The fear of the Lord is to hate evil: pride, and arrogancy, and the evil way, and the froward mouth, do I hate."*

- *2 Corinthians 7:1 (KJV) - "Having therefore these promises, dearly beloved, let us cleanse ourselves from all filthiness of the flesh and spirit, perfecting holiness in the fear of God."*

It is a Foundation of Life:

- *Prov. 14:27 (KJV) - "The fear of the Lord is a fountain of life, to depart from the snares of death."*

Example:

- Joseph: Genesis 39:8-9 (KJV) - "But he refused, and said unto his master's wife, Behold, my master wotteth not what is with me in the house, and he hath committed all that he hath to my hand; There is none greater in this house than I; neither hath he kept back any thing from me but thee, because thou art his wife: how then can I do this great wickedness, and sin against God?"

Its Reward:

- a. No Want: Psalm 34:9 - *"O fear the Lord, ye his saints: for there is no want to them that fear him."*

- b. Protection: Psalm 33:18 - *"Behold, the eye of the Lord is upon them that fear him, upon them that hope in his mercy;"*

- c. Provision: Psalm 111:5 - *"He hath given meat unto them that fear him: he will ever be mindful of his covenant."*

Example:

- The Mid-wife: Exodus 1:20-21 - *"Therefore God dealt well with the midwives: and the people multiplied, and waxed very mighty. And it came to pass, because the midwives feared God, that he made them houses."*

Self Denial.

Text: Mark 8:34 - *"And when he had called the people unto him with his disciples also, he said unto them, Whosoever will come after me, let him deny himself, and take up his cross, and follow me."*

Will Take Away the World and Give You Only Jesus:

- Cost of Discipleship*: Luke 9:23-26 - "And he said to them all, If any man will come after me, let him deny himself, and take up his cross daily, and follow me. For whosoever will save his life shall lose it: but whosoever will lose his life for my sake, the same shall save it. For what is a man advantaged, if he gain the whole world, and lose himself, or be cast away? For whosoever shall be ashamed of me and of my words, of him shall the Son of man be ashamed, when he shall come in his own glory, and in his Father's, and of the holy angels."*

- 2 Timothy 3:12 - *"Yea, and all that will live godly in Christ Jesus shall suffer persecution."*

- Mat. 19:27-30 - *"Then answered Peter and said unto him, Behold, we have forsaken all, and followed thee; what shall we have therefore? And Jesus said unto them, Verily I say unto you, That ye which have followed me, in the regeneration when the Son of man shall sit in the throne of his glory, ye also shall sit upon twelve thrones, judging the twelve tribes of Israel. And every one that hath forsaken houses, or brethren, or sisters, or father, or mother, or wife, or children, or lands, for my name's sake, shall receive an hundredfold, and shall inherit everlasting life. But many that are first shall be last; and the last shall be first."*

Daniel: Daniel 1:8 - *"But Daniel purposed in his heart that he would not defile himself with the portion of the king's meat, nor with the wine which he drank: therefore he requested of the prince of the eunuchs that he might not defile himself."*

Holiness Is Power.

Text: Proverbs 28:1b (KJV) - *"... but the righteous are bold as a lion."*

The First Thing to Seek:

- The Need to Know Him: Philippians 3:10 - *"That I may know him, and the power of his resurrection, and the fellowship of his sufferings, being made conformable unto his death;"*

- Because the Gospel is the Power of God: Romans 1:16 - *"For I am not ashamed of the gospel of Christ: for it is the power of God unto salvation to every one that believeth; to the Jew first, and also to the Greek."*

The Three Hebrews:

- Their Boldness: Daniel 3:16-18 - *"Shadrach, Meshach, and Abednego, answered and said to the king, O Nebuchadnezzar, we are not careful to answer thee in this matter. If it be so, our God whom we serve is able to deliver us from the burning fiery furnace, and he will deliver us out of thine hand, O king. But if not, be it known unto thee, O king, that we will not serve thy gods, nor worship the golden image which thou hast set up."*

- Their Deliverance: Daniel 3:23-26 - *"And these three men, Shadrach, Meshach, and Abednego, fell down bound into the midst of the burning fiery furnace. Then Nebuchadnezzar the king was astonied, and rose up in haste, and spake, and said unto his counsellors, Did not we cast three men bound into the midst of the fire? They answered and said unto the king, True, O king. He answered and said, Lo, I see four men loose, walking in the midst of the fire, and they have no hurt; and the form of the fourth is like the Son of God."*

The Unchangeable Jesus:

- Heb. 13:8 - *"Jesus Christ the same yesterday, and to day, and for ever."*

- Heb. 7:25 - *"Wherefore he is able also to save them to the uttermost that come unto God by him, seeing he ever liveth to make intercession for them."*

Authority of Believers Over Devil.

Text: Luke 9:1 - *"Then he called his twelve disciples together, and gave them power and authority over all devils, and to cure diseases."*

It is Our Heritage:

- Isaiah 54:17 - *"No weapon that is formed against thee shall prosper; and every tongue that shall rise against thee in judgment thou shalt condemn. This is the heritage of the servants of the Lord, and their righteousness is of me, saith the Lord."*

- Luke 10:19 - *"Behold, I give unto you power to tread on serpents and scorpions, and over all the power of the enemy: and nothing shall by any means hurt you."*

- Mark 16:18 - *"They shall take up serpents; and if they drink any deadly thing, it shall not hurt them; they shall lay hands on the sick, and they shall recover."*

Devil Recognized Believer's Authority:

- Acts 19:15 - *"And the evil spirit answered and said, Jesus I know, and Paul I know; but who are ye?"*

Its Manifestation:

- Exodus 7:10-12 - *"And Moses and Aaron went in unto Pharaoh, and they did so as the Lord had commanded: and Aaron cast down his rod before Pharaoh, and before his servants, and it became a serpent. Then Pharaoh also called the wise men and the sorcerers: now the magicians of Egypt, they also did in like manner with their enchantments. For they cast down every man his rod, and they became serpents: but Aaron's rod swallowed up their rods."*

- Acts 8:9-11, 18-21 - *"But there was a certain man, called Simon, which beforetime in the same city used sorcery, and bewitched the people of Samaria, giving out that himself was some great one: To whom they all gave heed, from the least to the greatest, saying, This man is the great power of God. And to him they had regard, because that of long time he had bewitched them with sorceries... And when Simon saw that through laying on of the apostles' hands the Holy Ghost was given, he offered them money, Saying, Give me also this power, that on whomsoever I lay hands, he may receive the Holy Ghost. But Peter said unto him, Thy money perish with thee, because thou hast thought that the gift of God may be purchased with money."*

Hardness of Heart.

Text: Proverbs 29:1 - *"He, that being often reproved hardeneth his neck, shall suddenly be destroyed, and that without remedy."*

Why Reproof?

- God is Love: Hebrews 12:6 - *"For whom the Lord loveth he chasteneth, and scourgeth every son whom he receiveth."*

- For Perfection and Righteousness: 2 Timothy 3:16-17 - *"All scripture is given by inspiration of God, and is profitable for doctrine, for reproof, for correction, for instruction in righteousness: That the man of God may be perfect, thoroughly furnished unto all good works."*

- Warning: Psalm 95:8 - *"Harden not your heart, as in the provocation, and as in the day of temptation in the wilderness:"; Hebrews 3:13b (KJV) - "But exhort one another daily, while it is called To day; lest any of you be hardened through the deceitfulness of sin."*

Danger:

- Prov. 28:14 - *"Happy is the man that feareth alway: but he that hardeneth his heart shall fall into mischief."*

Challenge:

- Luke 24:32 - *"And they said one to another, Did not our heart burn within us, while he talked with us by the way, and while he opened to us the scriptures?"*

- Openness: Luke 24:45 - *"Then opened he their understanding, that they might understand the scriptures,"*

Consider Your Latter End.

Text: Deuteronomy 32:29 (KJV) - *"O that they were wise, that they understood this, that they would consider their latter end!"*

Wisdom of the Wise:

- Psalm 39:4 - *"Lord, make me to know mine end, and the measure of my days, what it is; that I may know how frail I am."*

- Psalm 90:12 - *"So teach us to number our days, that we may apply our hearts unto wisdom."*

The Truth You Need to Consider:

- Death is Very Sure: Hebrews 9:27 - *"And as it is appointed unto men once to die, but after this the judgment.";*

- Ecclesiastes 9:10 - *"Whatsoever thy hand findeth to do, do it with thy might; for there is no work, nor device, nor knowledge, nor wisdom, in the grave, whither thou goest."*

- You Own Nothing at Last: 1 Timothy 6:7 - *"For we brought nothing into this world, and it is certain we can carry nothing out."*

The Sure Goal:

- Numbers 23:10 - *"Who can count the dust of Jacob, and the number of the fourth part of Israel? Let me die the death of the righteous, and let my last end be like his!"*

- Numbers 22:16-18 - *"And they came to Balaam, and said to him, Thus saith Balak the son of Zippor, Let nothing, I pray thee, hinder thee from coming unto me: For I will promote thee unto very great honour, and I will do whatsoever thou sayest unto me: come therefore, I pray thee, curse me this people. And Balaam answered and said unto the servants of Balak, If Balak would give me his house full of silver and gold, I cannot go beyond the word of the Lord my God, to do less or more."*

Those That Did Not Considered:

- *Samson, the Rich Man, Judas, Demas.*

   Challenge:

   What Shall It Profit a Man Give in Exchange for His Soul:

   Mark 8:36-37 - *"For what shall it profit a man, if he shall gain the whole world, and lose his own soul? Or what shall a man give in exchange for his soul?"*

The Greatest Power.

Text: Matthew 28:18 - *"And Jesus came and spake unto them, saying, All power is given unto me in heaven and in earth."*

The Power That Saves, Heals, and Delivers:

- *Isaiah 9:6 (KJV) - "For unto us a child is born, unto us a son is given: and the government shall be upon his shoulder: and his name shall be called Wonderful, Counsellor, The mighty God, The everlasting Father, The Prince of Peace."*

- *Romans 1:16 (KJV) - "For I am not ashamed of the gospel of Christ: for it is the power of God unto salvation to every one that believeth; to the Jew first, and also to the Greek."*

- *Hebrews 7:25 (KJV) - "Wherefore he is able also to save them to the uttermost that come unto God by him, seeing he ever liveth to make intercession for them."*

- *John 1:12 (KJV) - "But as many as received him, to them gave he power to become the sons of God, even to them that believe on his name:"*

The Need to Know Him:

- *Philippians 3:10 (KJV) - "That I may know him, and the power of his resurrection, and the fellowship of his sufferings, being made conformable unto his death;"*

The Church Today is a Perverse Generation:

- *Matthew 17:17 (KJV) - "Then Jesus answered and said, O faithless and perverse generation, how long shall I be with you? how long shall I suffer you? bring him hither to me."*

Unbelief and Fear:

- *2 Timothy 1:7 (KJV) - "For God hath not given us the spirit of fear; but of power, and of love, and of a sound mind."*

- *1 John 4:18 (KJV) - "There is no fear in love; but perfect love casteth out fear: because fear hath torment. He that feareth is not made perfect in love."*

Remove the Stones of Unbelief:

- *John 11:39-44 (KJV) - "Jesus said, Take ye away the stone. Martha, the sister of him that was dead, saith unto him, Lord, by this time he stinketh: for he hath been dead four days."*

Power of Resurrection.

Text: Philippians 3:10 - *"That I may know him, and the power of his resurrection, and the fellowship of his sufferings, being made conformable unto his death;"*

Jesus is Resurrection and Life:

- *John 11:25 (KJV) - "Jesus said unto her, I am the resurrection, and the life: he that believeth in me, though he were dead, yet shall he live:"*

Jesus' Resurrection from the Dead is Not Secret:

- *Matthew 28:2-6 (KJV) - "And, behold, there was a great earthquake: for the angel of the Lord descended from heaven, and came and rolled back the stone from the door, and sat upon it...He is not here: for he is risen, as he said. Come, see the place where the Lord lay."*

His Resurrection Makes a Difference:

- *1 Corinthians 15:17-18 (KJV) - "And if Christ be not raised, your faith is vain; ye are yet in your sins. Then they also which are fallen asleep in Christ are perished."*

- *It Brings Salvation, Healing, Deliverance, and Total Victory to Mankind:*

    - Matthew 27:50-54

    - Romans 8:11

    - Matthew 28:18 & 20b

Sell Not Yourself to Satan.

Text: Numbers 22:18 - *"And Balaam answered and said unto the servants of Balak, If Balak would give me his house full of silver and gold, I cannot go beyond the word of the Lord my God, to do less or more."*

Satan's Offer:

- *Numbers 22:16-17 (KJV) - "And they came to Balaam, and said to him, Thus saith Balak the son of Zippor, Let nothing, I pray thee, hinder thee from coming unto me: For I will promote thee unto very great honour, and I will do whatsoever thou sayest unto me: come therefore, I pray thee, curse me this people."*

Looking Unto Jesus:

- *Hebrews 12:2 (KJV) - "Looking unto Jesus the author and finisher of our faith; who for the joy that was set before him endured the cross, despising the shame, and is set down at the right hand of the throne of God."*

Jesus Rejects Satan's Offer:

- *Luke 4:6-7 (KJV) - "And the devil said unto him, All this power will I give thee, and the glory of them: for that is delivered unto me; and to whomsoever I will I give it. If thou therefore wilt worship me, all shall be thine."*

Mindful of the Word:

- *Luke 4:8 (KJV) - "And Jesus answered and said unto him, Get thee behind me, Satan: for it is written, Thou shalt worship the Lord thy God, and him only shalt thou serve."*

Satan is a Liar and Father of It:

- *John 8:44 (KJV) - "Ye are of your father the devil, and the lusts of your father ye will do. He was a murderer from the beginning, and abode not in the truth, because there is no truth in him. When he speaketh a lie, he speaketh of his own: for he is a liar, and the father of it."*

Who Owns the Power? Jesus:

- 1 Chronicles 29:11-12 (KJV) - "Thine, O Lord, is the greatness, and the power, and the glory, and the victory, and the majesty: for all that is in the heaven and in the earth is thine; thine is the kingdom, O Lord, and thou art exalted as head above all. Both riches and honour come of thee, and thou reignest over all; and in thine hand is power and might; and in thine hand it is to make great, and to give strength unto all."

- Colossians 1:15-17 (KJV) - "Who is the image of the invisible God, the firstborn of every creature: For by him were all things created, that are in heaven, and that are in earth, visible and invisible, whether they be thrones, or dominions, or principalities, or powers: all things were created by him, and for him: And he is before all things, and by him all things consist."

- *Matthew 28:18 (KJV) - "And Jesus came and spake unto them, saying, All power is given unto me in heaven and in earth."*

Reject Satan's Offer.

Text: Luke 4:8 - *"And Jesus answered and said unto him, Get thee behind me, Satan: for it is written, Thou shalt worship the Lord thy God, and him only shalt thou serve."*

What Was the Offer?

- *Luke 4:6-7 (KJV) - "And the devil said unto him, All this power will I give thee, and the glory of them: for that is delivered unto me; and to whomsoever I will I give it. If thou therefore wilt worship me, all shall be thine."*

Satan is a Liar and Father of It:

- *John 8:44b (KJV) - "...He was a murderer from the beginning, and abode not in the truth, because there is no truth in him. When he speaketh a lie, he speaketh of his own: for he is a liar, and the father of it."*

Power Belongs to Jesus:

- *Balaam Did Not Sell Himself:* Numbers 22:16-18

Only Remembered by What They Have Done.

Text: Matthew 26:13 - *"Verily I say unto you, Wheresoever this gospel shall be preached in the whole world, there shall also this, that this woman hath done, be told for a memorial of her."*

Memory of the Just:

- *Psalm 112:6 "Surely he shall not be moved for ever: the righteous shall be in everlasting remembrance."

- *Proverbs 10:7 - "The memory of the just is blessed: but the name of the wicked shall rot."

Examples:

- The Grandmother of Timothy: 2 Timothy 1:5 - *"When I call to remembrance the unfeigned faith that is in thee, which dwelt first in thy grandmother Lois, and thy mother Eunice; and I am persuaded that in thee also."*

- Dorcas: Acts 9:39 - *"Then Peter arose and went with them. When he was come, they brought him into the upper chamber: and all the widows stood by him weeping, and shewing the coats and garments which Dorcas made, while she was with them."*

- The Rich Man: Luke 16:25 - *"But Abraham said, Son, remember that thou in thy lifetime receivedst thy good things, and likewise Lazarus evil things: but now he is comforted, and thou art tormented."*

All Will Be Remembered:

- Matthew 12:36 - *"But I say unto you, That every idle word that men shall speak, they shall give account thereof in the day of judgment."*

- 2 Corinthians 5:10 - *"For we must all appear before the judgment seat of Christ; that every one may receive the things done in his body, according to that he hath done, whether it be good or bad."*

Challenge:

- Ecclesiastes 9:10 - *"Whatsoever thy hand findeth to do, do it with thy might; for there is no work, nor device, nor knowledge, nor wisdom, in the grave, whither thou goest."*

Awake Out of Sleep.

Text: Ephesians 5:14 (KJV) - "Wherefore he saith, Awake thou that sleepest, and arise from the dead, and Christ shall give thee light."

Reasons for the Church Falling Asleep:

- *The Bridegroom Tarried:* Matthew 25:5 (KJV) - "While the bridegroom tarried, they all slumbered and slept."

The Need to Awake:

- *Time Is at Hand:* Romans 13:11 (KJV) - "And that, knowing the time, that now it is high time to awake out of sleep: for now is our salvation nearer than when we believed."

- *Jesus Is Coming Very Soon:* Hebrews 10:37-39 (KJV) - "For yet a little while, and he that shall come will come, and will not tarry."

Awake from:

- *Sins, Worldliness, Self-Will, Apathy, Anti-Holiness:* Romans 13:12-14 (KJV) - "The night is far spent, the day is at hand: let us therefore cast off the works of darkness, and let us put on the armour of light."

Example:

- *Samson:* Judges 16:19 (KJV) - "And she made him sleep upon her knees; and she called for a man, and she caused him to shave off the seven locks of his head; and she began to afflict him, and his strength went from him."

Challenge:

- *Awake to Righteousness:* 1 Corinthians 15:34 (KJV) - "Awake to righteousness, and sin not; for some have not the knowledge of God: I speak this to your shame."

The Anti-holiness.

Text: Jeremiah 6:16b - *"But they said, We will not walk therein."*

The True Child of God:

- John 8:31 - *"Then said Jesus to those Jews which believed on him, If ye continue in my word, then are ye my disciples indeed."*

Stubbornness in the Church Today:

- *Exodus 32:9-10 - *"And the Lord said unto Moses, I have seen this people, and, behold, it is a stiffnecked people: Now therefore let me alone, that my wrath may wax hot against them, and that I may consume them: and I will make of thee a great nation."*

- *1 Samuel 8:19 - *"Nevertheless the people refused to obey the voice of Samuel; and they said, Nay; but we will have a king over us."*

- *Zechariah 7:11 - *"But they refused to hearken, and pulled away the shoulder, and stopped their ears, that they should not hear."*

- *Acts 7:51 - *"Ye stiffnecked and uncircumcised in heart and ears, ye do always resist the Holy Ghost: as your fathers did, so do ye."*

Jesus' Challenge:

- *Luke 6:46 - *"And why call ye me, Lord, Lord, and do not the things which I say?"*

The Key to Revival.

Text: Psalm 110:3 - *"Thy people shall be willing in the day of thy power, in the beauties of holiness from the womb of the morning: thou hast the dew of thy youth."*

What is the Key?

- *Willingness and Obedience:* Isaiah 1:19 - *"If ye be willing and obedient, ye shall eat the good of the land."*

- 2 Chronicles 7:14 - *"If my people, which are called by my name, shall humble themselves, and pray, and seek my face, and turn from their wicked ways; then will I hear from heaven, and will forgive their sin, and will heal their land."*

Examples:

- *The Children of Israel:* Joshua 1:16-18 - *"And they answered Joshua, saying, All that thou commandest us we will do, and whithersoever thou sendest us, we will go. According as we hearkened unto Moses in all things, so will we hearken unto thee: only the Lord thy God be with thee, as he was with Moses."*

- *The First Church:* Luke 24:49 (KJV) - *"And, behold, I send the promise of my Father upon you: but tarry ye in the city of Jerusalem, until ye be endued with power from on high."*

The Eyes of the Lord.

Text: 2 Chronicles 16:9 - *"For the eyes of the Lord run to and fro throughout the whole earth, to shew himself strong in the behalf of them whose heart is perfect toward him..."*

Looking for a Perfect Heart:

- *Psalm 34:15 - "The eyes of the Lord are upon the righteous, and his ears are open unto their cry."*

In the Day of God's Power:

- *Psalm 110:3 - "Thy people shall be willing in the day of thy power, in the beauties of holiness from the womb of the morning: thou hast the dew of thy youth."*

- *2 Chronicles 7:14 - "If my people, which are called by my name, shall humble themselves, and pray, and seek my face, and turn from their wicked ways; then will I hear from heaven, and will forgive their sin, and will heal their land."*

Why?

- God is in great need, looking for ONE: Ezekiel 22:30 - *"And I sought for a man among them, that should make up the hedge, and stand in the gap before me for the land, that I should not destroy it: but I found none."*

Challenge:

- Be willing and give up to God: Acts 6:4 - *"But we will give ourselves continually to prayer, and to the ministry of the word."*

The Church Needs Another Elijah.

Text: James 5:17 - *"Elias was a man subject to like passions as we are, and he prayed earnestly that it might not rain: and it rained not on the earth by the space of three years and six months."*

Elijah Kind of Prayer:

- Prayed until there was an answer:

  1 Kings 18:42-45 - *"So Ahab went up to eat and to drink. And Elijah went up to the top of Carmel; and he cast himself down upon the earth, and put his face between his knees, And said to his servant, Go up now, look toward the sea. And he went up, and looked, and said, There is nothing. And he said, Go again seven times. And it came to pass at the seventh time, that he said, Behold, there ariseth a little cloud out of the sea, like a man's hand. And he said, Go up, say unto Ahab, Prepare thy chariot, and get thee down, that the rain stop thee not."*

Man of Action:

- Challenged the prophets of Baal:

  1 Kings 18:27-29 - *"And it came to pass at noon, that Elijah mocked them, and said, Cry aloud: for he is a god; either he is talking, or he is pursuing, or he is in a journey, or peradventure he sleepeth, and must be awaked. And they cried aloud, and cut themselves after their manner with knives and lancets, till the blood gushed out upon them. And it came to pass, when midday was past, and they prophesied until the time of the offering of the evening sacrifice, that there was neither voice, nor any to answer, nor any that regarded."*

Prayed Down the Power of God:

- God of fire:

  1 Kings 18:38 - *"Then the fire of the Lord fell, and consumed the burnt sacrifice, and the wood, and the stones, and the dust, and licked up the water that was in the trench."*

- 2 Chronicles 7:1 - *"Now when Solomon had made an end of praying, the fire came down from heaven, and consumed the burnt offering and the sacrifices; and the glory of the Lord filled the house."*

Fear of God

Text: Proverbs 9:10 - *"The fear of the Lord is the beginning of wisdom: and the knowledge of the holy is understanding."*

Lack of Fear Leads to Sin:

- *Psalm 66:18 - *"If I regard iniquity in my heart, the Lord will not hear me."*

- *Romans 6:1-2 - *"What shall we say then? Shall we continue in sin, that grace may abound? God forbid. How shall we, that are dead to sin, live any longer therein?"*

- *Luke 6:46 - *"And why call ye me, Lord, Lord, and do not the things which I say?"*

Sin Hinders Revival:

- 2 Chronicles 7:14 - *"If my people, which are called by my name, shall humble themselves, and pray, and seek my face, and turn from their wicked ways; then will I hear from heaven, and will forgive their sin, and will heal their land."*

Godly Fear:

- Joshua 24:14 - *"Now therefore fear the Lord, and serve him in sincerity and in truth: and put away the gods which your fathers served on the other side of the flood, and in Egypt; and serve ye the Lord."*

- Genesis 39:9b - *"... how then can I do this great wickedness, and sin against God?"*

Godly Fear Leads to Hatred of Sin:

- Examples:

  - The Midwives: Exodus 1:17-21 - They feared God and did not obey Pharaoh's command to kill Hebrew male babies.

  - Cornelius: Acts 10:2 (KJV) - *"A devout man, and one that feared God with all his house, which gave much alms to the people, and prayed to God alway."*

Revival Promotes Fear of God in the Church:

- Acts 5:11-14 - *"And great fear came upon all the church, and upon as many as heard these things."*

- Acts 9:31 - *"Then had the churches rest throughout all Judaea and Galilee and Samaria, and were edified; and walking in the fear of the Lord, and in the comfort of the Holy Ghost, were multiplied."*

In the Presence of God.

Text: Habakkuk 2:20 (KJV) - *"But the Lord is in his holy temple: let all the earth keep silence before him."*

Christ's Promise:

- Matthew 18:20 - *"For where two or three are gathered together in my name, there am I in the midst of them."*

- Matthew 28:20) - *"Teaching them to observe all things whatsoever I have commanded you: and, lo, I am with you alway, even unto the end of the world. Amen."*

The Importance of His Presence:

- Comfort in Trials: *Isaiah 43:2 (KJV) - "When thou passest through the waters, I will be with thee; and through the rivers, they shall not overflow thee: when thou walkest through the fire, thou shalt not be burned; neither shall the flame kindle upon thee."*

- Reference to Martha in John 11:21 - Martha expressed her faith in Jesus' power, even in the midst of grief over her brother Lazarus's death.

Seeking God Wholeheartedly.

Text: Jeremiah 29:13 (KJV) - *"And ye shall seek me, and find me, when ye shall search for me with all your heart."*

Deuteronomy 4:29 - *"But if from thence thou shalt seek the Lord thy God, thou shalt find him, if thou seek him with all thy heart and with all thy soul."*

The Need for Serious Prayer:

- 2 Chronicles 16:9 - *"For the eyes of the Lord run to and fro throughout the whole earth, to shew himself strong in the behalf of them whose heart is perfect toward him."*

Heaven-Sent Revival:

- Right Time: Hosea 10:12 - *"Sow to yourselves in righteousness, reap in mercy; break up your fallow ground: for it is time to seek the Lord, till he come and rain righteousness upon you."*

- Promise of Revival: Jeremiah 29:10-12 - *"For thus saith the Lord, That after seventy years be accomplished at Babylon I will visit you, and perform my good word toward you, in causing you to return to this place. For I know the thoughts that I think toward you, saith the Lord, thoughts of peace, and not of evil, to give you an expected end. Then shall ye call upon me, and ye shall go and pray unto me, and I will hearken unto you."*

Because of Satan.

Text: 1 Peter 5:8 - *"Be sober, be vigilant; because your adversary the devil, as a roaring lion, walketh about, seeking whom he may devour."*

Reasons for Needing Revival:

- 1 Peter 5:8-9 - *"Be sober, be vigilant; because your adversary the devil, as a roaring lion, walketh about, seeking whom he may devour: Whom resist stedfast in the faith, knowing that the same afflictions are accomplished in your brethren that are in the world."*

- Ephesians 6:12 - *"For we wrestle not against flesh and blood, but against principalities, against powers, against the rulers of the darkness of this world, against spiritual wickedness in high places."*

Revival Means Putting on the Whole Armor of God:

- Ephesians 6:10-11 & 13 - *"Finally, my brethren, be strong in the Lord, and in the power of his might. Put on the whole armour of God, that ye may be able to stand against the wiles of the devil... Wherefore take unto you the whole armour of God, that ye may be able to withstand in the evil day, and having done all, to stand."*

Prayer for Revival:

- Zechariah 10:1 - *"Ask ye of the Lord rain in the time of the latter rain; so the Lord shall make bright clouds, and give them showers of rain, to every one grass in the field."*

Redeeming the Time:

- Ephesians 5:16 - *"Redeeming the time, because the days are evil."*

Call to Pray for Revival:

- Encouragement to persevere in prayer, even in the face of difficulty, until revival breaks out.

Vision to Pray.

Text: Acts 6:4a - *"But we will give ourselves continually to prayer, and to the ministry of the word."*

Importance of Vision in Prayer:

- Prov. 29:18 - *"Where there is no vision, the people perish: but he that keepeth the law, happy is he."*

Examples of Prayerful Visionaries:

- Job: Job 13:15 - *"Though he slay me, yet will I trust in him: but I will maintain mine own ways before him."*

- David: Psalm 85:6-8 - *"Wilt thou not revive us again: that thy people may rejoice in thee? Shew us thy mercy, O Lord, and grant us thy salvation. I will hear what God the Lord will speak: for he will speak peace unto his people, and to his saints: but let them not turn again to folly."*

- Daniel: Daniel 6:11, 21-23 - *"Then these men assembled, and found Daniel praying and making supplication before his God... Then said Daniel unto the king, O king, live for ever. My God hath sent his angel, and hath shut the lions' mouths, that they have not hurt me: forasmuch as before him innocency was found in me; and also before thee, O king, have I done no hurt."*

- Anna: Luke 2:36-37 - *"And there was one Anna, a prophetess... which departed not from the temple, but served God with fastings and prayers night and day."*

Example from the Early Church:

- Acts 12:5 - *"Peter therefore was kept in prison: but prayer was made without ceasing of the church unto God for him."*

Challenge to Seek Revival Through Prayer:

- 2 Chronicles 7:14 - *"If my people, which are called by my name, shall humble themselves, and pray, and seek my face, and turn from their wicked ways; then will I hear from heaven, and will forgive their sin, and will heal their land."*

Change Your Garment.

Text: Genesis 35:2 - *"Then Jacob said unto his household, and to all that were with him, Put away the strange gods that are among you, and be clean, and change your garments:"*

Return to Bethel:

- Genesis 35:1 - *"And God said unto Jacob, Arise, go up to Bethel, and dwell there: and make there an altar unto God, that appeared unto thee when thou fleddest from the face of Esau thy brother."*

- Genesis 28:16-17 - *"And Jacob awaked out of his sleep, and he said, Surely the Lord is in this place; and I knew it not. And he was afraid, and said, How dreadful is this place! this is none other but the house of God, and this is the gate of heaven."*

Need for the Church to Return to the Cross:

- Genesis 35:4-5 - *"And they gave unto Jacob all the strange gods which were in their hand, and all their earrings which were in their ears; and Jacob hid them under the oak which was by Shechem. And they journeyed: and the terror of God was upon the cities that were round about them, and they did not pursue after the sons of Jacob."*

- Reference to Jeremiah 6:16 and James 4:4 regarding rebellion and enmity against God.

- Emphasis on repentance from sin and hindrances to revival.

Sleeping Church.

Text: Luke 22:40 - *"And when he was at the place, he said unto them, Pray that ye enter not into temptation."*

Reasons for Church Sleeping:

- Sleeping due to sorrow: Luke 22:45 - *"And when he rose up from prayer, and was come to his disciples, he found them sleeping for sorrow."*

- Parallel drawn with Jonah fleeing from the presence of God: Jonah 1:5b - *"But Jonah was gone down into the sides of the ship; and he lay, and was fast asleep."*

Serious Challenge for the Church:

- Church compared to the situation in Jonah 1:6 - *"So the shipmaster came to him, and said unto him, What meanest thou, O sleeper? arise, call upon thy God, if so be that God will think upon us, that we perish not."*

Adversaries Against the Church:

- Reference to Psalm 74:9-10 (KJV) regarding adversaries afflicting the sanctuary.

The Expectation from Prayers.

Text: Acts 9:31 - *"Then had the churches rest throughout all Judaea and Galilee and Samaria, and were edified; and walking in the fear of the Lord, and in the comfort of the Holy Ghost, were multiplied."*

Expected Results from 3 Month Prayers:

1. Rest throughout the churches

2. Edification of the church: Acts 2:42 - *"And they continued steadfastly in the apostles' doctrine and fellowship, and in breaking of bread, and in prayers."*

3. Walking in the fear of the Lord: Acts 5:11 - *"And great fear came upon all the church, and upon as many as heard these things."*

4. Comfort of the Holy Ghost

5. Multiplication of believers: Acts 2:47 - *"Praising God, and having favour with all the people. And the Lord added to the church daily such as should be saved."*

Always on Prayer Fire.

Text: Leviticus 6:13 - *"The fire shall ever be burning upon the altar; it shall never go out."*

Continued in Prayer:

- Encouragement to continue in prayer: Colossians 4:2 - *"Continue in prayer, and watch in the same with thanksgiving."*

Devotion to Prayer:

- Emphasis on giving oneself to prayer and dedicating time to it: Acts 6:4 (KJV) - *"But we will give ourselves continually to prayer, and to the ministry of the word."*

Persistency in Prayer:

- Command to give God no rest: Isaiah 62:7 - *"And give him no rest, till he establish, and till he make Jerusalem a praise in the earth."*

- Similarly, giving oneself no rest in prayer: Isaiah 62:6 - *"I have set watchmen upon thy walls, O Jerusalem, which shall never hold their peace day nor night: ye that make mention of the LORD, keep not silence."*

Perseverance in Prayer:

- Illustration from Genesis 32:24-26 (KJV) of Jacob wrestling with the angel until he received a blessing.

Unity in Prayer:

- Reference to lifting up the hands of prayer as seen in Exodus 17:10-13 (KJV) during the battle with Amalek.

Have No Man.

Text: John 5:7 (KJV) - *"The impotent man answered him, Sir, I have no man, when the water is troubled, to put me into the pool: but while I am coming, another steppeth down before me."*

Jesus as the True Friend:

- Description of Jesus as the real true friend: Proverbs 18:24 - *"A man that hath friends must shew himself friendly: and there is a friend that sticketh closer than a brother."*

- Reference to John 15:13-15 (KJV) highlighting Jesus' sacrificial love and friendship towards his disciples.

Jesus as the Present Help:

- Assurance of Jesus being a present help in time of troubles: Psalm 46:1 - *"God is our refuge and strength, a very present help in trouble."*

Reliance on Jesus in Troubles:

- Acknowledgment that anything may happen but Jesus will be with us: Psalm 46:2-5 - *"Therefore will not we fear, though the earth be removed, and though the mountains be carried into the midst of the sea; Though the waters thereof roar and be troubled, though the mountains shake with the swelling thereof. Selah. There is a river, the streams whereof shall make glad the city of God, the holy place of the tabernacles of the most High. God is in the midst of her; she shall not be moved: God shall help her, and that right early."*

Jesus' Presence in Troubles:

- Illustration from Matthew 14:22-29 (KJV) of Jesus walking on water and rescuing Peter from the storm.

Salvation is a Must.

Text: John 3:3 (KJV) - *"Jesus answered and said unto him, Verily, verily, I say unto thee, Except a man be born again, he cannot see the kingdom of God."*

What Salvation Is Not:

- Correct religious practices do not guarantee salvation: John 3:1, 9-10 - *"There was a man of the Pharisees, named Nicodemus, a ruler of the Jews...Nicodemus answered and said unto him, How can these things be? Jesus answered and said unto him, Art thou a master of Israel, and knowest not these things?"*

- Baptism alone does not ensure salvation: Mark 16:16 - *"He that believeth and is baptized shall be saved; but he that believeth not shall be damned."*

- Relying on good works for salvation is insufficient: Titus 3:5 - *"Not by works of righteousness which we have done, but according to his mercy he saved us, by the washing of regeneration, and renewing of the Holy Ghost."*

The Church's Issue:

- The problem in the contemporary church is the presence of the unsaved within its congregations.

- Contrast with the early church's model in Acts 2:47 (KJV) where the Lord added to the church daily those who were being saved.

Nature of Salvation:

- Salvation entails a radical transformation of the heart: Romans 10:9-10 - *"That if thou shalt confess with thy mouth the Lord Jesus, and shalt believe in thine heart that God hath raised him from the dead, thou shalt be saved. For with the heart man believeth unto righteousness; and with the mouth confession is made unto salvation."*

- It involves a spiritual rebirth symbolized by baptism: John 3:1-7 - *"Jesus answered, Verily, verily, I say unto thee, Except a man be born of water and of the Spirit, he cannot enter into the kingdom of God."*

- Salvation brings deliverance from sin's bondage: 1 John 3:9 - *"Whosoever is born of God doth not commit sin; for his seed remaineth in him: and he cannot sin, because he is born of God."*

- It signifies a new life: 2 Corinthians 5:17 - *"Therefore if any man be in Christ, he is a new creature: old things are passed away; behold, all things are become new."*

How to Attain Salvation:

- Believe in and accept Jesus: Acts 16:30-31 - *"And brought them out, and said, Sirs, what must I do to be saved? And they said, Believe on the Lord Jesus Christ, and thou shalt be saved, and thy house."*

- Repentance is crucial: Acts 3:19 - *"Repent ye therefore, and be converted, that your sins may be blotted out, when the times of refreshing shall come from the presence of the Lord."*

- Salvation offers deliverance from the consequences of hellfire: John 3:17 (KJV) - *"For God sent not his Son into the world to condemn the world; but that the world through him might be saved."*

The Danger of Neglecting Great Salvation.

Text: Hebrews 2:3 (KJV) - *"How shall we escape, if we neglect so great salvation; which at the first began to be spoken by the Lord, and was confirmed unto us by them that heard him."*

God's Desire for Salvation:

- God's desire is for all to be saved: 2 Peter 3:9b - *"The Lord is not slack concerning his promise, as some men count slackness; but is longsuffering to us-ward, not willing that any should perish, but that all should come to repentance."*

- Jesus came to save sinners: Matthew 1:21 - *"And she shall bring forth a son, and thou shalt call his name Jesus: for he shall save his people from their sins."*

Illustration: Sodom and Gomorrah:

- Example of the consequences of neglecting salvation: Genesis 19:5-7, 24-26 - Describes the destruction of Sodom and Gomorrah due to their wickedness and neglect of God's warning.

Path to Salvation:

- Repentance is essential: Mark 1:15 (KJV) - *"And saying, The time is fulfilled, and the kingdom of God is at hand: repent ye, and believe the gospel."*

- Hope for the lost is found in Jesus: Hebrews 7:25 - *"Wherefore he is able also to save them to the uttermost that come unto God by him, seeing he ever liveth to make intercession for them."*

Labour Lost.

Text: 1 Timothy 6:7 (KJV) - *"For we brought nothing into this world, and it is certain we can carry nothing out."*

The Futility of Earthly Labor:

- The toil and labor of life ultimately amount to nothing: Ecclesiastes 2:11, 18-19, 22-23 - *"Then I looked on all the works that my hands had wrought, and on the labour that I had laboured to do: and, behold, all was vanity and vexation of spirit, and there was no profit under the sun...Yea, I hated all my labour which I had taken under the sun: because I should leave it unto the man that shall be after me. And who knoweth whether he shall be a wise man or a fool? yet shall he have rule over all my labour wherein I have laboured, and wherein I have shewed myself wise under the sun. This is also vanity."*

- What can one exchange for their soul?: Mark 8:36-37 - *"For what shall it profit a man, if he shall gain the whole world, and lose his own soul? Or what shall a man give in exchange for his soul?"*

Warning and Invitation:

- God warns against neglecting salvation: Psalm 146:4 - *"His breath goeth forth, he returneth to his earth; in that very day his thoughts perish."*

- Invitation to find rest in Christ: Matthew 11:28 - *"Come unto me, all ye that labour and are heavy laden, and I will give you rest."*

For if We Sin Willfully.

Text: Hebrews 10:26 (KJV) - *"For if we sin wilfully after that we have received the knowledge of the truth, there remaineth no more sacrifice for sins."*

Consequences of Willful Sin:

- Ignorance is preferable to turning away from the truth: Acts 17:30 - *"And the times of this ignorance God winked at; but now commandeth all men every where to repent."*

- Fearful judgment awaits those who sin willfully: Hebrews 10:27-31 - Describes the severity of God's judgment upon those who reject His truth.

Illustration: Samson:

- Example of Samson's willful disobedience and its consequences: Judges 16:7, 11, 13, 16:19-21 - Depicts Samson's disregard for God's commands, leading to his downfall and captivity.

Challenge:

- The warning against neglecting great salvation: Hebrews 2:3 - *"How shall we escape, if we neglect so great salvation; which at the first began to be spoken by the Lord, and was confirmed unto us by them that heard him."*

God is in This Place.

Text: Genesis 28:16 - *"And Jacob awaked out of his sleep, and he said, Surely the Lord is in this place; and I knew it not."*

Knowing God:

- Those who know their God will be strong: Daniel 11:32b - *"but the people that do know their God shall be strong, and do exploits."*

And Began to Publish Jesus.

Text: Mark 5:20 (KJV) - *"And he departed, and began to publish in Decapolis how great things Jesus had done for him: and all men did marvel."*

Becoming Witnesses:

- Witnessing begins when we encounter Jesus and continues afterward: Illustrated through various examples.

  - The Samaritan woman at the well: John 4:28-29 - Describes her testimony to the townspeople, leading to their belief.

  - The Gadarene demoniac: Mark 5:15, 18-19 - After being delivered, he is instructed by Jesus to share his testimony.

- Peter and the apostles: Acts 4:13-20 - Despite opposition, they boldly testify to the resurrection of Jesus.

Believe God and His Prophets.

Text: 2 Chronicles 20:20b (KJV) - *"...Believe in the Lord your God, so shall ye be established; believe his prophets, so shall ye prosper."*

Importance of Belief:

- Belief in God and His prophets brings blessings and good: Job 5:27 - *"Lo this, we have searched it, so it is; hear it, and know thou it for thy good."*

- It has rewards, but disbelief brings danger: Prov. 29:18, Mat. 10:41 - Highlighting the consequences of unbelief and the rewards of belief.

- Illustration of Jesus' rejection in Nazareth due to unbelief: Mark 6:1-6 - Despite witnessing miracles, the people's unbelief hindered God's blessings.

- God blesses through His prophets: Luke 4:24-27, 2 Kings 6:1-7 - Demonstrating how God uses prophets to bless and provide for His people.

They Lost Jesus.

Text: Luke 2:43b - *"And when they had fulfilled the days, as they returned, the child Jesus tarried behind in Jerusalem; and Joseph and his mother knew not of it."*

Why Jesus was Lost:

- Carelessness: Joseph and Mary assumed Jesus was with their relatives or friends. (Luke 2:44)

Restitution and Commitment:

- Returning to Jerusalem: Luke 2:45 - Seeking diligently until they found Him.

- Seriousness in seeking: Luke 2:46-49 - Illustrating the earnestness in finding Jesus.

- Comparison with Samson: Judges 16:20b - Samson lost God's favor unknowingly due to carelessness.

- Commitment to find: Judges 16:28-30 - Samson's ultimate commitment led to his restoration.

- Losing God means losing His blessings: Encouragement to seek diligently to avoid losing God's favor. (2 Chronicles 15:4)

Repentance.

Text: Mark 1:15 - *"And saying, The time is fulfilled, and the kingdom of God is at hand: repent ye, and believe the gospel."*

Commanded Repentance:

- Commanded by Jesus Himself: Luke 24:47, Acts 3:19 - Emphasizing the importance of repentance.

- Purpose: To call sinners to repentance and lead them to salvation: Luke 5:32, Acts 17:30.

- Repentance brings joy in Heaven: Luke 15:10 (KJV), Acts 17:30 (KJV).

The Only Savior.

Text: Mat. 1:21 - *"And she shall bring forth a son, and thou shalt call his name JESUS: for he shall save his people from their sins."*

Key Points:

1. **God-Given Savior:** John 3:16, Phil. 2:9-11 (KJV) - Emphasizing Jesus as the Savior provided by God Himself.

2. **Payment for Sin:** Isaiah 53:5, 1Pet. 2:24 (KJV) - Jesus paid the penalty for sin through His sacrifice on the cross.

3. **Exclusive Way to Heaven:** John 14:6, John 1:12 (KJV) - Jesus is the only way to attain salvation and access to heaven.

4. **Intercessor:** Heb. 7:25 (KJV) - Jesus serves as the mediator between God and humanity, offering salvation to all who come to Him.

5. **Call to Salvation:** John 3:14-15 (KJV) - Encouraging people to look to Jesus for salvation and eternal life.

Healing the Sick.

Text: Luke 9:2 - *"And he sent them to preach the kingdom of God, and to heal the sick."*

Key Points:

1. **Dual Ministry of Salvation and Healing:** Luke 9:2 - Jesus commissioned His disciples to preach the gospel and heal the sick, emphasizing the holistic nature of His ministry.

2. **Redemptive Work:** Psalm 103:2-3, Gal. 3:13 - Highlighting healing as part of the redemptive work of Christ.

3. **Jesus' Ministry:** Mat. 4:23-24, John 14:12 - Jesus performed numerous healing miracles during His earthly ministry, demonstrating His authority and power.

4. **For Believers:** Mark 16:15-18 - Healing is promised to those who believe in Jesus and His power.

5. **Freedom in Christ:** John 8:36 - Jesus came to set humanity free from all forms of bondage, including sickness and disease.

Bunch of Blessings.

Text: Romans 8:32 (KJV) - *"He that spared not his own Son, but delivered him up for us all, how shall he not with him also freely give us all things?"*

Salvation Plus:

- God's abundant provision for His children: Romans 8:32 assures us that if God did not spare His own Son but gave Him up for us, He will also graciously give us all things.

- Freely Given: Matthew 6:33 - *"But seek ye first the kingdom of God, and his righteousness; and all these things shall be added unto you."*

Conditions for Enjoying God's Blessings:

- Genuine Born-Again Experience: Those who are truly born again can fully enjoy God's blessings. Without salvation, the richness of God's blessings cannot be fully appreciated: Psalm 103:2-3 - *"Bless the Lord, O my soul, and forget not all his benefits: Who forgiveth all thine iniquities; who healeth all thy diseases."*

Psalm 34:9-10 - *"O fear the Lord, ye his saints: for there is no want to them that fear him. The young lions do lack, and suffer hunger: but they that seek the Lord shall not want any good thing."*

Psalm 37:25 - *"I have been young, and now am old; yet have I not seen the righteous forsaken, nor his seed begging bread."*

Encouragement to Salvation:

- Emphasizing the importance of salvation as the gateway to receiving God's abundant blessings.

Able God.

Text: Luke 1:37 (KJV) - *"For with God nothing shall be impossible."*

Attributes of God's Ability:

- Creator of the Whole World: Genesis 1:1-3 - *"In the beginning God created the heaven and the earth. And the earth was without form, and void; and darkness was upon the face of the deep. And the Spirit of God moved upon the face of the waters. And God said, Let there be light: and there was light."*

- All Power Belongs to Jesus: Matthew 28:18 - *"And Jesus came and spake unto them, saying, All power is given unto me in heaven and in earth."*

Demonstrations of God's Ability:

- Parting the Red Sea:

    Exodus 14:16-17, 21-22 - *"But lift thou up thy rod, and stretch out thine hand over the sea, and divide it: and the children of Israel shall go on dry ground through the midst of the sea... And Moses stretched out his hand over the sea; and the Lord caused the sea to go back by a strong east wind all that night, and made the sea dry land, and the waters were divided."*

- Daniel in the Lion's Den:

    Daniel 6:21-22 (KJV) - *"Then said Daniel unto the king, O king, live for ever. My God hath sent his angel, and hath shut the lions' mouths, that they have not hurt me: forasmuch as before him innocency was found in me; and also before thee, O king, have I done no hurt."*

- Raising Lazarus from the Dead:

John 11:39-44 - *"Jesus said, Take ye away the stone. Martha, the sister of him that was dead, saith unto him, Lord, by this time he stinketh: for he hath been dead four days... And he that was dead came forth, bound hand and foot with graveclothes: and his face was bound about with a napkin. Jesus saith unto them, Loose him, and let him go."*

Conclusion:

- Ephesians 3:20 - *"Now unto him that is able to do exceeding abundantly above all that we ask or think, according to the power that worketh in us,"* emphasizing God's limitless ability to accomplish the impossible.

The Kingdom of God.

Text: Mark 1:14 - *"Now after that John was put in prison, Jesus came into Galilee, preaching the gospel of the kingdom of God,"*

Key Points:

1. **Eternity - The Ultimate Goal:**

   - Prioritizing the kingdom of God over all worldly desires:

     Matthew 6:33 - *"But seek ye first the kingdom of God, and his righteousness; and all these things shall be added unto you."*

   - The Kingdom Beyond Materialism:

     Romans 14:17 - *"For the kingdom of God is not meat and drink; but righteousness, and peace, and joy in the Holy Ghost."*

   - Eternal Life:

     Matthew 19:16 - *"And, behold, one came and said unto him, Good Master, what good thing shall I do, that I may have eternal life?"*

2. **Total Surrender to Enter the Kingdom:**

   - Forsaking All: Matthew 19:20-26 - Jesus' dialogue with the rich young ruler highlights the necessity of forsaking all to inherit the kingdom.

   - The Forceful Advance of the Kingdom:

     Matthew 11:12 - *"And from the days of John the Baptist until now the kingdom of heaven suffereth violence, and the violent take it by force."*

   - No Exchange for the Soul:

Mark 8:36-37 - *"For what shall it profit a man, if he shall gain the whole world, and lose his own soul? Or what shall a man give in exchange for his soul?"*

3. **Mandatory Preaching of the Kingdom:**

   - Jesus' Command:

   Mark 1:15 - *"And saying, The time is fulfilled, and the kingdom of God is at hand: repent ye, and believe the gospel."*

   - Leaving All to Follow:

   Matthew 19:27 - *"Then answered Peter and said unto him, Behold, we have forsaken all, and followed thee; what shall we have therefore?"*

Do This in Remembrance of Me.

Text: Luke 22:19b - *"This do in remembrance of me."*

Significance of the Lord's Supper:

- Instituted by Jesus: Luke 22:13-18 - Jesus' preparation for the Last Supper emphasizes the importance of remembering His sacrifice.

Examination and Reflection:

- Self-Examination: 1 Corinthians 11:28 - *"But let a man examine himself, and so let him eat of that bread, and drink of that cup,"* highlighting the need for introspection and reflection during the observance of the Lord's Supper.

The Spirit of Seriousness.

Text: Ecclesiastes 9:10 - *"Whatsoever thy hand findeth to do, do it with thy might; for there is no work, nor device, nor knowledge, nor wisdom, in the grave, whither thou goest."*

Key Points:

1. **Displaying the Spirit of God:**

- Reflection of God's Creation: Genesis 1:1-3, 31; 2:1-2 (KJV) - The seriousness with which God created the world serves as an example for believers.

- Ezra's Dedication: Ezra 7:10 - *"For Ezra had prepared his heart to seek the law of the Lord, and to do it, and to teach in Israel statutes and judgments."*

- Jacob's Determination: Genesis 32:26 - *"And he said, Let me go, for the day breaketh. And he said, I will not let thee go, except thou bless me."*

- Job's Resolve: Job 13:15 - *"Though he slay me, yet will I trust in him: but I will maintain mine own ways before him."*

- Jabez's Prayer: 1 Chronicles 4:9-10 - Jabez's earnest prayer demonstrates a spirit of seriousness in seeking God's blessing.

- Solomon's Dedication: 2 Chronicles 7:1-2 - Solomon's reverence and seriousness during the dedication of the temple set a powerful example.

2. **Urgency and Commitment:**

- The Imperative of Seriousness: Ecclesiastes 9:10 - Urging believers to approach their tasks with diligence and commitment.

Contentment

Text: 1 Timothy 6:6 (KJV) - *"But godliness with contentment is great gain."*

Key Points:

1. **Understanding Contentment:**

- The Transience of Material Possessions: Luke 12:15 - Jesus warns against the pursuit of earthly possessions, highlighting their temporary nature.

- Vanity of Life:

  1 Timothy 6:7 - *"For we brought nothing into this world, and it is certain we can carry nothing out."*

- Finding Contentment in God:

  Hebrews 13:5 - *"Let your conversation be without covetousness; and be content with such things as ye have: for he hath said, I will never leave thee, nor forsake thee."*

2. **Dangers of Covetousness:**

   - The Love of Money:

     1 Timothy 6:10 - *"For the love of money is the root of all evil: which while some coveted after, they have erred from the faith, and pierced themselves through with many sorrows."*

3. **Goal of the Believer:**

   - Pursuing Righteousness:

     1 Timothy 6:11 - *"But thou, O man of God, flee these things; and follow after righteousness, godliness, faith, love, patience, meekness."*

Glad Tidings.

Text: Mark 16:15 (KJV) - *"And he said unto them, Go ye into all the world, and preach the gospel to every creature."*

Key Points:

1. **The Mandate to Preach:**

   - Compulsion to Share:

     1 Corinthians 9:16 - *"For though I preach the gospel, I have nothing to glory of: for necessity is laid upon me; yea, woe is unto me, if I preach not the gospel!"*

   - Urgency of the Message:

   - 2 Kings 7:10 - *"So they came and called unto the porter of the city: and they told them, saying, We came to the camp of the Syrians, and, behold, there was no man there, neither voice of man, but horses tied, and asses tied, and the tents as they were."*

2. **The Great Commission:**

   - Commanded by Jesus: Mark 16:15-20, Matthew 28:19-20 - Jesus instructs his disciples to spread the gospel to all nations.

3. **Impact of Glad Tidings:**

   - Bringing Joy: Acts 8:5-8 - Philip's preaching in Samaria brings great joy and deliverance from unclean spirits.

- Power of the Gospel:

  Romans 1:16 - *"For I am not ashamed of the gospel of Christ: for it is the power of God unto salvation to every one that believeth; to the Jew first, and also to the Greek."*

Consider Your Latter End.

Text: Deuteronomy 32:29 - *"O that they were wise, that they understood this, that they would consider their latter end!"*

1. **Reflection on Mortality:**

   - A Call to Reflection:

     Psalm 39:4, 90:12 (KJV) - Reflecting on the brevity of life and the need for wisdom in light of mortality.

   - Inevitability of Death:

     Hebrews 9:27 (KJV) - *"And as it is appointed unto men once to die, but after this the judgment:"*

2. **Spiritual Priority:**

   - The Kingdom of Heaven:

     2 Corinthians 5:10 (KJV) - Believers are urged to live with the understanding that they will be judged for their deeds.

   - Material Possessions:

     John 6:26-27 - Jesus highlights the importance of seeking spiritual sustenance over material gain.

   - No Exchange for Eternal Life:

     Mark 8:36-37 (KJV) - *"For what shall it profit a man, if he shall gain the whole world, and lose his own soul?"*

3. **Illustrative Warnings:**

   - Judas' Betrayal: Matthew 26:14-15 (KJV), Matthew 27:3-5 (KJV) - The tragic fate of Judas serves as a warning against betraying Christ for earthly gain.

- Parable of the Rich Man and Lazarus: Luke 16:22-25 - Jesus' parable illustrates the consequences of a life lived without consideration of eternity.

Don't Give Up!

Text: Job 13:15 - *"Though he slay me, yet will I trust in him: but I will maintain mine own ways before him."*

Psalm 34:19 - *"Many are the afflictions of the righteous: but the Lord delivereth him out of them all."*

Key Points:

1. **Perseverance of Abraham:**

   - Initial Doubt: Genesis 11:29-30 - Despite his doubts and advanced age, Abraham receives God's promise.

   - God's Promise: Genesis 12:3-4 - God promises to bless Abraham and make him a great nation.

   - Fulfillment of Promise: Genesis 21:5 - Abraham's faith is rewarded when Sarah conceives and bears a son in their old age.

   - Bonus Blessings: Genesis 25:1-7 - God continues to bless Abraham with children and prosperity even in his old age.

2. **Encouragement from Jesus:**

   - Healing at the Pool of Bethesda: John 5:5-9 - Jesus encourages the invalid man to persevere and take up his bed and walk.

He Believed the Word.

Text: John 4:50b (KJV) - *"...And the man believed the word that Jesus had spoken unto him, and he went his way."*

1. **Faith in God's Word:**

   - Healing Through Faith:

Psalm 107:20 - *"He sent his word, and healed them, and delivered them from their destructions."*

- Faith Comes by Hearing:

  Romans 10:17 - *"So then faith cometh by hearing, and hearing by the word of God."*

- Example of the Official's Faith:

  John 4:48-54 (KJV) - A royal official's son is healed because of his father's faith in Jesus' words.

2. **Belief and Obedience:**

   - Results of Belief:

     Romans 10:11 - *"For the scripture saith, Whosoever believeth on him shall not be ashamed."*

   - Obedience to Jesus' Words:

     Luke 6:46 - *"And why call ye me, Lord, Lord, and do not the things which I say?"*

War Against Poverty.

Text: Proverbs 30:8b - *"Give me neither poverty nor riches; feed me with food convenient for me."*

Key Points:

1. **Understanding Poverty:**

   - Poverty is described as a portion of sinners in Ecclesiastes 2:26, highlighting its negative spiritual connotations.

2. **Obedience to God's Word and Faith:**

   - Romans 12:11 - *"Not slothful in business; fervent in spirit; serving the Lord."*

   - Trusting in God's promises and diligently obeying His Word are emphasized as crucial in overcoming poverty.

3. **Salvation Plus:**

- Psalm 34:9-10 - *"O fear the Lord, ye his saints: for there is no want to them that fear him. The young lions do lack, and suffer hunger: but they that seek the Lord shall not want any good thing."*

- Matthew 6:33 - *"But seek ye first the kingdom of God, and his righteousness; and all these things shall be added unto you."*

- Romans 8:32 - *"He that spared not his own Son, but delivered him up for us all, how shall he not with him also freely give us all things?"*

4. **Antidote to Poverty:**

   - Encouragement to have faith and pray earnestly, trusting in God's provision as seen in the example of Jabez (1 Chronicles 4:9-10).

5. **Diligence and Hard Work:**

   - Proverbs 12:11 - *"He that tilleth his land shall be satisfied with bread: but he that followeth vain persons is void of understanding."*

   - Laziness is discouraged, and believers are urged to work diligently, recognizing that God blesses the work of their hands.

Conclusion:

- Poverty can also be seen as a condition often associated with spiritual deficiency, necessitating obedience to God's Word and faith in His promises. The assurance of salvation plus God's provision for those who seek Him is emphasized, along with the importance of prayer, faith, and hard work in overcoming poverty.

The Spirit of Un-thankfulness.

Text: Romans 1:21 - *"Because that, when they knew God, they glorified him not as God, neither were thankful; but became vain in their imaginations, and their foolish heart was darkened."*

Key Points:

1. **Un-thankfulness as a Dangerous Sin:**

   - Romans 1:21 highlights the failure to glorify God and be thankful as a serious sin leading to spiritual darkness.

2. **Perilous Times and God's Command:**

   - 2 Timothy 3:2b - *"For men shall be lovers of their own selves, covetous, boasters, proud, blasphemers, disobedient to parents, unthankful, unholy..."*

- Psalm 100:4 - *"Enter into his gates with thanksgiving, and into his courts with praise: be thankful unto him, and bless his name."*

3. **Salvation and Joy Through Thankfulness:**

   - Luke 10:19-20 - Jesus emphasizes the joy of salvation and the authority over spiritual enemies.

   - Psalm 103:2-3 - *"Bless the Lord, O my soul, and forget not all his benefits: Who forgiveth all thine iniquities; who healeth all thy diseases..."*

4. **Jesus' Displeasure with Un-thankfulness:**

   - Luke 17:17 - Jesus expresses displeasure when healing ten lepers, and only one, a Samaritan, returns to give thanks.

5. **The Root of Un-thankfulness:**

   - Un-thankfulness stems from failing to recognize and appreciate the blessings received from God.

Conclusion:

- Un-thankfulness is a dangerous sin leading to spiritual darkness. The message emphasizes the importance of gratitude as commanded by God, highlighting the joy and benefits of salvation that come through thankfulness. Jesus' response to un-thankfulness serves as a warning, urging believers to count their blessings and always express gratitude to God.

Man Second to None, Man Like God.

Text: Ezekiel 22:30 (KJV) - *"And I sought for a man among them, that should make up the hedge, and stand in the gap before me for the land, that I should not destroy it: but I found none."*

Examples of Men Like God:

i. **Job:**

- Job 1:8 - *"And the Lord said unto Satan, Hast thou considered my servant Job, that there is none like him in the earth, a perfect and an upright man, one that feareth God, and escheweth evil?"*

- Job 1:20-22 - *"Then Job arose, and rent his mantle, and shaved his head, and fell down upon the ground, and worshipped, And said, Naked came I out of my mother's womb, and naked shall I return thither: the Lord gave, and the Lord hath taken away; blessed be the name of the Lord. In all this Job sinned not, nor charged God foolishly."*

- Job 2:7-10 - *"So went Satan forth from the presence of the Lord, and smote Job with sore boils from the sole of his foot unto his crown. And he took him a potsherd to scrape himself withal; and he sat down among the ashes. Then said his wife unto him, Dost thou still retain thine integrity? curse God, and die. But he said unto her, Thou speakest as one of the foolish women speaketh. What? shall we receive good at the hand of God, and shall we not receive evil? In all this did not Job sin with his lips."*

ii. **Noah:**

- Genesis 6:5-8 - *"And God saw that the wickedness of man was great in the earth, and that every imagination of the thoughts of his heart was only evil continually. And it repented the Lord that he had made man on the earth, and it grieved him at his heart. And the Lord said, I will destroy man whom I have created from the face of the earth; both man, and beast, and the creeping thing, and the fowls of the air; for it repenteth me that I have made them. But Noah found grace in the eyes of the Lord."*

iii. **Enoch:**

- Genesis 5:24 - *"And Enoch walked with God: and he was not; for God took him."*

- Hebrews 11:5 - *"By faith Enoch was translated that he should not see death; and was not found, because God had translated him: for before his translation he had this testimony, that he pleased God."*

iv. **Hannah:**

- Luke 2:36-38 - *"And there was one Anna, a prophetess, the daughter of Phanuel, of the tribe of Aser: she was of a great age, and had lived with an husband seven years from her virginity; And she was a widow of about fourscore and four years, which departed not from the temple, but served God with fastings and prayers night and day. And she coming in that instant gave thanks likewise unto the Lord, and spake of him to all them that looked for redemption in Jerusalem."*

v. **The Centurion:**

- Matthew 8:5-13 (KJV) - *"And when Jesus was entered into Capernaum, there came unto him a centurion, beseeching him, And saying, Lord, my servant lieth at home sick of the palsy, grievously tormented. And Jesus saith unto him, I will come and heal him. The centurion answered and said, Lord, I am not worthy that thou shouldest come under my roof: but speak the word only, and my servant shall be healed... When Jesus heard it, he marvelled, and said to them that followed, Verily I say unto you, I have not found so great faith, no, not in Israel."*

- Matthew 19:27-30 - *"Then answered Peter and said unto him, Behold, we have forsaken all, and followed thee; what shall we have therefore?... And every one that hath forsaken houses, or brethren, or sisters, or father, or mother, or wife, or children, or lands, for my name's sake, shall receive an hundredfold, and shall inherit everlasting life. But many that are first shall be last; and the last shall be first."*

- Matthew 5:48 - *"Be ye therefore perfect, even as your Father which is in heaven is perfect."*

- John 6:60, 66-67 - *"Many therefore of his disciples, when they had heard this, said, This is an hard saying; who can hear it?... From that time many of his disciples went back, and walked no more with him. Then said Jesus unto the twelve, Will ye also go away?"*

Obedience, the Entrance to God's Miracle.

Text: Isaiah 1:19 (KJV) - *"If ye be willing and obedient, ye shall eat the good of the land."*

Obedience, the Entrance to God's Miracle:

- Obedience to God's Word, Obedience is Great Faith.

- The Fall of Jericho:

  - Joshua 6:1 - *"Now Jericho was straitly shut up because of the children of Israel: none went out, and none came in."*

  - Joshua 6:2 - *"And the Lord said unto Joshua, See, I have given into thine hand Jericho, and the king thereof, and the mighty men of valour."*

  - Joshua 6:3-5 - *"And ye shall compass the city, all ye men of war, and go round about the city once. Thus shalt thou do six days. And seven priests shall bear before the ark seven trumpets of rams' horns: and the seventh day ye shall compass the city seven times, and the priests shall blow with the trumpets. And it shall come to pass, that when they make a long blast with the ram's horn, and when ye hear the sound of the trumpet, all the people shall shout with a great shout; and the wall of the city shall fall down flat, and the people shall ascend up every man straight before him."*

  - Joshua 6:10 - *"And Joshua had commanded the people, saying, Ye shall not shout, nor make any noise with your voice, neither shall any word proceed out of your mouth, until the day I bid you shout; then shall ye shout."*

- Joshua 6:14-16 - *"And the second day they compassed the city once, and returned into the camp: so they did six days. And it came to pass on the seventh day, that they rose early about the dawning of the day, and compassed the city after the same manner seven times: only on that day they compassed the city seven times. And it came to pass at the seventh time, when the priests blew with the trumpets, Joshua said unto the people, Shout; for the Lord hath given you the city."*

Miracle Happened after Obedience:

- Joshua 6:20 (KJV) - "So the people shouted when the priests blew with the trumpets: and it came to pass, when the people heard the sound of the trumpet, and the people shouted with a great shout, that the wall fell down flat, so that the people went up into the city, every man straight before him, and they took the city."

Victory Follows:

- Joshua 6:20 (KJV) - "So the people shouted when the priests blew with the trumpets: and it came to pass, when the people heard the sound of the trumpet, and the people shouted with a great shout, that the wall fell down flat, so that the people went up into the city, every man straight before him, and they took the city."

Holy Ghost and Fire.

Text: Luke 3:16b (KJV) - *"he shall baptize you with the Holy Ghost and with fire."*

Why Church is No More Alive, Dried Bones, Slumbered Asleep:

- Mat. 25:5 - *"While the bridegroom tarried, they all slumbered and slept."*

- Ezekiel 37:1-3 - *"The hand of the Lord was upon me, and carried me out in the spirit of the Lord, and set me down in the midst of the valley which was full of bones, And caused me to pass by them round about: and, behold, there were very many in the open valley; and, lo, they were very dry. And he said unto me, Son of man, can these bones live? And I answered, O Lord God, thou knowest."*

No More Fire on the Altar in the Church:

- Psalm 74:9 - *"We see not our signs: there is no more any prophet: neither is there among us any that knoweth how long."*

Seriousness is a Thing of the Past:

- Acts 1:14 - *"These all continued with one accord in prayer and supplication, with the women, and Mary the mother of Jesus, and with his brethren."*

- Acts 2:1-5 - *"And when the day of Pentecost was fully come, they were all with one accord in one place. And suddenly there came a sound from heaven as of a rushing mighty wind, and it filled all the house where they were sitting. And there appeared unto them cloven tongues like as of fire, and it sat upon each of them. And they were all filled with the Holy Ghost, and began to speak with other tongues, as the Spirit gave them utterance."*

Work of the Holy Spirit:

- John 16:8 - *"And when he is come, he will reprove the world of sin, and of righteousness, and of judgment."*

Repentance and Asking:

- Acts 2:38 - *"Then Peter said unto them, Repent, and be baptized every one of you in the name of Jesus Christ for the remission of sins, and ye shall receive the gift of the Holy Ghost."*

- Luke 11:13 - *"If ye then, being evil, know how to give good gifts unto your children: how much more shall your heavenly Father give the Holy Spirit to them that ask him?"*

I Will Heal Their Land.

Text: 2 Chronicles 7:14 (KJV) - *"If my people, which are called by my name, shall humble themselves, and pray, and seek my face, and turn from their wicked ways; then will I hear from heaven, and will forgive their sin, and will heal their land."*

Time of Trouble:

- 2 Chronicles 7:12-13 - *"And the Lord appeared to Solomon by night, and said unto him, I have heard thy prayer, and have chosen this place to myself for an house of sacrifice. If I shut up heaven that there be no rain, or if I command the locusts to devour the land, or if I send pestilence among my people;"*

God the Healer:

- Exodus 15:26 - *"And said, If thou wilt diligently hearken to the voice of the Lord thy God, and wilt do that which is right in his sight, and wilt give ear to his commandments, and keep all his statutes, I will put none of these diseases upon thee, which I have brought upon the Egyptians: for I am the Lord that healeth thee."*

Healeth All Thy Diseases:

- Psalm 103:2-3 - *"Bless the Lord, O my soul, and forget not all his benefits: Who forgiveth all thine iniquities; who healeth all thy diseases;"*

- Mark 16:17-18 - *"And these signs shall follow them that believe; In my name shall they cast out devils; they shall speak with new tongues; They shall take up serpents; and if they drink any deadly thing, it shall not hurt them; they shall lay hands on the sick, and they shall recover."*

- Matthew 10:7-8 - *"And as ye go, preach, saying, The kingdom of heaven is at hand. Heal the sick, cleanse the lepers, raise the dead, cast out devils: freely ye have received, freely give."*

The Situation of This City is Pleasant, But.

Text: 2 Kings 2:19 - *"And the men of the city said unto Elisha, Behold, I pray thee, the situation of this city is pleasant, as my lord seeth: but the water is naught, and the ground barren."*

Something is Missing:

- 2 Kings 2:19-22 - *"And the men of the city said unto Elisha, Behold, I pray thee, the situation of this city is pleasant, as my lord seeth: but the water is naught, and the ground barren. And he said, Bring me a new cruse, and put salt therein. And they brought it to him. And he went forth unto the spring of the waters, and cast the salt in there, and said, Thus saith the Lord, I have healed these waters; there shall not be from thence any more death or barren land. So the waters were healed unto this day, according to the saying of Elisha which he spake."*

They Saw Their Needs:

- Water is Naught and the Ground Barren.

God's Promise: I Will Heal Their Land:

- Christ is the Healer - Mat. 4:23-24 - *"And Jesus went about all Galilee, teaching in their synagogues, and preaching the gospel of the kingdom, and healing all manner of sickness and all manner of disease among the people. And his fame went throughout all Syria: and they brought unto him all sick people that were taken with divers diseases and torments, and those which were possessed with devils, and those which were lunatick, and those that had the palsy; and he healed them."*

Healing Night.

Text: Mark 1:32 (KJV) - *"And at even, when the sun did set, they brought unto him all that were diseased, and them that were possessed with devils."*

Not Permit Them to Speak:

- Mark 1:33-34 - *"And all the city was gathered together at the door. And he healed many that were sick of divers diseases, and cast out many devils; and suffered not the devils to speak, because they knew him."*

They Know Him:

- Jesus' Ministry is Healing - Acts 10:38 - *"How God anointed Jesus of Nazareth with the Holy Ghost and with power: who went about doing good, and healing all that were oppressed of the devil; for God was with him."*

That Also Applies to Believers:

- John 14:12 - *"Verily, verily, I say unto you, He that believeth on me, the works that I do shall he do also; and greater works than these shall he do; because I go unto my Father."*

- Mark 16:15-18 - *"And he said unto them, Go ye into all the world, and preach the gospel to every creature. He that believeth and is baptized shall be saved; but he that believeth not shall be damned. And these signs shall follow them that believe; In my name shall they cast out devils; they shall speak with new tongues; They shall take up serpents; and if they drink any deadly thing, it shall not hurt them; they shall lay hands on the sick, and they shall recover."*

God's Power Always Present to Heal:

- Luke 5:17 - *"And it came to pass on a certain day, as he was teaching, that there were Pharisees and doctors of the law sitting by, which were come out of every town of Galilee, and Judaea, and Jerusalem: and the power of the Lord was present to heal them."*

Faith for Healing.

Text: Acts 14:9 - *"The same heard Paul speak: who stedfastly beholding him, and perceiving that he had faith to be healed."*

Faith Cometh By:

- Rom. 10:17 - *"So then faith cometh by hearing, and hearing by the word of God."*

- Heb. 11:6 (KJV) - *"But without faith it is impossible to please him: for he that cometh to God must believe that he is, and that he is a rewarder of them that diligently seek him."*

Faith in God:

- Faith in God's Word.

Faith to be Healed:

- God Sends His Word - Psalm 107:20 - *"He sent his word, and healed them, and delivered them from their destructions."*

- Power in the Word - Must be Preached and Believed - Jesus Saw Their Faith - Mark 2:5, Mark 2:2-5, Mark 2:11-12 - *"When Jesus saw their faith, he said unto the sick of the palsy, Son, thy sins be forgiven thee."*

Healing from Poverty and Wants.

Text: Psalm 34:10 - "The young lions do lack, and suffer hunger: but they that seek the Lord shall not want any good thing."

Why?

- Because It is the Sinner's Portion - Eccl 2:26 - *"For God giveth to a man that is good in his sight wisdom, and knowledge, and joy: but to the sinner he giveth travail, to gather and to heap up, that he may give to him that is good before God. This also is vanity and vexation of spirit."*

It is a Curse:

- Deut. 28:15-16 - *"But it shall come to pass, if thou wilt not hearken unto the voice of the Lord thy God, to observe to do all his commandments and his statutes which I command thee this day; that all these curses shall come upon thee, and overtake thee: Cursed shalt thou be in the city, and cursed shalt thou be in the field."*

Redeemed from Curse:

- Gal. 3:13 - *"Christ hath redeemed us from the curse of the law, being made a curse for us: for it is written, Cursed is every one that hangeth on a tree."*

Salvation Plus:

- Rom. 8:32 - *"He that spared not his own Son, but delivered him up for us all, how shall he not with him also freely give us all things?"*

God's Promise:

- Psalm 23:1, Psalm 37:25-26 - *"The Lord is my shepherd; I shall not want. I have been young, and now am old; yet have I not seen the righteous forsaken, nor his seed begging bread."*

Antidote Over Poverty and Wants:

- Faith Prayer - Jabez: 1Cro. 4:9-10, Prov. 30:8 - *"And Jabez was more honourable than his brethren: and his mother called his name Jabez, saying, Because I bare him with sorrow. And Jabez called on the God of Israel, saying, Oh that thou wouldest bless me indeed, and enlarge my coast, and that thine hand might be with me, and that thou wouldest keep me from evil, that it may not grieve me! And God granted him that which he requested."*

Power of God Present to Heal.

Text: Luke 5:17 - *"And it came to pass on a certain day, as he was teaching, that there were Pharisees and doctors of the law sitting by, which were come out of every town of Galilee, and Judaea, and Jerusalem: and the power of the Lord was present to heal them."*

His Promise:

- Mat. 18:20 - *"For where two or three are gathered together in my name, there am I in the midst of them."*

To Be Aware of It:

- Gen. 28:16 - *"And Jacob awaked out of his sleep, and he said, Surely the Lord is in this place; and I knew it not."*

God in His Only Temple:

- Faith in God's Promises - Mark 5:28 - *"For she said, If I may touch but his clothes, I shall be whole."*

I Will Go, Touch, and I Will Be Healed:

- Have Faith in God for Your Healing.

The Children's Bread.

Text: Mark 7:27 - *"But Jesus said unto her, Let the children first be filled: for it is not meet to take the children's bread, and to cast it unto the dogs."*

Who Are the Children:

- 2John 1:12 - *"Having many things to write unto you, I would not write with paper and ink: but I trust to come unto you, and speak face to face, that our joy may be full."*

- The Redeemed Born of God - 1John 3:9 (Sin Not).

The Children of God's Benefit:

- Psalm 103:2-3 - *"Bless the Lord, O my soul, and forget not all his benefits: Who forgiveth all thine iniquities; who healeth all thy diseases."*

Free:

- Healing - James 5:14-15, Mark 16:17-18, Mat. 10:7-8, 3John 2 (KJV) - *"Beloved, I wish above all things that thou mayest prosper and be in health, even as thy soul prospereth."*

You Need the Power.

Text: Ephesians 6:10 - *"Finally, my brethren, be strong in the Lord, and in the power of his might."*

Why?

- Because of the devil and his forces: Luke 29:49 - *"And, behold, I send the promise of my Father upon you: but tarry ye in the city of Jerusalem, until ye be endued with power from on high."*

- To be an effective Christian and bold witness of Christ: Acts 1:8 (KJV) - *"But ye shall receive power, after that the Holy Ghost is come upon you: and ye shall be witnesses unto me both in Jerusalem, and in all Judaea, and in Samaria, and unto the uttermost part of the earth."*

- It takes holy living: Romans 12:1-2 - *"I beseech you therefore, brethren, by the mercies of God, that ye present your bodies a living sacrifice, holy, acceptable unto God, which is your reasonable service. And be not conformed to this world: but be ye transformed by the renewing of your mind, that ye may prove what is that good, and acceptable, and perfect, will of God."*

- And seriousness: Acts 4:29-31 - *"And now, Lord, behold their threatenings: and grant unto thy servants, that with all boldness they may speak thy word, By stretching forth thine hand to heal; and that signs and wonders may be done by the name of thy holy child Jesus. And when they had prayed, the place was shaken where they were assembled together; and they were all filled with the Holy Ghost, and they spake the word of God with boldness."*

- Acts 2:1-4 - *"And when the day of Pentecost was fully come, they were all with one accord in one place. And suddenly there came a sound from heaven as of a rushing mighty wind, and it filled all the house where they were sitting. And there appeared unto them cloven tongues like as of fire, and it sat upon each of them. And they were all filled with the Holy Ghost, and began to speak with other tongues, as the Spirit gave them utterance."*

Clean Vessels.

Text: Isaiah 52:11 - *"Depart ye, depart ye, go ye out from thence, touch no unclean thing; go ye out of the midst of her; be ye clean, that bear the vessels of the Lord."*

Why Clean Vessels?

- Unclean vessel cannot serve a Holy God: Isaiah 6:1-8 (KJV) - *"In the year that king Uzziah died I saw also the Lord sitting upon a throne, high and lifted up, and his train filled the temple. Above it stood the seraphims: each one had six wings; with twain he covered his face, and with twain he covered his feet, and with twain he did fly. And one cried unto another, and said, Holy, holy, holy, is the Lord of hosts: the whole earth is full of his glory. And the posts of the door moved at the voice of him that cried, and the house was filled with smoke. Then said I, Woe is me! for I am undone; because I am a man of unclean lips, and I dwell in the midst of a people of unclean lips: for mine eyes have seen the King, the Lord of hosts. Then flew one of the seraphims unto me, having a live coal in his hand, which he had taken with the tongs from off the altar: And he laid it upon my mouth, and said, Lo, this hath touched thy lips; and thine iniquity is taken away, and thy sin purged. Also I heard the voice of the Lord, saying, Whom shall I send, and who will go for us? Then said I, Here am I; send me."*

God Wants Vessels of Honor:

2 Timothy 2:19-21 - *"Nevertheless the foundation of God standeth sure, having this seal, The Lord knoweth them that are his. And, Let every one that nameth the name of Christ depart from iniquity. But in a great house there are not only vessels of gold and of silver, but also of wood and of earth; and some to honour, and some to*

dishonour. If a man therefore purge himself from these, he shall be a vessel unto honour, sanctified, and meet for the master's use, and prepared unto every good work."

Need to Be Cleaned:

Ezekiel 22:26 - *"Her priests have violated my law, and have profaned mine holy things: they have put no difference between the holy and profane, neither have they shewed difference between the unclean and the clean, and have hid their eyes from my sabbaths, and I am profaned among them."*

Isaiah 1:16 - *"Wash you, make you clean; put away the evil of your doings from before mine eyes; cease to do evil."*

Obedience, Great Faith.

Text: Isaiah 1:19 (KJV) - *"If ye be willing and obedient, ye shall eat the good of the land."*

Obedience is the Gateway to God's Blessings and Miracles:

Obedience to God's Word is paramount.

The Centurion's Great Faith:

Matthew 8:5-13 narrates the story of the centurion who displayed remarkable faith. Despite being a Gentile, he approached Jesus, acknowledging His authority and expressing faith in His ability to heal his servant.

His faith was so profound that Jesus marveled at it (Matthew 8:10).

Power in Authority:

The centurion recognized the authority Jesus held, understanding that His mere word could bring about healing (Matthew 8:9).

Belief, Obedience, and Action:

- The centurion demonstrated his faith by believing in Jesus' word, obeying His instructions, and acting accordingly (Matthew 8:13).

The Consequences of Disobedience:

- Isaiah 1:20 warns of the consequences of disobedience, emphasizing the importance of aligning with God's will.

Peter's Obedience to Jesus' Word:

- Luke 5:5-6 recounts Peter's obedience when Jesus instructed him to cast his nets for a catch, despite having toiled all night without success. His obedience led to a miraculous catch of fish.

Active Faith, Faith in Action.

Text: James 2:17 - *"Even so faith, if it hath not works, is dead, being alone."*

An Active Faith Woman:

- The narrative of the woman with the issue of blood in Mark 5:25-34 illustrates active faith in action. Despite her condition, she believed in Jesus' healing power and took action by touching His garment, resulting in her complete healing.

Faith in God's Word:

- She believed in what she had heard about Jesus and acted upon that faith, demonstrating her confidence in God's ability to heal (Mark 5:25-34).

Speaking Words of Faith:

- Mark 5:34 records Jesus' affirmation of her faith, declaring that her faith had made her whole. This highlights the power of faith-filled words spoken in alignment with God's promises (Hebrews 11:1, 6; Mark 10:27; Mark 11:22).

Conclusion:

- Active faith, coupled with belief in God's Word and corresponding actions, leads to miraculous outcomes and wholeness.

Earnestly Contend for the Faith.

Text: Jude 3 - *"Beloved, when I gave all diligence to write unto you of the common salvation, it was needful for me to write unto you, and exhort you that ye should earnestly contend for the faith which was once delivered unto the saints."*

The Faith Delivered to the Saints:

- Jude urges believers to contend fervently for the faith that was entrusted to the early saints, emphasizing the importance of defending the truth.

Fighting for the Truth of Old-Time Faith:

- It entails upholding the faith of our fathers, as depicted in Psalm 34:19, and not neglecting the salvation offered through Christ (Hebrews 2:3).

No Compromise on Holiness Standards:

- Upholding holiness standards, adhering to the truth of God's Word without compromise (John 8:31; 1 Timothy 4:1).

Preserving the Ancient Landmarks:

- Proverbs 22:28 warns against removing the ancient landmarks, signifying the importance of preserving the foundational truths of the faith.

Preaching the Word and Holiness:

- 2 Timothy 4:2 emphasizes the need to preach the Word, upholding holiness forever, without succumbing to preaching another gospel (Galatians 1:9).

Examples of Contending for the Faith:

- The apostles in Acts 4:17-20 and Acts 5:27-29 stood firm in the face of opposition, even at the risk of persecution.

- Stephen's steadfastness in Acts 7:59, and the faith of those mentioned in Hebrews 11:13, who endured trials and remained faithful.

The Trial of Faith.

Text: 1 Peter 1:7 (KJV) - *"That the trial of your faith, being much more precious than of gold that perisheth, though it be tried with fire, might be found unto praise and honour and glory at the appearing of Jesus Christ."*

Trials as Inevitable:

- Peter reminds believers that trials are inevitable but assures them that God will provide a way of escape (1 Peter 4:12; 1 Corinthians 10:13).

Example of Job's Faith:

- Job serves as a prime example of enduring faith amidst trials (James 5:11). Despite suffering immense loss and affliction, he remained steadfast, never denying God (Job 2:9-10).

Personal Faith in God:

- Job's unwavering faith in God, demonstrated in his statements of trust (Job 13:15) and eventual restoration (Job 42:10-12), underscores the importance of personal faith in times of trial.

Conclusion:

- Both Jude and Peter emphasize the necessity of contending for and enduring in the faith, even amid trials and opposition, as exemplified by the faithful throughout Scripture.

-

Ye Have Not So Learned of Christ.

Text: Ephesians 4:20 - *"But ye have not so learned Christ;"*

What Did the Gospel Teach Us?

- Repentance: Mark 1:15 - *"And saying, The time is fulfilled, and the kingdom of God is at hand: repent ye, and believe the gospel."*

  Acts 3:19 - *"Repent ye therefore, and be converted, that your sins may be blotted out, when the times of refreshing shall come from the presence of the Lord."*

- Not to walk as Gentiles: Ephesians 4:17-19 - *"This I say therefore, and testify in the Lord, that ye henceforth walk not as other Gentiles walk, in the vanity of their mind, Having the understanding darkened, being alienated from the life of God through the ignorance that is in them, because of the blindness of their heart: Who being past feeling have given themselves over unto lasciviousness, to work all uncleanness with greediness."*

- To be transformed and changed: Romans 12:2 - *"And be not conformed to this world: but be ye transformed by the renewing of your mind, that ye may prove what is that good, and acceptable, and perfect, will of God."* Ephesians 4:22-31 - *"That ye put off concerning the former conversation the old man, which is corrupt according to the deceitful lusts; And be renewed in the spirit of your mind; And that ye put on the new man, which after God is created in righteousness and true holiness."*

Challenge:

- Judgment first in the house of God: 1 Peter 4:17-18 - *"For the time is come that judgment must begin at the house of God: and if it first begin at us, what shall the end be of them that obey not the gospel of God? And if the righteous scarcely be saved, where shall the ungodly and the sinner appear?"*

Christmas Bonus.

Text: Romans 8:32 (KJV) - *"He that spared not his own Son, but delivered him up for us all, how shall he not with him also freely give us all things?"*

Christmas or the Birth of Jesus:

- Glad tidings of great joy to the whole world: Luke 2:9-11 (KJV) - "And, lo, the angel of the Lord came upon them, and the glory of the Lord shone round about them: and they were sore afraid. And the angel said unto them, Fear not: for, behold, I bring you good tidings of great joy, which shall be to all people. For unto you is born this day in the city of David a Saviour, which is Christ the Lord."

- Reasons for His Birth: Matthew 1:21 (KJV) - "And she shall bring forth a son, and thou shalt call his name Jesus: for he shall save his people from their sins." Luke 19:10 (KJV) - "For the Son of man is come to seek and to save that which was lost."

- Christmas Time is Time to Preach the Good Tidings of Great Joy: Mark 16:15-20 (KJV) - "And he said unto them, Go ye into all the world, and preach the gospel to every creature."

- Christmas Plus: Matthew 6:33 (KJV) - "But seek ye first the kingdom of God, and his righteousness; and all these things shall be added unto you." Romans 8:32 (KJV) - "He that spared not his own Son, but delivered him up for us all, how shall he not with him also freely give us all things?"

Not Time to Enjoy Sins:

- Hebrews 11:24-25 (KJV) - "By faith Moses, when he was come to years, refused to be called the son of Pharaoh's daughter; Choosing rather to suffer affliction with the people of God, than to enjoy the pleasures of sin for a season."

Last Minute Miracles.

Text: Genesis 22:13 (KJV) - *"And Abraham lifted up his eyes, and looked, and behold behind him a ram caught in a thicket by his horns: and Abraham went and took the ram, and offered him up for a burnt offering in the stead of his son."*

Faith in God, Faith in God's Word, and Faith Testimony:

- Genesis 2:3, 4 - *"And God blessed the seventh day, and sanctified it: because that in it he had rested from all his work which God created and made. These are the generations of the heavens and of the earth when they were created, in the day that the Lord God made the earth and the heavens."*

- Obedient Word of Faith: Genesis 22:5 - *"And Abraham said unto his young men, Abide ye here with the ass; and I and the lad will go yonder and worship, and come again to you."*

- Faith in God: Genesis 22:8 - *"And Abraham said, My son, God will provide himself a lamb for a burnt offering: so they went both of them together."*

Obedient to the Last Minute:

- Genesis 22:9-10 - *"And they came to the place which God had told him of; and Abraham built an altar there, and laid the wood in order, and bound Isaac his son, and laid him on the altar upon the wood. And Abraham stretched forth his hand, and took the knife to slay his son."*

- Romans 4:20 - *"He staggered not at the promise of God through unbelief; but was strong in faith, giving glory to God;"*

Miracles Follow Obedience:

- Genesis 22:11-13 (KJV) - *"And the angel of the Lord called unto him out of heaven, and said, Abraham, Abraham: and he said, Here am I. And he said, Lay not thine hand upon the lad, neither do thou any thing unto him: for now I know that thou fearest God, seeing thou hast not withheld thy son, thine only son from me. And Abraham lifted up his eyes, and looked, and behold behind him a ram caught in a thicket by his horns: and Abraham went and took the ram, and offered him up for a burnt offering in the stead of his son."*

Last Minute Obedience Gives Birth to Last Minute Miracles. Praise the Lord!

War of Disobedience.

Text: Jeremiah 6:16 - *"Thus saith the Lord, Stand ye in the ways, and see, and ask for the old paths, where is the good way, and walk therein, and ye shall find rest for your souls. But they said, We will not walk therein."*

The Fall of Man:

- Disobedience: Genesis 2:16-17 (KJV) - *"And the Lord God commanded the man, saying, Of every tree of the garden thou mayest freely eat: But of the tree of the knowledge of good and evil, thou shalt not eat of it: for in the day that thou eatest thereof thou shalt surely die."*

- Genesis 3:6-7 (KJV) - *"And when the woman saw that the tree was good for food, and that it was pleasant to the eyes, and a tree to be desired to make one wise, she took of the fruit thereof, and did eat, and gave also unto her husband with her; and he did eat. And the eyes of them both were opened, and they knew that they were naked; and they sewed fig leaves together, and made themselves aprons."*

Obedience is Key to God's Blessing:

- Isaiah 1:19 - *"If ye be willing and obedient, ye shall eat the good of the land:"*

- John 2:5 - *"His mother saith unto the servants, Whatsoever he saith unto you, do it."*

Obedience is Great Faith:

- John 8:31 - *"Then said Jesus to those Jews which believed on him, If ye continue in my word, then are ye my disciples indeed;"*

- James 1:22 - *"But be ye doers of the word, and not hearers only, deceiving your own selves."*

Jesus' Challenge:

- Luke 6:46 - *"And why call ye me, Lord, Lord, and do not the things which I say?"*

You Do Not Believe Until You Obey the Word of God:

- John 11:40 - *"Jesus saith unto her, Said I not unto thee, that, if thou wouldest believe, thou shouldest see the glory of God?"*

Women of Old.

Text: 1 Peter 3:5 (KJV) - *"For after this manner in the old time the holy women also, who trusted in God, adorned themselves, being in subjection unto their own husbands:"*

They were Holy:

- 1 Peter 3:5-6 - *"For after this manner in the old time the holy women also, who trusted in God, adorned themselves, being in subjection unto their own husbands: Even as Sara obeyed Abraham, calling him lord: whose daughters ye are, as long as ye do well, and are not afraid with any amazement."*

Special Distinction of Women:

- Last at the Cross: Mark 15:47 - *"And Mary Magdalene and Mary the mother of Joses beheld where he was laid."*

- Last at the Tomb: John 20:1 - *"The first day of the week cometh Mary Magdalene early, when it was yet dark, unto the sepulchre, and seeth the stone taken away from the sepulchre."*

- First to Proclaim the Resurrection: Matthew 28:8 - *"And they departed quickly from the sepulchre with fear and great joy; and did run to bring his disciples word."*

- Handle First Prayer Meeting: Acts 1:14 - *"These all continued with one accord in prayer and supplication, with the women, and Mary the mother of Jesus, and with his brethren."*

- First to Preach to the Jews: Luke 2:37-38 - *"And she was a widow of about fourscore and four years, which departed not from the temple, but served God with fastings and prayers night and day. And she coming in that instant gave thanks likewise unto the Lord, and spake of him to all them that looked for redemption in Jerusalem."*

- First to Greet Missionaries: Paul & Silas in Europe: Acts 16:13 - *"And on the sabbath we went out of the city by a river side, where prayer was wont to be made; and we sat down, and spake unto the women which resorted thither."*

- First European Convert: Acts 16:14 - *"And a certain woman named Lydia, a seller of purple, of the city of Thyatira, which worshipped God, heard us: whose heart the Lord opened, that she attended unto the things which were spoken of Paul."*

Women to be Followers of God:

- Ephesians 5:1 - *"Be ye therefore followers of God, as dear children;"*

Obedience.

Text: John 2:5 (KJV) - *"His mother saith unto the servants, Whatsoever he saith unto you, do it."*

Obedience is Great Faith:

- Matthew 8:8-9 - *"The centurion answered and said, Lord, I am not worthy that thou shouldest come under my roof: but speak the word only, and my servant shall be healed. For I am a man under authority, having soldiers under me: and I say to this man, Go, and he goeth; and to another, Come, and he cometh; and to my servant, Do this, and he doeth it."*

- Matthew 7:24-27 - *"Therefore whosoever heareth these sayings of mine, and doeth them, I will liken him unto a wise man, which built his house upon a rock: And the rain descended, and the floods came, and the winds blew, and beat upon that house; and it fell not: for it was founded upon a rock. And every one that heareth these sayings of mine, and doeth them not, shall be likened unto a foolish man, which built his house upon the sand: And the rain descended, and the floods came, and the winds blew, and beat upon that house; and it fell: and great was the fall of it."*

Obedience Leads to God's Miracle:

- If you believe God, you must do what God says.

- Lazarus: John 11:40 - *"Jesus saith unto her, Said I not unto thee, that, if thou wouldest believe, thou shouldest see the glory of God?"*

- James 1:22 - *"But be ye doers of the word, and not hearers only, deceiving your own selves."*

Challenge:

- Why do you worship God whom you do not trust? - Luke 6:46 (KJV) - *"And why call ye me, Lord, Lord, and do not the things which I say?"*

Believe His Prophet.

Text: 2 Chronicles 20:20b - *"...Believe in the LORD your God, so shall ye be established; believe his prophets, so shall ye prosper."*

God Speaks Through His Servants:

2 Peter 1:21 - *"For the prophecy came not in old time by the will of man: but holy men of God spake as they were moved by the Holy Ghost."*

Ephesians 4:11 - *"And he gave some, apostles; and some, prophets; and some, evangelists; and some, pastors and teachers;"*

Danger Where There is No Prophet:

Proverbs 29:18 - *"Where there is no vision, the people perish: but he that keepeth the law, happy is he."*

Psalm 74:9 - *"We see not our signs: there is no more any prophet: neither is there among us any that knoweth how long."*

God Will Not Send an Angel:

- Rich Man: Luke 16:27-30 - *"Then he said, I pray thee therefore, father, that thou wouldest send him to my father's house: For I have five brethren; that he may testify unto them, lest they also come into this place of torment. Abraham saith unto him, They have Moses and the prophets; let them hear them. And he said, Nay, father Abraham: but if one went unto them from the dead, they will repent."*

God Still Sends His Word:

Romans 10:17 - *"So then faith cometh by hearing, and hearing by the word of God."*

Elijah: 2 Kings 7:1-2, 19-20 - *"Then Elisha said, Hear ye the word of the LORD; Thus saith the LORD, To morrow about this time shall a measure of fine flour be sold for a shekel, and two measures of barley for a shekel, in the gate of Samaria."*

Apostles:

Acts 2:41-42 - *"Then they that gladly received his word were baptized: and the same day there were added unto them about three thousand souls. And they continued stedfastly in the apostles' doctrine and fellowship, and in breaking of bread, and in prayers."*

Deceiving Spirit:

1 Timothy 4:1 (KJV) - "Now the Spirit speaketh expressly, that in the latter times some shall depart from the faith, giving heed to seducing spirits, and doctrines of devils."

Galatians 3:1 (KJV) - "O foolish Galatians, who hath bewitched you, that ye should not obey the truth, before whose eyes Jesus Christ hath been evidently set forth, crucified among you?"

<u>The Word of the Prophet.</u>

Text: 2 Chronicles 20:20b **-** *"...Believe in the LORD your God, so shall ye be established; believe his prophets, so shall ye prosper."*

The Lord Gives:

Ephesians 4:11 - *"And he gave some, apostles; and some, prophets; and some, evangelists; and some, pastors and teachers;"*

Need of Prophets:

Proverbs 29:18 - *"Where there is no vision, the people perish: but he that keepeth the law, happy is he."*

Psalm 74:9 - *"We see not our signs: there is no more any prophet: neither is there among us any that knoweth how long."*

God Sends His Word Through His Prophets:

2 Peter 1:21 - *"For the prophecy came not in old time by the will of man: but holy men of God spake as they were moved by the Holy Ghost."*

Preach the True Word of God:

2 Timothy 4:2 - *"Preach the word; be instant in season, out of season; reprove, rebuke, exhort with all longsuffering and doctrine."*

Elisha: 2 Kings 7:1-2 - *"Then Elisha said, Hear ye the word of the LORD; Thus saith the LORD, To morrow about this time shall a measure of fine flour be sold for a shekel, and two measures of barley for a shekel, in the gate of Samaria."*

<u>Whosoever is Born of God.</u>

Text: 1 John 3:9 **-** *"Whosoever is born of God doth not commit sin; for his seed remaineth in him: and he cannot sin, because he is born of God."*

Need to Be Born Again:

John 3:3 - *"Jesus answered and said unto him, Verily, verily, I say unto thee, Except a man be born again, he cannot see the kingdom of God."*

He That Committeth Sin is of the Devil:

1 John 3:8 - *"He that committeth sin is of the devil; for the devil sinneth from the beginning. For this purpose the Son of God was manifested, that he might destroy the works of the devil."*

Born of God is to Transform and Change of Heart:

Acts 3:19 - *"Repent ye therefore, and be converted, that your sins may be blotted out, when the times of refreshing shall come from the presence of the Lord;"*

Ephesians 4:22-24 - *"That ye put off concerning the former conversation the old man, which is corrupt according to the deceitful lusts; And be renewed in the spirit of your mind; And that ye put on the new man, which after God is created in righteousness and true holiness."*

2 Corinthians 5:17 - *"Therefore if any man be in Christ, he is a new creature: old things are passed away; behold, all things are become new."*

Acts 16:30-35 (KJV) - "And brought them out, and said, Sirs, what must I do to be saved? And they said, Believe on the Lord Jesus Christ, and thou shalt be saved, and thy house."

Say No to Sin, Yes to Jesus:

- Great Joy in Heaven: Luke 15:7 - *"I say unto you, that likewise joy shall be in heaven over one sinner that repenteth, more than over ninety and nine just persons, which need no repentance."*
- Born Again, Spirit-Filled Child of God: John 1:12 - *"But as many as received him, to them gave he power to become the sons of God, even to them that believe on his name:"*

1 John 3:1 - *"Behold, what manner of love the Father hath bestowed upon us, that we should be called the sons of God: therefore the world knoweth us not, because it knew him not."*

Sleeping in Bale.

Text: Jonah 1:5b - *"But Jonah was gone down into the sides of the ship; and he lay, and was fast asleep."*

What Causes It?

- Away from God's Presence: Jonah 1:3a - *"But Jonah rose up to flee unto Tarshish from the presence of the LORD, and went down to Joppa; and he found a ship going to Tarshish: so he paid the fare thereof, and went down into it, to go with them unto Tarshish from the presence of the LORD."*

Why?

Mat. 25:5 - *"While the bridegroom tarried, they all slumbered and slept."*

Sleeping in Time of Crises:

Jonah 1:5 - *"Then the mariners were afraid, and cried every man unto his god, and cast forth the wares that were in the ship into the sea, to lighten it of them. But Jonah was gone down into the sides of the ship; and he lay, and was fast asleep."*

Samson:

Judges 16:19 - *"And she made him sleep upon her knees; and she called for a man, and she caused him to shave off the seven locks of his head; and she began to afflict him, and his strength went from him."*

Challenge:

2 Samuel 1:25, 27 - *"How are the mighty fallen in the midst of the battle! O Jonathan, thou wast slain in thine high places... How are the mighty fallen, and the weapons of war perished!"*

Wake Up:

1 Peter 5:8-9 - *"Be sober, be vigilant; because your adversary the devil, as a roaring lion, walketh about, seeking whom he may devour: Whom resist stedfast in the faith, knowing that the same afflictions are accomplished in your brethren that are in the world."*

Sin Makes One to Be Deaf:

Judges 16:6 - *"And Delilah said to Samson, Tell me, I pray thee, wherein thy great strength lieth, and wherewith thou mightest be bound to afflict thee."*

Sign of Last Day:

Mat. 24:12, Mat. 25:5 - *"And because iniquity shall abound, the love of many shall wax cold... While the bridegroom tarried, they all slumbered and slept."*

Satan is Not Playing.

Text: Judges 16:6 (KJV) - *"And Delilah said to Samson, Tell me, I pray thee, wherein thy great strength lieth, and wherewith thou mightest be bound to afflict thee."*

He Means Business:

- 1 Peter 5:8-9 - *"Be sober, be vigilant; because your adversary the devil, as a roaring lion, walketh about, seeking whom he may devour: Whom resist stedfast in the faith, knowing that the same afflictions are accomplished in your brethren that are in the world."*

Samson Lied Until He Was Defeated:

- Judges 16:16-17 - *"And it came to pass, when she pressed him daily with her words, and urged him, so that his soul was vexed unto death; That he told her all his heart, and said unto her, There hath not come a razor upon mine head; for I have been a Nazarite unto God from my mother's womb: if I be shaven, then my strength will go from me, and I shall become weak, and be like any other man."*

Slept in Sin:

- Judges 16:19 - *"And she made him sleep upon her knees; and she called for a man, and she caused him to shave off the seven locks of his head; and she began to afflict him, and his strength went from him."*

He Lost His Power:

- Judges 16:20 - *"And she said, The Philistines be upon thee, Samson. And he awoke out of his sleep, and said, I will go out as at other times before, and shake myself. And he wist not that the LORD was departed from him."*

Tormented:

- Judges 16:21 - *"But the Philistines took him, and put out his eyes, and brought him down to Gaza, and bound him with fetters of brass; and he did grind in the prison house."*

Prayed Back Power:

- Judges 16:28-30 - *"And Samson called unto the LORD, and said, O Lord GOD, remember me, I pray thee, and strengthen me, I pray thee, only this once, O God, that I may be at once avenged of the Philistines for my two eyes. And Samson took hold of the two middle pillars upon which the house stood, and on which it was borne up, of the one with his right hand, and of the other with his left. And Samson said, Let me die with the Philistines. And he bowed himself with all his might; and the house fell upon the lords, and upon all the people that were therein. So the dead which he slew at his death were more than they which he slew in his life."*

Satan Does Not Play and Jesus Never Deceives His Church:

- Luke 24:49 - *"And, behold, I send the promise of my Father upon you: but tarry ye in the city of Jerusalem, until ye be endued with power from on high."*

The Need of Another Elijah.

Text: James 5:17 (KJV) - *"Elias was a man subject to like passions as we are, and he prayed earnestly that it might not rain: and it rained not on the earth by the space of three years and six months."*

He Prayed Through:

- 1 Kings 18:42-45 - *"So Ahab went up to eat and to drink. And Elijah went up to the top of Carmel; and he cast himself down upon the earth, and put his face between his knees, And said to his servant, Go up now, look toward the sea. And he went up, and looked, and said, There is nothing. And he said, Go again seven times. And it came to pass at the seventh time, that he said, Behold, there ariseth a little cloud out of the sea, like a man's hand. And he said, Go up, say unto Ahab, Prepare thy chariot, and get thee down, that the rain stop thee not."*

Man of Action:

- 1 Kings 18:21 - *"And Elijah came unto all the people, and said, How long halt ye between two opinions? if the LORD be God, follow him: but if Baal, then follow him. And the people answered him not a word."*

Challenge the Prophets of Baal:

- 1 Kings 18:27-29 - *"And it came to pass at noon, that Elijah mocked them, and said, Cry aloud: for he is a god; either he is talking, or he is pursuing, or he is in a journey, or peradventure he sleepeth, and must be awaked. And they cried aloud, and cut themselves after their manner with knives and lancets, till the blood gushed out upon them. And it came to pass, when midday was past, and they prophesied until the time of the offering of the evening sacrifice, that there was neither voice, nor any to answer, nor any that regarded."*

Prayed Down God's Power:

- 1 Kings 18:36-37 - *"And it came to pass at the time of the offering of the evening sacrifice, that Elijah the prophet came near, and said, LORD God of Abraham, Isaac, and of Israel, let it be known this day that thou art God in Israel, and that I am thy servant, and that I have done all these things at thy word. Hear me, O LORD, hear me, that this people may know that thou art the LORD God, and that thou hast turned their heart back again."*

God of Fire:

- 1 Kings 18:38 - *"Then the fire of the LORD fell, and consumed the burnt sacrifice, and the wood, and the stones, and the dust, and licked up the water that was in the trench."*

- 2 Chronicles 7:1-2 - *"Now when Solomon had made an end of praying, the fire came down from heaven, and consumed the burnt offering and the sacrifices; and the glory of the LORD filled the house. And the priests could not enter into the house of the LORD, because the glory of the LORD had filled the LORD'S house."*

Spirit of Fear.

Text: 2 Timothy 1:7 - *"For God hath not given us the spirit of fear; but of power, and of love, and of a sound mind."*

It is of Devil Inherited from Adam:

Genesis 3:10 - *"And he said, I heard thy voice in the garden, and I was afraid, because I was naked; and I hid myself."*

Deliverance:

Luke 1:74 - "That he would grant unto us, that we being delivered out of the hand of our enemies might serve him without fear,"

Has to Ment:

1 John 4:18b - *"There is no fear in love; but perfect love casteth out fear: because fear hath torment. He that feareth is not made perfect in love."*

Sinner's Portion:

Proverbs 28:1 - *"The wicked flee when no man pursueth: but the righteous are bold as a lion."*

God's Power to the Believers:

Matthew 28:18-20 - *"And Jesus came and spake unto them, saying, All power is given unto me in heaven and in earth. Go ye therefore, and teach all nations, baptizing them in the name of the Father, and of the Son, and of the Holy Ghost:* Teaching them to observe all things whatsoever I have commanded you: and, lo, I am with you always, even unto the end of the world. Amen."

- 1 John 4:4 - *"Ye are of God, little children, and have overcome them: because greater is he that is in you, than he that is in the world."*

Build on the Rock:

Matthew 16:18 - *"And I say also unto thee, That thou art Peter, and upon this rock I will build my church; and the gates of hell shall not prevail against it."*

Isaiah 54:17 - *"No weapon that is formed against thee shall prosper; and every tongue that shall rise against thee in judgment thou shalt condemn. This is the heritage of the servants of the LORD, and their righteousness is of me, saith the LORD."*

Luke 10:19 - *"Behold, I give unto you power to tread on serpents and scorpions, and over all the power of the enemy: and nothing shall by any means hurt you."*

Bold as Lion:

- Proverbs 28:1b - *"...but the righteous are bold as a lion."*

God's Provision

Text: Genesis 22:8 - *"And Abraham said, My son, God will provide himself a lamb for a burnt offering: so they went both of them together."*

Faith in God and His Word Knowing God:

Daniel 11:32b - *"...but the people that do know their God shall be strong, and do exploits."*

Holiness Gateway to God's Provision:

Philippians 3:10 - *"That I may know him, and the power of his resurrection, and the fellowship of his sufferings, being made conformable unto his death;"*

Psalm 34:9 - *"O fear the LORD, ye his saints: for there is no want to them that fear him."*

Philippians 4:19 - *"But my God shall supply all your need according to his riches in glory by Christ Jesus."*

Ram:

Genesis 22:13 - *"And Abraham lifted up his eyes, and looked, and behold behind him a ram caught in a thicket by his horns: and Abraham went and took the ram, and offered him up for a burnt offering in the stead of his son."*

Obedience:

Genesis 22:3 - *"And Abraham rose up early in the morning, and saddled his ass, and took two of his young men with him, and Isaac his son, and clave the wood for the burnt offering, and rose up, and went unto the place of which God had told him."*

Fear of God:

Genesis 22:12 - *"And he said, Lay not thine hand upon the lad, neither do thou any thing unto him: for now I know that thou fearest God, seeing thou hast not withheld thy son, thine only son from me."*

Bread and Meat:

1 Kings 17:6 - *"And the ravens brought him bread and flesh in the morning, and bread and flesh in the evening; and he drank of the brook."*

Obedience - 1 Kings 17:5 - *"So he went and did according unto the word of the LORD: for he went and dwelt by the brook Cherith, that is before Jordan."*

The Royal Provider:

Psalm 37:25 - *"I have been young, and now am old; yet have I not seen the righteous forsaken, nor his seed begging bread."*

Thief in the House of God.

Text: Malachi 3:8 (KJV) - *"Will a man rob God? Yet ye have robbed me. But ye say, Wherein have we robbed thee? In tithes and offerings."*

Law of God:

Exodus 20:15 - *"Thou shalt not steal."*

Matthew 5:17-18 - *"Think not that I am come to destroy the law, or the prophets: I am not come to destroy, but to fulfil. For verily I say unto you, Till heaven and earth pass, one jot or one tittle shall in no wise pass from the law, till all be fulfilled."*

God's Command:

Malachi 3:10 - *"Bring ye all the tithes into the storehouse, that there may be meat in mine house, and prove me now herewith, saith the LORD of hosts, if I will not open you the windows of heaven, and pour you out a blessing, that there shall not be room enough to receive it."*

Failure is a Curse:

Malachi 3:9 - *"Ye are cursed with a curse: for ye have robbed me, even this whole nation."*

Examples in the Bible:

Abraham - Genesis 14:20 - *"And blessed be the most high God, which hath delivered thine enemies into thy hand. And he gave him tithes of all."*

Jacob - Genesis 28:22 - *"And this stone, which I have set for a pillar, shall be God's house: and of all that thou shalt give me I will surely give the tenth unto thee."*

The Pharisees - Matthew 5:20 - *"For I say unto you, That except your righteousness shall exceed the righteousness of the scribes and Pharisees, ye shall in no case enter into the kingdom of heaven."*

Challenge of Christ:

Luke 18:12 - *"I fast twice in the week, I give tithes of all that I possess."*

Early Church:

Acts 2:45 - *"And sold their possessions and goods, and parted them to all men, as every man had need."*

Acts 4:34-35 - *"Neither was there any among them that lacked: for as many as were possessors of lands or houses sold them, and brought the prices of the things that were sold, And laid them down at the apostles' feet: and distribution was made unto every man according as he had need."*

Challenge: Given All - Luke 21:1-4

Time to Seek God's Power.

Text: 2 Chronicles 16:9 (KJV) - *"For the eyes of the LORD run to and fro throughout the whole earth, to shew himself strong in the behalf of them whose heart is perfect toward him. Herein thou hast done foolishly: therefore from henceforth thou shalt have wars."*

Believers Need God's Power:

Joel 2:28 - *"And it shall come to pass afterward, that I will pour out my spirit upon all flesh; and your sons and your daughters shall prophesy, your old men shall dream dreams, your young men shall see visions."*

Acts 1:8 - *"But ye shall receive power, after that the Holy Ghost is come upon you: and ye shall be witnesses unto me both in Jerusalem, and in all Judaea, and in Samaria, and unto the uttermost part of the earth."*

Luke 24:49 - *"And, behold, I send the promise of my Father upon you: but tarry ye in the city of Jerusalem, until ye be endued with power from on high."*

Prayed Down Fire:

2 Chronicles 7:1 - *"Now when Solomon had made an end of praying, the fire came down from heaven, and consumed the burnt offering and the sacrifices; and the glory of the LORD filled the house."*

Acts 4:29-31 - *"And now, Lord, behold their threatenings: and grant unto thy servants, that with all boldness they may speak thy word, By stretching forth thine hand to heal; and that signs and wonders may be done by the name of thy holy child Jesus. And when they had prayed, the place was shaken where they were assembled together; and they were all filled with the Holy Ghost, and they spake the word of God with boldness."*

Luke 11:13 - *"If ye then, being evil, know how to give good gifts unto your children: how much more shall your heavenly Father give the Holy Spirit to them that ask him?"*

Gospel is Power of God:

Romans 1:16 - *"For I am not ashamed of the gospel of Christ: for it is the power of God unto salvation to every one that believeth; to the Jew first, and also to the Greek."*

John 1:12 - *"But as many as received him, to them gave he power to become the sons of God, even to them that believe on his name."*

Saved by the Power:

John 1:12 - *"But as many as received him, to them gave he power to become the sons of God, even to them that believe on his name."*

Additional Note:

Seek God's power through prayer, reliance on the Holy Spirit, and boldness in proclaiming the Gospel.

They that Know God.

Text: Daniel 11:32 - *"And such as do wickedly against the covenant shall he corrupt by flatteries: but the people that do know their God shall be strong, and do exploits."*

God's Expectation:

1 John 3:6 - *"Whosoever abideth in him sinneth not: whosoever sinneth hath not seen him, neither known him."*

John 17:3 - *"And this is life eternal, that they might know thee the only true God, and Jesus Christ, whom thou hast sent."*

Knowing Scriptures:

2 Timothy 3:15 - *"And that from a child thou hast known the holy scriptures, which are able to make thee wise unto salvation through faith which is in Christ Jesus."*

John 7:17 - *"If any man will do his will, he shall know of the doctrine, whether it be of God, or whether I speak of myself."*

Philippians 3:10 - *"That I may know him, and the power of his resurrection, and the fellowship of his sufferings, being made conformable unto his death;"*

Belief in the Word:

Hebrews 11:6 - *"But without faith it is impossible to please him: for he that cometh to God must believe that he is, and that he is a rewarder of them that diligently seek him."*

Challenge to Philip:

John 14:9 - *"Jesus saith unto him, Have I been so long time with you, and yet hast thou not known me, Philip? he that hath seen me hath seen the Father; and how sayest thou then, Shew us the Father?"*

John 14:12 - *"Verily, verily, I say unto you, He that believeth on me, the works that I do shall he do also; and greater works than these shall he do; because I go unto my Father."*

The 3 Hebrews:

Daniel 3:16-18 - *"Shadrach, Meshach, and Abednego, answered and said to the king, O Nebuchadnezzar, we are not careful to answer thee in this matter. If it be so, our God whom we serve is able to deliver us from the burning fiery furnace, and he will deliver us out of thine hand, O king. But if not, be it known unto thee, O king, that we will not serve thy gods, nor worship the golden image which thou hast set up."*

Abraham:

Genesis 22:7-8 - *"And Isaac spake unto Abraham his father, and said, My father: and he said, Here am I, my son. And he said, Behold the fire and the wood: but where is the lamb for a burnt offering? And Abraham said, My son, God will provide himself a lamb for a burnt offering: so they went both of them together."*

Genesis 22:10-13 - *"And Abraham stretched forth his hand, and took the knife to slay his son. And the angel of the LORD called unto him out of heaven, and said, Abraham, Abraham: and he said, Here am I. And he said, Lay not thine hand upon the lad, neither do thou any thing unto him: for now I know that thou fearest God, seeing thou hast not withheld thy son, thine only son from me. And Abraham lifted up his eyes, and looked, and behold behind him a ram caught in a thicket by his horns: and Abraham went and took the ram, and offered him up for a burnt offering in the stead of his son."*

Do It Quickly.

Text: John 13:27b - *"That thou doest, do quickly."*

Act Now, Time is Short:

Hebrews 9:27 - *"And as it is appointed unto men once to die, but after this the judgment:"*

Ecclesiastes 9:10 - *"Whatsoever thy hand findeth to do, do it with thy might; for there is no work, nor device, nor knowledge, nor wisdom, in the grave, whither thou goest."*

John 9:4 - *"I must work the works of him that sent me, while it is day: the night cometh, when no man can work."*

No Delay:

John 4:35 - *"Say not ye, There are yet four months, and then cometh harvest? behold, I say unto you, Lift up your eyes, and look on the fields; for they are white already to harvest."*

It Is Now:

2 Chronicles 6:2 - *"But I have built an house of habitation for thee, and a place for thy dwelling for ever."*

Careless Soul, Heed God's Warning:

Psalm 146:4 - *"His breath goeth forth, he returneth to his earth; in that very day his thoughts perish."*

Don't Be a Fool:

Luke 12:16-20 - *"And he spake a parable unto them, saying, The ground of a certain rich man brought forth plentifully: And he thought within himself, saying, What shall I do, because I have no room where to bestow my fruits? And he said, This will I do: I will pull down my barns, and build greater; and there will I bestow all my fruits and my goods. And I will say to my soul, Soul, thou hast much goods laid up for many years; take thine ease, eat, drink, and be merry. But God said unto him, Thou fool, this night thy soul shall be required of thee: then whose shall those things be, which thou hast provided?"*

Forget Not All His Benefits.

Text: Psalm 103:2 - *"Bless the Lord, O my soul, and forget not all his benefits:"*

Spirit of Appreciation:

Psalm 100:4- *"Enter into his gates with thanksgiving, and into his courts with praise: be thankful unto him, and bless his name."*

That We Know God:

Luke 10:20 - *"Notwithstanding in this rejoice not, that the spirits are subject unto you; but rather rejoice, because your names are written in heaven."*

His Benefits:

Psalm 103:3-5 - *"Who forgiveth all thine iniquities; who healeth all thy diseases; Who redeemeth thy life from destruction; who crowneth thee with lovingkindness and tender mercies; Who satisfieth thy mouth with good things; so that thy youth is renewed like the eagle's."*

The Greatest Sin is Unthankful:

Romans 1:21 - *"Because that, when they knew God, they glorified him not as God, neither were thankful; but became vain in their imaginations, and their foolish heart was darkened."*

Count Your Blessings One by One.

The Resurrection of Christ.

Text: Mat. 28:6 - *"He is not here: for he is risen, as he said. Come, see the place where the Lord lay."*

Satan Failed All Round:

Matthew 27:62-66 - Details the account of the chief priests and Pharisees securing the tomb of Jesus.

Matthew 28:11-15 - Describes the bribing of the guards by the chief priests and elders.

Enough Proof:

Acts 1:2-3 - *"Until the day in which he was taken up, after that he through the Holy Ghost had given commandments unto the apostles whom he had chosen: To whom also he shewed himself alive after his passion by many infallible proofs, being seen of them forty days, and speaking of the things pertaining to the kingdom of God."*

Resurrection the Only Hope:

1 Corinthians 15:14 - *"And if Christ be not risen, then is our preaching vain, and your faith is also vain."*

All Power Belongs to Jesus:

Matthew 28:18 - *"And Jesus came and spake unto them, saying, All power is given unto me in heaven and in earth."*

John 11:25 - *"Jesus said unto her, I am the resurrection, and the life: he that believeth in me, though he were dead, yet shall he live:"*

Need of Holy Spirit:

Acts 1:4 - *"And, being assembled together with them, commanded them that they should not depart from Jerusalem, but wait for the promise of the Father, which, saith he, ye have heard of me."*

Romans 8:11 - *"But if the Spirit of him that raised up Jesus from the dead dwell in you, he that raised up Christ from the dead shall also quicken your mortal bodies by his Spirit that dwelleth in you."*

Able to Save and to Deliver:

Hebrews 7:25 - *"Wherefore he is able also to save them to the uttermost that come unto God by him, seeing he ever liveth to make intercession for them."*

Resurrection's Benefit:

> Psalm 103:2-3 - *"Bless the Lord, O my soul, and forget not all his benefits: Who forgiveth all thine iniquities; who healeth all thy diseases;"*

> 1 Peter 2:24 - *"Who his own self bare our sins in his own body on the tree, that we, being dead to sins, should live unto righteousness: by whose stripes ye were healed."*

He Is Coming Back Again.

Man Disappointed God.

Text: Gen. 6:6 (KJV) - *"And it repented the Lord that he had made man on the earth, and it grieved him at his heart."*

1. **The Creation of Man:**

   > Gen. 2:7 - *"And the Lord God formed man of the dust of the ground, and breathed into his nostrils the breath of life, and man became a living soul."*

   > Gen. 1:26-27 - *"And God said, Let us make man in our image, after our likeness: and let them have dominion over the fish of the sea, and over the fowl of the air, and over the cattle, and over all the earth, and over every creeping thing that creepeth upon the earth. So God created man in his own image, in the image of God created he him; male and female created he them."*

2. **God's Care:**

   > Gen. 2:18 - *"And the Lord God said, It is not good that the man should be alone; I will make him an help meet for him."*

   > Gen. 2:19 - *"And out of the ground the Lord God formed every beast of the field, and every fowl of the air; and brought them unto Adam to see what he would call them: and whatsoever Adam called every living creature, that was the name thereof."*

3. **God's Work on Man:**

   > Gen. 2:21-22 - *"And the Lord God caused a deep sleep to fall upon Adam, and he slept: and he took one of his ribs, and closed up the flesh instead thereof; And the rib, which the Lord God had taken from man, made he a woman, and brought her unto the man."*

Violation of God's Command:

Gen. 2:16-17 - *"And the Lord God commanded the man, saying, Of every tree of the garden thou mayest freely eat: But of the tree of the knowledge of good and evil, thou shalt not eat of it: for in the day that thou eatest thereof thou shalt surely die."*

Gen. 3:6 - *"And when the woman saw that the tree was good for food, and that it was pleasant to the eyes, and a tree to be desired to make one wise, she took of the fruit thereof, and did eat, and gave also unto her husband with her; and he did eat."*

Saved by Grace:

Eph. 2:8 - *"For by grace are ye saved through faith; and that not of yourselves: it is the gift of God:"*

Luke 6:46 - *"And why call ye me, Lord, Lord, and do not the things which I say?"*

Willful Sin:

Heb. 10:26-27 - *"For if we sin wilfully after that we have received the knowledge of the truth, there remaineth no more sacrifice for sins, But a certain fearful looking for of judgment and fiery indignation, which shall devour the adversaries."*

Bastard in the House of God.

Text: Heb. 12:8b - *"then are ye bastards, and not sons."*

Be Without Chastisement, God Gave His Words:

The Bible for - 2Tim. 3:15-17 - *"And that from a child thou hast known the holy scriptures, which are able to make thee wise unto salvation through faith which is in Christ Jesus. All scripture is given by inspiration of God, and is profitable for doctrine, for reproof, for correction, for instruction in righteousness: That the man of God may be perfect, throughly furnished unto all good works."*

Chastisement:

Heb. 12:8-11 - *"But if ye be without chastisement, whereof all are partakers, then are ye bastards, and not sons. Furthermore we have had fathers of our flesh which corrected us, and we gave them reverence: shall we not much rather be in subjection unto the Father of spirits, and live? For they verily for a few days chastened us after their own pleasure; but he for our profit, that we might be partakers of his holiness. Now no chastening for the present seemeth to be joyous, but grievous: nevertheless afterward it yieldeth the peaceable fruit of righteousness unto them which are exercised thereby."*

Those That Commit Sin Are Bastards/Carnal Man:

1 John 3:8 - *"He that committeth sin is of the devil; for the devil sinneth from the beginning. For this purpose the Son of God was manifested, that he might destroy the works of the devil."*

Rom. 8:6-8 *"For to be carnally minded is death; but to be spiritually minded is life and peace. Because the carnal mind is enmity against God: for it is not subject to the law of God, neither indeed can be. So then they that are in the flesh cannot please God."*

The Children of God:

1 John 3:9 - *"Whosoever is born of God doth not commit sin; for his seed remaineth in him: and he cannot sin, because he is born of God."*

The Un-Converted Souls in the Church, The Worldly Christian, Carnal Believers:

Timothy 4:2 - *"Preach the word; be instant in season, out of season;*

He that Believeth on Him.

Text: John 3:18 - *"He that believeth on him is not condemned: but he that believeth not is condemned already, because he hath not believed in the name of the only begotten Son of God."*

Who are Those?

Sons of God: John 1:12 - *"But as many as received him, to them gave he power to become the sons of God, even to them that believe on his name:"*

Continues in His Word: John 8:31-32 - *"Then said Jesus to those Jews which believed on him, If ye continue in my word, then are ye my disciples indeed; And ye shall know the truth, and the truth shall make you free."*

Doers of the Word:

Doer of the Word: James 1:22 - *"But be ye doers of the word, and not hearers only, deceiving your own selves."*

Believe in Him – Do What He Says: Luke 9:1-2 - *"Then he called his twelve disciples together, and gave them power and authority over all devils, and to cure diseases. And he sent them to preach the kingdom of God, and to heal the sick."*

Miracles and Blessings: John 14:12 - *"Verily, verily, I say unto you, He that believeth on me, the works that I do shall he do also; and greater works than these shall he do; because I go unto my Father."*

Victory in Jesus.

Text: John 16:33 - *"These things I have spoken unto you, that in me ye might have peace. In the world ye shall have tribulation: but be of good cheer; I have overcome the world."*

Creation:

Genesis 1:1-2: *"In the beginning God created the heaven and the earth. And the earth was without form, and void; and darkness was upon the face of the deep. And the Spirit of God moved upon the face of the waters."*

Power of Creation:

Genesis 1:3: *"And God said, Let there be light: and there was light."*

Perfection:

Genesis 1:31: *"And God saw every thing that he had made, and, behold, it was very good. And the evening and the morning were the sixth day."*

The Victory in Jesus:

1 John 5:4: *"For whatsoever is born of God overcometh the world: and this is the victory that overcometh the world, even our faith."*

1 John 5:6: *"This is he that came by water and blood, even Jesus Christ; not by water only, but by water and blood. And it is the Spirit that beareth witness, because the Spirit is truth."*

Matthew 28:18-20: *"And Jesus came and spake unto them, saying, All power is given unto me in heaven and in earth. Go ye therefore, and teach all nations, baptizing them in the name of the Father, and of the Son, and of the Holy Ghost: Teaching them to observe all things whatsoever I have commanded you: and, lo, I am with you always, even unto the end of the world. Amen."*

Acts 1:3-4: *"To whom also he shewed himself alive after his passion by many infallible proofs, being seen of them forty days, and speaking of the things pertaining to the kingdom of God: And, being assembled together with them, commanded them that they should not depart from Jerusalem, but wait for the promise of the Father, which, saith he, ye have heard of me."*

Paul:

Acts 19:11-16: *"And God wrought special miracles by the hands of Paul: So that from his body were brought unto the sick handkerchiefs or aprons, and the diseases departed from them, and the evil spirits went out of them. Then certain of the vagabond Jews, exorcists, took upon them to call over them which had evil spirits the name of the Lord Jesus, saying, We adjure you by Jesus whom Paul preacheth. And there were seven sons of one Sceva, a Jew, and chief of the priests, which did so. And the evil spirit answered and said, Jesus I know, and Paul I know; but who are ye? And the man in whom the evil spirit was leaped on them, and overcame them, and prevailed against them, so that they fled out of that house naked and wounded."*

Praying Through:

John 16:24: *"Hitherto have ye asked nothing in my name: ask, and ye shall receive, that your joy may be full."*

Luke 24:49: *"And, behold, I send the promise of my Father upon you: but tarry ye in the city of Jerusalem, until ye be endued with power from on high."*

Acts 1:12-14: *"Then returned they unto Jerusalem from the mount called Olivet, which is from Jerusalem a sabbath day's journey. And when they were come in, they went up into an upper room, where abode both Peter, and James, and John, and Andrew, Philip, and Thomas, Bartholomew, and Matthew, James the son of Alphaeus, and Simon Zelotes, and Judas the brother of James. These all continued with one accord in prayer and supplication, with the women, and Mary the mother of Jesus, and with his brethren."*

Bad Works:

Acts 19:18: *"And many that believed came, and confessed, and shewed their deeds."*

<u>Victory through Faith.</u>

Text: 1 John 5:4 - *"For whatsoever is born of God overcometh the world: and this is the victory that overcometh the world, even our faith."*

Woman with the Issue of Blood:

- **Faith in Her Victory:** Mark 5:28 - *"For she said, If I may touch but his clothes, I shall be whole."*

- **Believed the Word:** Mark 5:25-34 - Describes the account of the woman with the issue of blood who believed that if she touched Jesus' garment, she would be healed.

- **Action into Faith Determination:** She was determined, saying, *"I will go."* (Mark 5:28)

- **Speaking It:** Mark 5:34 (KJV) - *"And he said unto her, Daughter, thy faith hath made thee whole; go in peace, and be whole of thy plague."*

Perfection - By Faith, Victory Is Sure

<u>Victory in the Word.</u>

Text: Psalm 107:20 - *"He sent his word, and healed them, and delivered them from their destructions."*

Power of the Word:

Genesis 1:3: *"And God said, Let there be light: and there was light."*

John 1:3: *"All things were made by him; and without him was not any thing made that was made."*

In the Beginning with God: John 1:2 - *"The same was in the beginning with God."*

Jesus is the Word: John 1:1 - *"In the beginning was the Word, and the Word was with God, and the Word was God."*

In the Word of God:

The Centurion: Matthew 8:8 - *"The centurion answered and said, Lord, I am not worthy that thou shouldest come under my roof: but speak the word only, and my servant shall be healed."*

Elijah Speak the Word

Elisha Speak the Word

Moses Speak the Word

The Apostles: Mark 16:20 - *"And they went forth, and preached every where, the Lord working with them, and confirming the word with signs following. Amen."*

The Church: Matthew 18:18 - *"Verily I say unto you, Whatsoever ye shall bind on earth shall be bound in heaven: and whatsoever ye shall loose on earth shall be loosed in heaven."*

With Signs Following.

Text: Mark 16:20 - *"And they went forth, and preached every where, the Lord working with them, and confirming the word with signs following. Amen."*

The signs following signify victory in Jesus. However, today, we may not see signs as spoken of in Psalm 74:9.

Hindrances to Signs:

Unbelief: Matthew 17:19-20 - Jesus said unto them, *"Because of your unbelief: for verily I say unto you, If ye have faith as a grain of mustard seed, ye shall say unto this mountain, Remove hence to yonder place; and it shall remove; and nothing shall be impossible unto you."*

Faithless and Perverse Generation: Mark 9:19 (KJV) - Jesus answered him, and said, *"O faithless generation, how long shall I be with you? how long shall I suffer you? bring him unto me."*

No Mighty Miracles in Nazareth:

Reason: Unbelief

Victory in Jesus with Signs Following:

Mark 16:17-20 - *"And these signs shall follow them that believe; In my name shall they cast out devils; they shall speak with new tongues; They shall take up serpents; and if they drink any deadly thing, it shall not hurt them; they shall lay hands on the sick, and they shall recover."*

Challenge:

Unbelievers in the Believing Churches

Faith in Healing: Acts 14:8-10 - *"And there sat a certain man at Lystra, impotent in his feet, being a cripple from his mother's womb, who never had walked: The same heard Paul speak: who steadfastly beholding him, and perceiving that he had faith to be healed, Said with a loud voice, Stand upright on thy feet. And he leaped and walked."*

In Jesus' Name.

Text: Mark 16:17 - *"And these signs shall follow them that believe; In my name shall they cast out devils; they shall speak with new tongues."*

Victory in Jesus' name is emphasized. God has highly exalted the name of Jesus above other names (Philippians 2:9-10).

The Name of Jesus:

Only for the Righteous: Proverbs 18:10 - "The name of the LORD is a strong tower: the righteous runneth into it, and is safe."

Peter and John at the Beautiful Gate: Acts 3:6-8 - Peter said, *"Silver and gold have I none; but such as I have give I thee: In the name of Jesus Christ of Nazareth rise up and walk."*

Through Faith in His Name: Acts 3:16 - *"And his name through faith in his name hath made this man strong, whom ye see and know: yea, the faith which is by him hath given him this perfect soundness in the presence of you all."*

Anything Asked in Jesus' Name: John 14:13 - *"And whatsoever ye shall ask in my name, that will I do, that the Father may be glorified in the Son."*

Able God.

Text: Hebrews 7:25 - *"Wherefore he is able also to save them to the uttermost that come unto God by him, seeing he ever liveth to make intercession for them."*

God is omnipotent, able to do all things (Mark 10:27). It's crucial to know Him:

- **To Have Faith in Him:** Daniel 11:32b, Mark 11:22 - *"And Jesus answering saith unto them, Have faith in God."*

- **Examples of Faith:** Shadrach, Meshach, and Abednego in the fiery furnace (Daniel 3:16-18).

- **Experience of Victory:** Daniel 3:27 - *"And the princes, governors, and captains, and the king's counsellors, being gathered together, saw these men, upon whose bodies the fire had no power, nor was an hair of their head singed, neither were their coats changed, nor the smell of fire had passed on them."*

- **Trust in God:** They trusted in God.

Perfection.

Text: Genesis 2:2 - *"And on the seventh day God ended his work which he had made; and he rested on the seventh day from all his work which he had made."*

Perfection is exemplified in various instances, such as Jericho's conquest (Joshua 6:1-3, 14).

Victory was achieved (Joshua 6:20).

Additional Points:

Laying Hands on the Sick: Mark 16:17-18 - *"And these signs shall follow them that believe; In my name shall they cast out devils; they shall speak with new tongues; They shall take up serpents; and if they drink any deadly thing, it shall not hurt them; they shall lay hands on the sick, and they shall recover."*

Completeness in Jesus: Philippians 1:6 - *"Being confident of this very thing, that he which hath begun a good work in you will perform it until the day of Jesus Christ."*

Celebration.

Text: Psalm 126:3 - *"The Lord hath done great things for us; whereof we are glad."*

Of What?

- Beginning of New Things - Isaiah 43:19 - *"Behold, I will do a new thing; now it shall spring forth; shall ye not know it? I will even make a way in the wilderness, and rivers in the desert."*

Appreciation of God's Love and Blessings:

- Children of Israel Celebrated Their Victories - Exodus 15:1-3, 9-12, 20-21 - *"Then sang Moses and the children of Israel this song unto the Lord, and spake, saying, I will sing unto the Lord, for he hath triumphed gloriously: the horse and his rider hath he thrown into the sea. The Lord is my strength and song, and he is become my salvation: he is my God, and I will prepare him an habitation; my father's God, and I will exalt him."*

The Entrance to New Things is Obedience to God and His Word –

Isaiah 1:19 - *"If ye be willing and obedient, ye shall eat the good of the land:"*

Word of Prophets:

Matthew. 10:41 - *"He that receiveth a prophet in the name of a prophet shall receive a prophet's reward; and he that receiveth a righteous man in the name of a righteous man shall receive a righteous man's reward."*

2Chronicles 20:20 - *"And they rose early in the morning, and went forth into the wilderness of Tekoa: and as they went forth, Jehoshaphat stood and said, Hear me, O Judah, and ye inhabitants of Jerusalem; Believe in the Lord your God, so shall ye be established; believe his prophets, so shall ye prosper."*

Warning:

- 2King 7:19-20 - "And that lord answered the man of God, and said, Now, behold, if the Lord should make windows in heaven, might such a thing be? And he said, Behold, thou shalt see it with thine eyes, but shalt not eat thereof. And so it fell out unto him: for the people trode upon him in the gate, and he died." (Excerpt)

  1-2 - *"Then Elisha said, Hear ye the word of the Lord; Thus saith the Lord, To morrow about this time shall a measure of fine flour be sold for a shekel, and two measures of barley for a shekel, in the gate of Samaria."*

The Fear of God.

Text: Proverb. 1:7 - *"The fear of the Lord is the beginning of knowledge: but fools despise wisdom and instruction."*

Hate Evil:

- Proverb 8:13 - *"The fear of the Lord is to hate evil: pride, and arrogancy, and the evil way, and the froward mouth, do I hate."*

Fountain of Life:

- Proverb 14:27 - *"The fear of the Lord is a fountain of life, to depart from the snares of death."*

Examples:

- Joseph - Genesis 39:8-9 - *"But he refused, and said unto his master's wife, Behold, my master wotteth not what is with me in the house, and he hath committed all that he hath to my hand; There is none greater in this house than I; neither hath he kept back any thing from me but thee, because thou art his wife: how then can I do this great wickedness, and sin against God?"*

- Mid-wife - Exodus 1:17 - *"But the midwives feared God, and did not as the king of Egypt commanded them, but saved the men children alive."*

Rewards:

- No Want - Psalm 34:9 - *"O fear the Lord, ye his saints: for there is no want to them that fear him."*

- Protection - Psalm 33:18 - *"Behold, the eye of the Lord is upon them that fear him, upon them that hope in his mercy;"*

- Provision - Psalm 111:5 - *"He hath given meat unto them that fear him: he will ever be mindful of his covenant."*

Example: The Mid-wife - Exodus 1:21 - *"And it came to pass, because the midwives feared God, that he made them houses."*

Challenge:

- Do You Fear God? If You Do, You Will Keep God's Commandments - Psalm 66:18, Hebrew 12:28, Psalm 119:11, Colossians. 3:16

But Ye Shall Receive Power.

Text: Acts 1:8 - *"But ye shall receive power, after that the Holy Ghost is come upon you: and ye shall be witnesses unto me both in Jerusalem, and in all Judaea, and in Samaria, and unto the uttermost part of the earth."*

Promise of God:

Luke 24:49 - *"And, behold, I send the promise of my Father upon you: but tarry ye in the city of Jerusalem, until ye be endued with power from on high."*

The Church on the Rock:

Matthew 16:18 - *"And I say also unto thee, That thou art Peter, and upon this rock I will build my church; and the gates of hell shall not prevail against it."*

Power of Disciples:

Luke 9:1 - *"Then he called his twelve disciples together, and gave them power and authority over all devils, and to cure diseases."*

The Need of Power:

To Live a Victorious Life - Ephesians. 6:10-11 - *"Finally, my brethren, be strong in the Lord, and in the power of his might. Put on the whole armour of God, that ye may be able to stand against the wiles of the devil."*

Not for Sinners and Un-repented but for Repented Sinless, Serious Christians:

2Chronicles. 7:1 - *"Now when Solomon had made an end of praying, the fire came down from heaven, and consumed the burnt offering and the sacrifices; and the glory of the Lord filled the house."*

Acts 4:31 - *"And when they had prayed, the place was shaken where they were assembled together; and they were all filled with the Holy Ghost, and they spake the word of God with boldness."*

Sell Not Your Birthright.

Text: Gen. 25:33 - *"And Jacob said, Swear to me this day; and he sware unto him: and he sold his birthright unto Jacob."*

What is Birthright?

- Heritage

Heritage of God to His Children – Holiness – John 3:36a, 1Pet. 1;15-16 - *"But as he which hath called you is holy, so be ye holy in all manner of conversation; Because it is written, Be ye holy; for I am holy."*

God's Warning:

Luke 21:34-35 - *"And take heed to yourselves, lest at any time your hearts be overcharged with surfeiting, and drunkenness, and cares of this life, and so that day come upon you unawares. For as a snare shall it come on all them that dwell on the face of the whole earth."*

Heb. 12:16-17 - *"Lest there be any fornicator, or profane person, as Esau, who for one morsel of meat sold his birthright. For ye know how that afterward, when he would have inherited the blessing, he was rejected: for he found no place of repentance, though he sought it carefully with tears."*

Example:

Esau – Gen. 25:29-33 - *"And Jacob sod pottage: and Esau came from the field, and he was faint: And Esau said to Jacob, Feed me, I pray thee, with that same red pottage; for I am faint: therefore was his name called Edom. And Jacob said, Sell me this day thy birthright. And Esau said, Behold, I am at the point to die: and what profit shall this birthright do to me? And Jacob said, Swear to me this day; and he sware unto him: and he sold his birthright unto Jacob."*

Conclusion:

No Exchange: Mark 8:36-38 - *"For what shall it profit a man, if he shall gain the whole world, and lose his own soul? Or what shall a man give in exchange for his soul? Whosoever therefore shall be ashamed of me and of my words in this adulterous and sinful generation; of him also shall the Son of man be ashamed, when he cometh in the glory of his Father with the holy angels."*

What Lack I Yet.

Text: Mat. 19:20b - *"What lack I yet?"*

Eternity Question:

- Mat. 19:16 - *"And, behold, one came and said unto him, Good Master, what good thing shall I do, that I may have eternal life?"*

  A Very Religious Man – Mat. 19:18-20 - *"He saith unto him, Which? Jesus said, Thou shalt do no murder, Thou shalt not commit adultery, Thou shalt not steal, Thou shalt not bear false witness, Honour thy father and thy mother: and, Thou shalt love thy neighbour as thyself. The young man saith unto him, All these things have I kept from my youth up: what lack I yet?"*

  Sell Out for God – Mark 8:34, Mat. 19:21 - *"Then said Jesus unto his disciples, If any man will come after me, let him deny himself, and take up his cross, and follow me. Jesus said unto him, If thou wilt be perfect, go and sell that thou hast, and give to the poor, and thou shalt have treasure in heaven: and come and follow me."*

  Willingness Change of Heart to Be Perfect – Mat. 19:21 - *"Jesus said unto him, If thou wilt be perfect, go and sell that thou hast, and give to the poor, and thou shalt have treasure in heaven: and come and follow me."*

Did Not Want to Change – Mat. 19:22 - *"But when the young man heard that saying, he went away sorrowful: for he had great possessions."*

Those That Converted:

Acts 2:37-41,42 (KJV) - *"Now when they heard this, they were pricked in their heart, and said unto Peter and to the rest of the apostles, Men and brethren, what shall we do? Then Peter said unto them, Repent, and be baptized every one of you in the name of Jesus Christ for the remission of sins, and ye shall receive the gift of the Holy Ghost. ... Then they that gladly received his word were baptized: and the same day there were added unto them about three thousand souls. And they continued stedfastly in the apostles' doctrine and fellowship, and in breaking of bread, and in prayers."*

The Keeper of the Prison:

Acts 16:30-31, 32-34 - *"And brought them out, and said, Sirs, what must I do to be saved? And they said, Believe on the Lord Jesus Christ, and thou shalt be saved, and thy house. ... And they spake unto him the word of the Lord, and to all that were in his house. And he took them the same hour of the night, and washed their stripes; and was baptized, he and all his, straightway. And when he had brought them into his house, he set meat before them, and rejoiced, believing in God with all his house."*

Word of Faith:

Rom. 10:8-10 - *"But what saith it? The word is nigh thee, even in thy mouth, and in thy heart: that is, the word of faith, which we preach; That if thou shalt confess with thy mouth the Lord Jesus, and shalt believe in thine heart that God hath raised him from the dead, thou shalt be saved. For with the heart man believeth unto righteousness; and with the mouth confession is made unto salvation."*

Wake Up, Not Time to Sleep.

Text: Jonah 1:6 - *"So the shipmaster came to him, and said unto him, What meanest thou, O sleeper? arise, call upon thy God, if so be that God will think upon us, that we perish not."*

Sleeping in Wrong Time:

Jonah 1:5 - *"Then the mariners were afraid, and cried every man unto his god, and cast forth the wares that were in the ship into the sea, to lighten it of them. But Jonah was gone down into the sides of the ship; and he lay, and was fast asleep."*

For Sorrow:

Luke 22:45 - *"And when he rose up from prayer, and was come to his disciples, he found them sleeping for sorrow,"*

Time to Pray, Time to Be on Fire:

1Pet. 5:8-9 - *"Be sober, be vigilant; because your adversary the devil, as a roaring lion, walketh about, seeking whom he may devour: Whom resist stedfast in the faith, knowing that the same afflictions are accomplished in your brethren that are in the world."*

Wake Up:

Luke 22:40 - *"And when he was at the place, he said unto them, Pray that ye enter not into temptation."*

No Exchange of Man's Soul.

Text: Mark 8:37 - *"Or what shall a man give in exchange for his soul?"*

One Single Life with One Soul:

Psalm 146:4 - *"His breath goeth forth, he returneth to his earth; in that very day his thoughts perish."*

Heart – Deceitful:

Jer. 17:9 - *"The heart is deceitful above all things, and desperately wicked: who can know it?"*

Do Not Be Careless of Your Soul:

Mark 8:36 - *"For what shall it profit a man, if he shall gain the whole world, and lose his own soul?"*

For Fear Him Only:

Who? God – Mat. 10:28 - *"And fear not them which kill the body, but are not able to kill the soul: but rather fear him which is able to destroy both soul and body in hell."*

Eternity is Sure:

But Where Will You Spend Eternity? Rev. 20:15 - *"And whosoever was not found written in the book of life was cast into the lake of fire."*

Spirit of Fear.

Text: 2Tim. 1:7 - *"For God hath not given us the spirit of fear; but of power, and of love, and of a sound mind."*

God Wants Men to Serve Him:

Luke 1:74 - *"That he would grant unto us, that we being delivered out of the hand of our enemies might serve him without fear,"*

Sin Brought Fear:

Gen. 3:10 - *"And he said, I heard thy voice in the garden, and I was afraid, because I was naked; and I hid myself."*

Devil's Spirit:

It Has Torment – 1John 4:18b - *"There is no fear in love; but perfect love casteth out fear: because fear hath torment. He that feareth is not made perfect in love."*

It is for Sinners:

Prov. 28:1a - *"The wicked flee when no man pursueth: but the righteous are bold as a lion."*

Heb. 2:15 - *"And deliver them who through fear of death were all their lifetime subject to bondage."*

God's Power to Believers:

Mat. 28:18-20 - *"And Jesus came and spake unto them, saying, All power is given unto me in heaven and in earth. Go ye therefore, and teach all nations, baptizing them in the name of the Father, and of the Son, and of the Holy Ghost: Teaching them to observe all things whatsoever I have commanded you: and, lo, I am with you alway, even unto the end of the world. Amen."*

Christ in Us:

1John 4:4 - *"Ye are of God, little children, and have overcome them: because greater is he that is in you, than he that is in the world."*

Luke 9:1-2 - *"Then he called his twelve disciples together, and gave them power and authority over all devils, and to cure diseases. And he sent them to preach the kingdom of God, and to heal the sick."*

Luke 10:19 - *"Behold, I give unto you power to tread on serpents and scorpions, and over all the power of the enemy: and nothing shall by any means hurt you."*

Jesus – Fear Not, It is I:

Mat. 14:26-27 - *"And when the disciples saw him walking on the sea, they were troubled, saying, It is a spirit; and they cried out for fear. But straightway Jesus spake unto them, saying, Be of good cheer; it is I; be not afraid."*

I Am With You Always:

Mat. 28:20 - *"Teaching them to observe all things whatsoever I have commanded you: and, lo, I am with you alway, even unto the end of the world. Amen."*

When Thou Shalt Have Dominion.

Text: Gen. 27:40 - *"And by thy sword shalt thou live, and shalt serve thy brother; and it shall come to pass when thou shalt have the dominion, that thou shalt break his yoke from off thy neck."*

Dominion Comes Through Prevailing Prayer:

Gen. 32:26 - *"And he said, Let me go, for the day breaketh. And he said, I will not let thee go, except thou bless me."*

Jesus Promised It:

Luke 29:49 - *"And, behold, I send the promise of my Father upon you: but tarry ye in the city of Jerusalem, until ye be endued with power from on high."*

Acts 1:14 - *"These all continued with one accord in prayer and supplication, with the women, and Mary the mother of Jesus, and with his brethren."*

Believers' Prayer Must Be for Holy Ghost Power:

Acts 1:8 - *"But ye shall receive power, after that the Holy Ghost is come upon you: and ye shall be witnesses unto me both in Jerusalem, and in all Judaea, and in Samaria, and unto the uttermost part of the earth."*

Acts 4:29-34 - *(Excerpt) "And now, Lord, behold their threatenings: and grant unto thy servants, that with all boldness they may speak thy word... And with great power gave the apostles witness of the resurrection of the Lord Jesus: and great grace was upon them all."*

Acts 10:38 - *"How God anointed Jesus of Nazareth with the Holy Ghost and with power: who went about doing good, and healing all that were oppressed of the devil; for God was with him."*

Present Help.

Text: Psalm 46:1 - *"God is our refuge and strength, a very present help in trouble."*

When?:

In Time of Trouble, to Know God – Dan. 11:32 - *"And such as do wickedly against the covenant shall he corrupt by flatteries: but the people that do know their God shall be strong, and do exploits."*

His Promises and Stand on It:

Psalm 50:15 - *"And call upon me in the day of trouble: I will deliver thee, and thou shalt glorify me."*

John 16:33 - *"These things I have spoken unto you, that in me ye might have peace. In the world ye shall have tribulation: but be of good cheer; I have overcome the world."*

Psalm 43:2 - *"For thou art the God of my strength: why dost thou cast me off? why go I mourning because of the oppression of the enemy?"*

Examples:

Abraham – Gen. 22:10-13 – *"And Abraham stretched forth his hand, and took the knife to slay his son... And Abraham lifted up his eyes, and looked, and behold behind him a ram caught in a thicket by his horns: and Abraham went and took the ram, and offered him up for a burnt offering in the stead of his son."*

Jonah – Jonah 1:17 - *"Now the Lord had prepared a great fish to swallow up Jonah. And Jonah was in the belly of the fish three days and three nights."*

Call on God:

Psalm 107:28 - *"Then they cry unto the Lord in their trouble, and he bringeth them out of their distresses."*

Today Is a Special Day:

Today Will Be Special Mark It in Your Life.

God Heareth Not Sinners.

Text: John 9:31 - *"Now we know that God heareth not sinners: but if any man be a worshipper of God, and doeth his will, him he heareth."*

The Truth All Need to Know:

All unrighteousness is sin, sin hinders prayer – Isa. 59:1 - *"Behold, the Lord's hand is not shortened, that it cannot save; neither his ear heavy, that it cannot hear."*

Psalm 66:18 (KJV) - *"If I regard iniquity in my heart, the Lord will not hear me:"*

Un-confessed Sin:

Prov. 28:13 - *"He that covereth his sins shall not prosper: but whoso confesseth and forsaketh them shall have mercy."*

Examples:

Samson – Judges 16:20 - *"And she said, The Philistines be upon thee, Samson. And he awoke out of his sleep, and said, I will go out as at other times before, and shake myself. And he wist not that the Lord was departed from him."*

Prayer of the Righteous:

Prov. 28:1 - *"The wicked flee when no man pursueth: but the righteous are bold as a lion."*

Psalm 34:17 - *"The righteous cry, and the Lord heareth, and delivereth them out of all their troubles."*

James 5:16 - *"Confess your faults one to another, and pray one for another, that ye may be healed. The effectual fervent prayer of a righteous man availeth much."*

They Lost Jesus.

Text: Luke 2:40-43 - *[40] And the child grew, and waxed strong in spirit, filled with wisdom: and the grace of God was upon him. [41] Now his parents went to Jerusalem every year at the feast of the passover. [42] And when he was twelve years old, they went up to Jerusalem after the custom of the feast. [43] And when they had fulfilled the days, as they returned, the child Jesus tarried behind in Jerusalem; and Joseph and his mother knew not of it.*

I. Carelessness Leading to Loss:

Jesus was not lost, but they lost Him. They were careless in their awareness of His absence. Luke 2:43 - " *And when they had fulfilled the days, as they returned, the child Jesus tarried behind in Jerusalem; and Joseph and his mother knew not of it."*

II. The Challenge of False Assumptions:

Luke 2:44 - *"But they, supposing him to have been in the company, went a day's journey; and they sought him among their kinsfolk and acquaintance."*

III. Restitution and Seriousness in Seeking:

Recognising their mistake, they returned to Jerusalem: Luke 2:45 - *"And when they found him not, they turned back again to Jerusalem, seeking him."*

Seriousness in seeking Him: Luke 2:46-49 - *⁴⁶ And it came to pass, that after three days they found him in the temple, sitting in the midst of the doctors, both hearing them, and asking them questions. ⁴⁷ And all that heard him were astonished at his understanding and answers. ⁴⁸ And when they saw him, they were amazed: and his mother said unto him, Son, why hast thou thus dealt with us? behold, thy father and I have sought thee sorrowing. ⁴⁹ And he said unto them, How is it that ye sought me? wist ye not that I must be about my Father's business?*

IV. Lessons from Samson's Loss:

- Samson lost God unaware: Judges 16:20b - *And he wist not that the Lord was departed from him.*

- Samson's commitment to seek God: Judges 16:28-30 - *²⁸ And Samson called unto the Lord, and said, O Lord God, remember me, I pray thee, and strengthen me, I pray thee, only this once, O God, that I may be at once avenged of the Philistines for my two eyes. ²⁹ And Samson took hold of the two middle pillars upon which the house stood, and on which it was borne up, of the one with his right hand, and of the other with his left. ³⁰ And Samson said, Let me die with the Philistines. And he bowed himself with all his might; and the house fell upon the lords, and upon all the people that were therein. So the dead which he slew at his death were more than they which he slew in his life.*

V. The Consequences of Losing Jesus:

- When you lose Jesus, you lose His blessings: 2 Chronicles 15:4 (KJV) - *"But when they in their trouble did turn unto the Lord God of Israel, and sought him, he was found of them."*

My Messages

Made in the USA
Columbia, SC
23 October 2024

44552860R00139